Debating Higher Education: Philosophical Perspectives

Volume 5

Series Editors

Ronald Barnett, Institute of Education, University College London, London, UK
Søren S. E. Bengtsen, Aarhus University, Aarhus C, Denmark

Debating Higher Education: Philosophical Perspectives is a new book series launched by Springer and is motivated by two considerations.

Higher education has become a huge matter globally, both politically and socially, commanding massive resources, national and cross-national decision-making, and the hopes of many. In parallel, over the last four decades or so, there has been a growing interest in the academic literature in grappling with technical issues in and around higher education. In particular, work has developed drawing on philosophical perspectives and social theory. This is evident right across the world, especially in the journal literature and in research students' doctoral theses. In effect, we have witnessed the formation of a new sub-discipline, a shorthand of which is 'the philosophy of higher education', and which includes perspectives drawn not only from philosophy and social theory but also feminism, ethics, geopolitics, learning theory, and organizational studies.

Through this book series – the first of its kind – the editors want to encourage the further development of this literature. We are keen to promote lively volumes which are informed about changing practices and policy frameworks in higher education and which engage seriously and deeply with matters of public interest, and are written in an accessible style.

Books will take a variety of forms, and will include both sole-authored and multi-authored formats. Importantly, each volume will have a dialogical flavour, engaging explicitly in dialogue with contemporary debates and their contending positions and, where practicable, especially in volumes with many contributors, will themselves exemplify dialogue.

The editors are keen that the series is open to many approaches. We wish to include work that focuses directly on the university as a social institution and on higher education as an educational process; on the idea of the university and on higher education as a sector with political and policy frameworks; on students and learning, and on academics and academic knowledge; and on curricula and pedagogy, and on research and knowledge processes.

Volumes will examine policy and practical issues including, for example, internationalisation, higher education as a set of 'public goods', access and fairness, and the digital era and learning as well as more conceptual and theoretical issues such as academic freedom, ethics, wellbeing, and the philosophy of social organizations.

The editors very much welcome informal inquiries at any time.

Ronald Barnett, UCL Institute of Education – ron.barnett@ucl.ac.uk
Søren S.E. Bengtsen, Aarhus University – ssbe@tdm.au.dk

More information about this series at http://www.springer.com/series/15094

Nuraan Davids • Yusef Waghid

Academic Activism in Higher Education

A Living Philosophy for Social Justice

 Springer

Nuraan Davids (iD)
Stellenbosch University
Cape Town, South Africa

Yusef Waghid (iD)
Stellenbosch University
Cape Town, South Africa

ISSN 2366-2573   ISSN 2366-2581   (electronic)
Debating Higher Education: Philosophical Perspectives
ISBN 978-981-16-0339-6   ISBN 978-981-16-0340-2   (eBook)
https://doi.org/10.1007/978-981-16-0340-2

This Springer imprint is published by the registered company Springer Nature Singapore Pte Ltd.
The registered company address is: 152 Beach Road, #21-01/04 Gateway East, Singapore 189721, Singapore

Preface

We conceive this monograph at a time of immense uncertainty for the condition of what it means to be and act with humanity, and indeed, the state of our collective humanity beyond, for instance, a Covid-19 phenomenon. In South Africa, which serves as the context of this book, the current global pandemic has brought untold disruption and paralysis across all sectors and all forms of interactions. The context, which we describe here, is of course not unique or limited to South Africa. Much of the ensuing reflections, contentions and contestations with which we engage cut across various geopolitical contexts, highlighting significant global challenges in higher education. Some universities have been able to transition relatively easily to modes of online and blended learning, with minimal disruption to its academic programmes and the well-being of its academic and administrative staff and students. Most, however, have only been able to function minimally, as the socio-economic contexts of both universities and students come to bear on access to digital resources and infrastructure. While many debates have centred on how to salvage the academic year, the content of these debates has not only revealed different perceptions and experiences of higher education but has brought into disrepute the idea of a singular system of higher education in post-apartheid South Africa. With this in mind, it is important to clarify the intricacies of a South African context, which serve as the background to this book.

Setting the Scene

Prior to 1994, the differentiated higher education system comprised 26 public universities, 15 technikons (polytechnics), 120 colleges of education, 24 nursing colleges and 11 agricultural colleges, which all differed in terms of quality of academic provision, adequacy of infrastructure and facilities, and the level of state investment and funding (HESA, 2014: 9). With the advent of constitutional democracy in 1994 and the subsequent promulgation of the government's *White Paper 3: A Programme for the Transformation of Higher Education* by the then Department of Education

(DoE) in 1997, the higher education system was subsequently completely over-hauled as an integrated, 'single, national, co-ordinated system that would ensure diversity in its organisational form and the institutional landscape, mix of institutional missions and programmes commensurate with national and regional needs in social, cultural and economic development' (DoE, 1997: 2.3). To Badat (2010: 3), the social purposes that higher education was intended to serve, as identified in the *White Paper 3* (DoE, 1997), resonate with the core roles of higher education of disseminating knowledge and producing critical graduates, producing and applying knowledge through research and development activities, and contributing to economic and social development and democracy through learning and teaching, research, and community engagement.

By 2001, the colleges of education were either closed or incorporated into the universities and technikons, and the 36 higher education institutions (HEIs) were either merged, unbundled or incorporated to form 11 traditional (research) universities that mainly offer degree programmes, 6 comprehensive universities (one distance education institution in the form of the University of South Africa [Unisa]) and 6 universities of technology. In addition, two institutes of higher education were established in provinces without universities, namely the Northern Cape and Mpumalanga – two of nine provinces in the country – in 2013. Thus, it was envisaged that the post-1994 institutional restructuring would engender a differentiated, diverse and articulated higher education system that resonated with the knowledge and development needs of South Africa and the imperative of achieving social justice (HESA, 2014:10).

Despite notions of a 'single, national co-ordinated system' (DHET, 1997), South Africa's higher education system remains binary, which means that it continues to rely on a blend of training colleges, technical/vocational institutes, polytechnic-type institutions and universities. As a result, state Ng'ethe, Subotzky and Afeti (2008: 21), there are two opposing tendencies: 'one towards the traditional university type through academic drift and driven by aspirations for higher status, and the other towards institutional differentiation and diversity to accommodate a wider market. The latter includes vocational drift in universities in order to capture more of the lucrative short-term training market'.

A lack of policy clarity regarding the appropriate boundaries between polytechnics and universities in terms of their mission, purpose, curricula and programmes (and the knowledge underpinnings of these), has allowed the two-way drift to proceed unencumbered (Ng'ethe et al., 2008). Ng'ethe et al. (2008) contend that the strict binary divide, and the particularly narrow interpretation of polytechnic training within this, has been contested as technicist and divisive, and tends to inhibit debate on important issues such as equity, access, mobility and the relationship between education and training in general. With very few exceptions, continue Ng'ethe et al. (2008: 24), the overall public perception is that polytechnic education is of much lower status than university education.

As acknowledged by Higher Education South Africa (HESA), a new, differentiated higher education institutional landscape has not adequately and justifiably addressed the past inequities, more specifically as they relate to the educational, material, financial and geographical elements of the (white) advantaged and the (black) disadvantaged:

> The continued under-developed institutional capacities of historically black institutions must be emphasized; providing access to rural poor and working-class black students, inadequate state support for the historically black institutions to equalize the quality of undergraduate provision compromises their ability to facilitate equity of opportunity and outcomes (HESA, 2014: 11).

In line with global trends, higher education enrolments on the African continent, and particularly, sub-Saharan Africa, have grown faster than in any other region in the world – despite remaining the lowest in the world. The rapid growth in higher education enrolments in Sub-Saharan Africa can be ascribed to two main reasons: increased enrolment in primary and secondary education, which has created a rising demand for higher education; and a growing awareness on the part of African governments of the role of higher education in national economic productivity (Akalu, 2016; Mohamedbhai, 2008). In South Africa, the participation rate in higher education increased from 15% in 2000 to 18% in 2010, and it was expected that the 20% target would have been met by 2015/2016 (CHE, 2013).

By 2018, 'black' students constituted 70% of university students – a significant increase the onset of democracy, state Case, Marshall, McKenna and Mogashana (2018: 11), but still somewhat less than the population proportion of 80%. Moreover, while most historically advantaged ('white') universities now have a majority 'black' student body, historically disadvantaged 'black' universities remain almost exclusively populated by black students (Case et al., 2018). That being said, a shift in student demographics has not led to a shift in institutional culture. Instead, historically advantaged institutions have retained their historic racially and culturally defined identities and face ongoing criticism of perpetuating a culture of white privilege. As recently as 2015, through the '#FeesMustFall' and '#RhodesMustFall' campaigns, students have called for the end of domination by 'white, male, Western, capitalist, heterosexual, European world views' in higher education; and for the incorporation of other South African, African and global 'perspectives, experiences [and] epistemologies' as the central tenets of the curriculum, teaching, learning and research in the country (Shay, 2016).

Some of the most significant markers of transformation has occurred at the doctoral level. According to Cloete (2016), 'black' doctoral graduates increased from 58 in 1996 to 821 in 2012, an increase of 706% in the post-1996 period. By contrast, 'white' graduate numbers only grew by 71% (from 587 to 816). Over the same period, the proportion of 'black' doctoral graduates increased from 8% to 44%, and in 2012, the number of 'black' graduates exceeded those of 'whites' (Cloete, 2016). In turn, continues Cloete (2016), 'black' female graduates, starting from a very low base of 10 in 1996, increased by 960% to 106 in 2012, while 'black' male graduates increased by 356%. In contrast, the number of 'white' male graduates remained more or less constant – around 367 between 1996 and 2012; and 'white' female graduates increased from 219 in 1996 to 449 in 2012 (105%). These significant shifts in student demographics notwithstanding, students are drawn from a tiny proportion of schools in the system, specifically, schools which have retained a strong socio-economic standing. As Case et al. (2018: 11) observe, South Africa continues to operate along a two-tiered system, 'with the poor only having access to poorly resourced schools from which very few obtain the school results needed for access to higher education (and for those who do, it is mainly to lower status universities), while wealthier families access well-resourced public or private schools, and have good chances of access to higher status universities'.

Cloete (2016: 2) maintains that if transformation is counted as improvement in percentage change, then 'black' students, and especially 'black' female students, have attained spectacular gains when compared to 'white' males. 'We have not found another international example with such demographic changes in a national higher education system over such a short period (16 years)'. In a South African context, increasing student enrolments, or massification, particularly from historically marginalised 'black' communities is seen as critical to the democratisation of access by making higher education accessible to diverse sections of the population, and benefitting groups which, historically, have been excluded from the elite systems of higher education (Akalu, 2016).

The merging of institutions and massification have been accompanied by additional significant restructuring objectives. These include the establishment of a national quality assurance framework and infrastructure, which comprises of policies, mechanisms and initiatives concerning institutional audit; and programme accreditation, quality promotion and capacity development have been implemented (Badat, 2010). These achievements, however, run the risk of being diminished by a growing number of challenges, which appear to be fuelling the erosion of especially historically disadvantaged universities. While the idea of high student enrolment in the context of post-apartheid South Africa is assumed to imply transformation through diversification, there is disagreement, however, on whether it has redressed past inequalities. More specifically, it is unclear whether high student enrolment has addressed the dual concerns of democratisation of higher education through participation (Davids, 2019).

A Complexity of Dilemmas

First, despite the significant advances made in terms of massification, deemed as necessary for political and socio-economic redress, there is little evidence, however, that massification tackles social inequalities of access and participation – that is, inequalities in terms of access and success persist even in participation systems (Hornsby & Osman, 2014; Marginson, 2016).

The concerns raised by Badat (2010) remain unchanged 10 years later – namely, the extent that government and universities have sought to pursue social equity and redress and quality in higher education simultaneously, have given rise to difficult political and social dilemmas, choices, decisions and paradoxes, especially in the context of inadequate public finances and academic development initiatives to support underprepared students, who tend to be mostly black and/or of the working class or rural poor social origins. According to Badat (2010: 7):

> An exclusive concentration on social equity and redress without adequate public funding and academic development initiatives to support under-prepared students has negative implications for quality, compromises the production of high-quality graduates with the requisite knowledge, competencies and skills, and adversely affects economic development. Conversely, an exclusive focus on economic development and quality and 'standards', (especially when considered to be timeless and invariant and attached to a single, a-historical and universal model of higher education) result in equality being retarded or delayed with limited erosion of the racial and gender character of the high-level occupational structure.

The state, according to Badat (2016: 4), has indeed provided considerable funding for 'infrastructure and efficiency' to address backlogs and increase institutional capacities related to teaching, research and student accommodation at all universities, and especially the historically disadvantaged ('black') universities. However, the backlogs at historically disadvantaged universities are so severe, that the infrastructure funding has been inadequate to eliminate the range of conditions that impact on the quality of higher education provision. This, states Badat (2016), compromises equity of opportunity and outcomes for the students at the historically black universities, who are largely from working-class and rural low-income families.

Second, students, especially those who have been historically excluded from higher education, explains Tinto (2003: 2), are affected 'by the campus expectational climate and by their perceptions of the expectations that faculty and staff hold for their individual performance'. Central to this 'expectational climate', is the perpetuation of a curriculum, which is not only disconnected from the majority of students but from the political and social contexts of South African society. There is a profound irony in the retention of a curriculum, which, on the one hand, was used to oppress the majority of South Africans during apartheid, and on the other hand, affords scant regard for the inclusion of African knowledge and voices. There is an unavoidable connection between the retention of a colonialist curriculum and the existing institutional cultures of 'whiteness' at historically advantaged universities. In addition to curriculum content, students are required to adapt to particular institutional cultures, which are as prevalent in lecture theatres, tutorial groups, libraries and laboratories, as they are in student residences and any social gatherings. This transition and the pressure to assimilate to a dominant institutional culture is amplified when historically disadvantaged students enter the spaces of historically advantaged institutions (Davids, 2019).

Third, the high rate of student enrolment or massification has not necessarily translated into congruent student retention and graduation rates. A detailed analysis of the 2000 and 2006 cohorts, explains Cloete (2016), shows that the proportion of intake into contact institutions of students who are sufficiently prepared to complete undergraduate curricula within the intended time, is small: only 27%, or roughly only one in every four graduates. Performance is very poor for all groups across the three qualification types (diplomas, 3-year and 4-year degrees) with only 48% in contact universities graduating within 5 years (Cloete, 2016). It is estimated that 45% will never graduate. In terms of distance education, the statistics of the University of South Africa (UNISA) show that only 6% of students graduate within 5 years, and it is estimated that 78% will never graduate. By the end of the regulation time for all three qualification types, more students have been lost to failure and dropout than have graduated – more than twice as many in the case of African students and those in diploma courses (Cloete, 2016).

Fourth, a focused emphasis on massification has not necessarily included due regard for the specific identities, circumstances and experiences of students, particularly those who constitute cohorts of first-generation students. It is somewhat unsettling to propagate massification without, firstly, being cognisant of who students are and what they do or do not bring; and, secondly, without taking account of the need to cultivate the contexts in which high student enrolments might evolve into student belonging. It is disconcerting for students to come up against norms, traditions and ways of being, with which they do not identify. Accordingly, they feel disconnected from the academic and institutional cultures to which they gained external access.

There is an argument, according to Case et al. (2018: 3), 'that the forms of knowledge and associated literacy practices that are valued in the academy are those of privileged groups in society, and that the university mainly serves to prop up this privilege'. The majority of historically disadvantaged students struggle in finding their way and themselves, in the institutions that have offered them external access, but not internal inclusion (Davids, 2019). As Hlengwa, McKenna and Njovane (2018: 55) explain, students, who find themselves in such alienating campus environments, are effectively stripped of their heritage, norms, values and social practices. It is, therefore, unsurprising to find that students who feel estranged from their institutions and struggle to find points of resonance, subsequently detach themselves from their own learning (Davids, 2019).

Fifth, given its objective of massification as a manifestation of democratising university spaces, an overwhelming number of students, who are accessing are insufficiently prepared for the academic demands of higher education. The two-tiered system (historically advantaged and historically disadvantaged) is not limited to higher education. South Africa's primary and secondary schooling system presents profound complexities. Schools are wholly unequal in terms of infrastructure; resources; learner-to-teacher ratios; teacher qualifications and content knowledge; learning support programmes; leadership; management; governance; and parental support and involvement. While much of the discrepancies in the schooling sector can be ascribed to historical descriptors, which determined the levels of (apartheid) state support, the democratic government has shown a disturbing lack of political will in ensuring the necessary infrastructural and pedagogical reform desperately needed by historically disadvantaged schools.

As Case, Marshall and Grayson (2013: 1) observe, the level of preparation of first-year students for university studies has long been a concern, with the interface between school and higher education often characterised in terms of a discontinuity or 'articulation gap'. Many students require academic support if they are to participate equitably and graduate successfully (Badat, 2016). This concern continues to be neglected as historically disadvantaged universities, in particular, struggle in providing sufficient resources devoted to academic development programmes. Whatever resources have been provided to such programmes, contends Badat (2016), have been often used ineffectively by universities, which have lacked the necessary academic capacities to mount high-quality programmes.

The sixth point, which centres on funding, has already been touched on in the preceding discussions. It is worth adding, however, that the proportion of government funding to universities decreased from 49% in 2000 to 40% in 2014 (Cloete, 2016). The shortfall was made up through student fees, which increased by 42% from 2010 to 2014. This is an increase of 9% per annum in contrast to the 5% to 6% inflation rate. While most comparable countries are spending closer to 2% of GDP on higher education, South Africa spends less than 1% of GDP) and has not reached its own target of 1% on research and development – a figure which is well below international targets (Cloete, 2016).

Certainly, debates and conflicts centring on the role of higher education in relation to democracy, are not new. Many democracies, however, have not had to overcome the lasting effects of both colonialism and apartheid. And none have had to embark on a similar type of transformational path of political, social, economic and educational reform as South Africa. There are, therefore, particular developments and experiences, which provide the South African story with a definitive edge, which not only speaks to its broken and damaging history but which raises concerns about its ongoing fragility. This fragility resides in numerous intersectional points and discourses, as discussed above – equitable access and participation, curriculum reform, funding, alienating institutional cultures, academic inadequacies, and low student throughput rates. However, it also presents itself, most problematically, in increasing displays of violent student protests, which speak not only to intense student frustration and anger but to a hopelessness, which cannot be dismissed.

Unless, the narrative shifts to a greater focus on the role of higher education in relation to its responsibility in a democracy, as opposed to a minimalist emphasis on transformation in terms of numbers and representation, the existing fragility will lead to disrepair. One of the key considerations to draw upon in this regard are renewed conceptions and enactments of academic activism – that is, a willing acceptance of responsibilities, which extend beyond teaching, learning, research and writing, and which are critical to the development and sustenance of a democracy.

Why Academic Activism?

In his seminal essay, 'The responsibility of intellectuals' (1967), Noam Chomsky asserts:

With respect to the responsibility of intellectuals, there are still other, equally disturbing questions. Intellectuals are in a position to expose the lies of governments, to analyze actions according to their causes and motives and often hidden intentions. In the Western world, at least, they have the power that comes from political liberty, from access to information and freedom of expression. For a privileged minority, Western democracy provides the leisure, the facilities, and the training to seek the truth lying hidden behind the veil of distortion and misrepresentation, ideology and class interest, through which the events of current history are presented to us … IT IS THE RESPONSIBILITY of intellectuals to speak the truth and to expose lies. This, at least, may seem enough of a truism to pass over without comment.

The role of universities has always been looked at as having to extend beyond the immediate functions of the academy. This is because education enables intellectuals to grasp the entirety of the social and political structure and adopt 'a broader point of view' (Mannheim, 1991: 162). Moreover, the training of the intellectual 'has equipped him [her] to face the problems of the day in several perspectives and not only in one, as most participants in the controversies of their time do' (Mannheim, 1992: 105). By implication, intellectuals or academics, have the privilege not only of knowledge but should be able to exercise autonomy in terms of thinking and acting. Mannheim's (1992) description of a 'broader point of view' suggests a capacity to look at issues from varying perspectives, to be open to that which is different and unfamiliar, and to respond critically to whatever is encountered – within a university space, as well as the public sphere. Similar arguments have been extended by Said (1993), in that academics need to stand outside society and its institutions and actively disturb the status quo but at the same time address their concerns to as wide a public as possible. Moreover, by Barnett (2016: 9) who describes a university as being unafraid of confronting 'the dominant interests of our age'.

Seemingly, and probably more so in a time of a post-truth era, there is a need for a university to *be* and *do* more in relation and response to broader public debates and discontents. At stake, says Olsen (2005), are the university's purpose, work processes, organisation, system of governance and financial basis, as well as its role in the political system, the economy and society at large. One such recognition is vested in New Zealand's 1989 Education Act (section 162(4)(a)), which, in addition to affirming the characteristics of teaching, learning, research and knowledge, requires that all higher education institutions should 'accept a role as critic and conscience of society'. It is defined in the Act as the freedom of academic staff and students, within the law, to question and test received wisdom, to put forward new ideas and to state controversial or unpopular opinions (Education Act, 1989). Described as a statutory obligation, the role of the New Zealand academic is seen as vital to influencing democratic social change. The role of a 'critic and conscience', however, argues Grey (2013: 701), is not the same as being an activist in a social movement. To her, '[a]ctivism involves deliberately and consciously dissenting against the status quo, against hegemonic discourses. It is a role centred on engendering substantive democracy in all spheres of society…' (Grey, 2013: 701).

Grey (2013) cites particular instances of activism – such as the Greensboro lunch counter sit-ins and the anti-Vietnam war teach-ins – which she describes as idealised images of universities as the centre of radical activism. She also recalls the signing of the Port Huron Statement, which outlined how students sought to end poverty, racism and imperialism through non-violent protest, education and uniting student organisations and outside communities. The lunch counter sit-ins that would change American history began when four 'black' teenagers refused to leave a Woolworth's lunch counter in Greensboro, North Carolina. Within 3 days, they were joined by 300 others; the sit-ins had spread to more than 50 cities, leading to the rapid desegregation of lunch counters (Astor, 2018). The actions of the 'Greensboro Four' led directly to the creation of the 'Student Nonviolent Coordinating Committee' in April 1960, which coordinated the continuing sit-ins. Later, SNCC would play a significant role in the Freedom Rides and voter registration efforts across the South. Moreover, the momentum that began at the Woolworth's lunch counter would eventually contribute to the passage of the Civil Rights Act of 1964, which outlawed segregation in public spaces (Astor, 2018).

Elsewhere, the waves of protest, commonly referred to as the 'Arab Spring', which erupted in Tunisia in December 2010, followed by Egypt, Libya, Algeria, Bahrain, Lebanon, Kuwait, Jordan, Yemen and Morocco in 2011, firmly brought into question the purpose of higher education on the African continent. The self-immolation of Tunisian university graduate, Mohamed Bouazizi, quite literally sparked the flames of what would lead to massive civil unrest in the middle-eastern regions, in pursuit of democracy. Prior to the Arab Spring, studies of Middle Eastern politics had primarily centred on structural factors and political elites; very little research had focused on 'politics from below' – that is, the dynamics of mobilisation and change on the ground. The sudden emergence of popular coalitions between various social sectors that had been assumed ineffective or apolitical, explains Grimm (2018), turned into an opportunity for many researchers who had paid little attention to the region so far. On the one hand, scholars explored the similarities between the roundabout revolutions in Bahrain, Cairo, Sanaa and Tunis and the spatial occupations by the Occupy movement and the anti-austerity protesters in Southern Europe. On the other hand, students of revolutions compared the cross-class and cross-ideological coalitions of the Arab Spring to revolutionary movements in Eastern Europe and Latin America (Grimm, 2018).

As Grimm (2018) elaborates, the revolutions stirred feelings of solidarity, particularly among young researchers who could identify with the agents of change and their pluralist and emancipatory ideals – effectively propelling the discipline of Middle Eastern Studies from a niche existence to the centre of political science. In turn, between 2011 and 2013, Western policymakers fostered an active exchange with Arab activists and civil society organisations; in many Western capitals, researchers thereby functioned as international multipliers of the protest actors' voices and contributed to the dissemination of their demands (Grimm, 2018).

Then there are the more recent events in Turkey. As is the case in many other global contexts, academic independence and freedom in Turkey have long been under attack through the neoliberalisation of universities and state control of agenda in science and education (Acar & Canan, 2020). According to Tören and Kutun (2018: 105), 'There was injustice, state violence and fear among the majority of the academy resulting from injustice and state violence. Academics were facing the absence of the rule of law, precarious working conditions, an inflexible academic hierarchy, and, most importantly, repression from the government'. On 11 January 2016, a petition entitled 'We will not be party to this crime' – later commonly known as the 'peace petition' – was published with 1128 signatures from different universities under the umbrella of 'Academics for Peace' (Tören & Kutun, 2018: 105). The 'peace petition' called on the government to repeal the curfews in Kurdish towns and to restart the reconciliation process with Kurdish parties. Following the attempted coup in July 2016, the current Justice and Development Party government and its apparatuses reacted with harsh measures (Acar & Canan, 2020). These included clamping down on academic freedom and independence by threatening academics, opening legal cases against them, jailing them and firing them from universities. The decree-laws, explain Acar and Canan (2020: 389), have also meant that thousands of academics – including PhD students to those well established in their careers – have been dismissed from their positions, barred from working in any university in the country and, at times, prevented from leaving the country. In response, continue Acar and Canan (2020: 389), a number of academics sought to continue their scholarly activities outside the university.

Unemployed academics have established 'solidarity academies' and other academic collectives in various cities across Turkey. They see these collectives, explain Acar and Canan (2020: 389), as 'a catalyst for the politicization and organization of a new group of scholars, creating activism around learning, teaching, and acquiring knowledge practices in a way that could not be done in the more restrictive environment of Turkey's formal institutions'. Acar and Canan (2020: 389) describe the 'solidarity academies' as 'a new movement of scholar activism, albeit with roots in past practices, against rising inequality and systematic deprivations, with a critical reflection on the role of the academic as a catalyst for social change.

Given South Africa's turbulent political history, much has been written about its transition from an apartheid to a democratic state, with most discussions and debates centring on the role and contribution of civil and student activism. Unsurprisingly, these debates are embedded in South Africa's 'struggle politics', which, in turn, cannot be separated from broader social injustices and economic inequalities. In this regard, there are parallels to be drawn with other geopolitical contexts, such as the United States of America, where black student activism played a significant role and made distinctive contributions to the larger campaigns for social and political change (Franklin, 2003: 204).

At one level, there are clear similarities between South Africa's apartheid and legal segregation, as practised in the USA. As Franklin (2003) explains, in both contexts, authorities demanded that students who participated in protests be severely disciplined or expelled from the university; university expulsions triggered protests, marches, classes and other demonstrations that led to the closing of the universities; 'black' students in the USA and South Africa were willing to sacrifice and withdraw from the university altogether when their demands were not met; and improvements were not forthcoming. In many instances, continues Franklin (2003), these students never returned, or did not return until years later, opting instead to commit their lives to participate in larger freedom struggles and activism.

At another level, there are fundamental differences. Firstly, unlike the US context, which saw a significant decrease in student activism among 'black' and 'white' students during the 1980s and 1990s, 'black' student activism in South Africa continued. Franklin (2003: 214–215) explains that although many 'black' and 'white' American students participated in the South African 'divestment campaigns' and the 'Free South Africa movement', these activities were not as pervasive on college campuses as the earlier civil rights, anti-war and student rights campaigns that came to define American higher education in the 1960s. Secondly, whereas the 'Black Liberation Movement' in the USA sought the inclusion and recognition of African Americans as a distinct cultural group within the US political system, black political empowerment in South Africa would mean a shift in control of the political structures and institutions from the white minority to the black majority.

Certainly, the end of South Africa's political struggle has not translated into a struggle-free democracy. If anything, the country's transition to a democracy has amplified the demands for far-reaching reform and restoration. Not only is higher education highly stratified in terms of student and academic demographics, but there are significant incongruencies concerning academic offerings, resources, facilities, further hampered by high rates of student attrition and degree incompletion – brought about by financial constraints or inadequate academic support. Alongside these discrepancies and challenges are escalating problems pertaining to systemic institutional cultures of racism and marginalisation, leading to experiences of increasing alienation and displacement among both students and academics. Seemingly, the promises suggested by a democracy, as expressed in a litany of policy reform, has done little to redress historical inequalities – to the extent that it remains commonplace, 26 years after a democracy, to still refer to historically ('white') advantaged and historically ('black') disadvantaged institutions. As a result, we have seen a series of student protests – from #FeesMustFall, #RhodesMustFall, to calls for decolonisation and #AmINext? in response to the growing scourge of gender-based violence.

While these protests have forced renewed interest on the state of higher education, it would be wrong to think that the plight of students are new, or only started up in 2015, when the first set of protests flared up. What we are confronted with, is a continuation of a long-standing narrative, emanating from the dehumanising practices of first, colonialism, followed by apartheid. While the political contexts are different, the marginalisation and exclusion of students and citizens alike have remained intact. Any notion of activism, therefore, regardless of being located in the spaces of higher education, is necessarily tied to what it means for higher education to be in a democracy. The challenge and responsibility of academic activism are driven as much by a democratic imperative as it is by moral responsibility. And this provides clarity into what we see as the purpose of this book – one which delves into conceptions and practices of higher education, with a view to using a philosophy of higher education to remove the blinkers, shift the gaze, and re-imagine how things might be otherwise.

Through the Lens of a Philosophy of Higher Education

Every academic discipline comes with its inevitable dominant conceptions, discourses, debates, theorists and practitioners, not to mention its accompanying questions and scepticism. As academics who work in philosophy of higher education, we are often confronted with questions regarding the usefulness, and it would seem, activism, of a philosophy of higher education. Often one hears assertions and mutterings in university corridors that a philosophy of higher education is too vague and abstract and does not contribute to doing real research. We hear that a philosophy of higher education is disconnected from real-life experiences of people and hence, does not amount to plausible educational research. We even hear that a philosophy of higher education only deals with the conceptual and that the practical is seemingly blatantly ignored. Ironically, these criticisms are not too removed from the ones commonly levelled at the academe – reflective of perceptions that despite all the ivory tower chatter, nothing is actually done. There are many layers here – some that speak to erroneous dichotomous constructions between practice and theory; and some that speak to broader life concerns of education – ultimately, posing the question of what is the point of education, if what it does is not immediately realisable, visible, actionable? What, therefore, are the activities of the academic, the academe and, in our case, the philosopher of higher education?

The relative newness of South Africa's democracy has provided it with a particular kind of cushioning, which has allowed it, at times, to hide beneath the covers of not 'yet-knowing' and 'still learning'. Higher education is but one sector that continues to bear the brunt of a broken narrative. Deliberations on academic activism, however, has either been somewhat muted, or has been limited to contestations in relation to academic freedom. This is concerning for multiple reasons. Unless confronted, this narrative will persist, which is why academic activism is so critical to both higher education and democracy. While we draw upon and share the experiences of a South African context, we know that these experiences are not unique to one particular context. Although concerns about poverty and socio-economic disparity might be more pronounced in South Africa than it is in most other liberal democracies, issues of racism, marginalisation and exclusion are ubiquitous to all higher education settings, as are matters of gender-based violence. As such, this book should be as appealing to university management and governance structures and higher education policymakers, as it is to academics, researchers and students from across disciplines.

Our purpose, therefore, for producing this book does not involve only discounting spurious claims or doubts about philosophy of higher education but also to think differently about the discourse and offer some pathways as to how credible philosophy of higher education can be pursued, especially concerning contemporary malaises and dystopias.

In this monograph, firstly, we make an argument for renewed understandings of academic activism, understandings which conceive of the ideas, arguments and scholarship of the academe as embedded within the practices of what the academe does. Secondly, we examine the implications of these renewed understandings for a philosophy of higher education. Concomitant to this departure, we hold the view that higher education is a discourse that engenders practices in specific ways. Such practices of higher education involve teaching, learning, management, governance, research and service to communities outside of the university. Our focus would be on the theory-practices of teaching and learning, in particular how such pedagogical actions are guided by social, political and cultural influences outside of the university as a higher education institution.

By implication, our focus in this book is on curricular and institutional practices as instances of higher education discourse. Implicit in our argument is a view that academic activism ought to guide higher education and its curricular and institutional practices. In turn, we are interested in why and how a renewed notion of academic activism informs a philosophy of higher education specifically in relation to teaching and learning. Surely, it is enough just to get on with the hard practices of teaching, without the added complexities purportedly brought about by a philosophy of higher education and the influences of academic activism. Also, it seems as if the very notion of a philosophy of higher education is inappropriately linked to being too arcane, too technical, especially for academics and practitioners who endeavour to think deeply about their professional work – that is, to rethink their academic activism. As we listen to these oft-repeated questions and assertions, doubting the purpose of what it is we seek to do, we cannot help but notice, with some irony, how these questions serve to confirm the need for a renewed understanding of academic activism and how it might influence a philosophy of higher education. On the one hand, it would seem that questions about the purpose and usefulness of philosophy of higher education arise precisely because there are gaps and emptiness in understanding the complexities and dystopias of the world in which we find ourselves. This means, academic activism, as espoused in this book, is not disconnected from happenings in the metaphysical world, but rather influenced by it.

Likewise, we are often marginalised in an academic environment where a philosophy of higher education is perceived as being a luxury, especially for teachers and administrators, and that there is a disconnect between an academic activist in the first place and the somewhat abstract notion of philosophical thinking. The more these schisms present themselves, the more we are faced with the questions as to the role of academic activism in relation to a philosophy of higher education.

On the other hand, what these questions reveal is an ongoing misunderstanding of philosophy of higher education and its concomitant link with academic activism. It is neither abstract nor unrelated or additional to what teaching and learning require as higher education practices. Instead, a philosophy of higher education is entirely practical and relational – in endeavouring to make sense not only of teaching and learning, but of education in relation to societal, social, communal and global norms and tensions, in particular how such actions impact the notion of academic activism. For now, we enunciate academic activism in relation to the actions of university teachers and students, in particular how these pedagogical agents respond to claims of transformation in higher education settings. Such claims relate to critical academic agency that responds to the public relevance of their curricula offerings; student protestations about their disquiet towards ongoing repressive and discriminatory institutional actions; autonomous (in an enlightened sense) university management that encourages openness and reflexivity in curricula re-imaginings; post-human activism that endeavours to protect the integrity of the digital explosion of knowledge; and university teachers and students that aspire to maintain academic freedom so necessary during turbulent times.

Consider, for example, the global scramble among institutions of higher learning to suddenly transition from traditional contact sites to online nodes of teaching and learning. Not only is higher education confronted with the inherent challenges, which accompany teaching and learning through a digital discourse, but there are broader questions about why higher education, thus far, has persisted with traditional forms of teaching and learning when the world in which we find ourselves has for a long time lent itself to other forms of encounters. The point is, there is a seeming disconnect between academic activism and curricular developments. If not, why would problems persist? Encounters, which have, thus far, retained existing dichotomies of exclusion/inclusion; and allowed self-proclaimed ivy league institutions to maintain its elitism through the insistence of exorbitant tuition fees. In turn, shifts towards a digital discourse brings to the fore other forms of disparities as students find themselves reliant on their own, at times, impoverished private circumstances in trying to digitally meet the requirements of a degree. It also brings into renewed contestation the role and necessity of 'the teacher'. These are the concerns of a philosophy of higher education – it ponders on why it exists and how it unfolds around us, in search of renewed questions and contestations. Put differently, if academic activism is not present in higher education, the possibility that teaching and learning practices would suffer becomes real.

But more importantly, we want to develop an understanding of higher education and its practices in line with a defensible form of academic activism – one that takes seriously the concerns and plights of university teachers and students. We refer to philosophy of higher education as a discourse in a Foucauldian sense by analysing the multiple ways in which knowledge is constituted within social practices in relation to human subjectivity and power relations that underscore such knowledge and the ways it manifests in social practices. By delving into particular theoretical conceptions, we are interested in exploring the practices of how a philosophy of higher education can or should be applied, and most poignantly, if so, how a philosophy of higher education can contribute to enhancing academic activism and social justice education. Conversely, we are also interested in how a renewed understanding of academic activism can bring about reimagined views of higher education practices.

Organisation of the Book

In 10 interrelated chapters, we look at the ways academic activism guides the philosophy of higher education. We are intent upon drawing upon a rich array of prominent philosophers of education – philosophers, who have long espoused their own activism through their writing. We have been both systematic and deliberately provocative in ensuring the inclusion not only of particular theorists but certainly of particular concepts and arguments. To this end, we endeavour to contextualise, deconstruct and reconstruct in line with new considerations and arguments of how a philosophy of higher education might be considered anew in relation to conceptions, practices, tensions and responsibilities of academic activism.

Our encounters with academic activism have been significantly influenced and ruptured by at least three pertinent developments in South African higher education over at least the last three decades: Firstly, our witnessing of and participation in student protests as a way of resisting attempts to undermine a liberatory discourse of education; secondly, as historically marginalised academics intent on dissenting against pedagogical exclusion in the higher education sector; and thirdly, as social change agents who use community platforms to espouse more substantive forms of human living commensurable with an education for socio-political justice. Academics, who work in the extraordinary and privileged environment of a university, make their living through acts of expositing, pronouncing and justifying – actions that have a bearing on what it means to be human. In a neo-Aristotelian fashion, academics are those diligent human beings who are fortunate to work in a university context where the pursuit of knowledge for its own sake has remained their private and public interest for some while now. Coupling the practice of activism with the epistemological labour of academics is a very courageous reminder that academics are neither complacent nor only occupied with the pursuit of knowledge for its own sake. Instead, they are influenced by and are responsive to the world in which they find themselves; they are prepared to disrupt taken-for-granted understandings and show an openness to re-conceive and reconsider their perspectives and engagements with their contexts and those around them.

Chapter 1, therefore, commences with an awareness of the complexities that underlie the landscape and language of academic activism. We explore some philosophical reflection on the notion of academic activism, as espoused through our human experiences, as academics, in relation to the practice of encounters. Concurrently, we show how these practices of academic activism connect with a philosophical paradigm of interpretivism that gives activism its rigorous potency. Thereafter, we show how the notion of the philosophy of higher education should be reconsidered in line with a more tenable understanding of academic activism.

Remaining with the interpretivist paradigm, established in Chap. 1, we turn to Seyla Benhabib's theory of critique in Chap. 2. Standing in the traditions of Kant and Habermas, Benhabib (1986) articulates an understanding of critique, which makes a necessary connection between rationality and autonomy. That is, any form of analysis of the social world is an act of philosophy (of higher education) and that such an analysis is dependent upon 'its commitment to the dignity and autonomy of the rational subject' (Benhabib, 1986: 15). Using this understanding as our foundation, we are specifically interested in how a critical-social educational theory can most appropriately advance human existence. To this end, we draw on Seyla Benhabib's (1986) re-articulation of Jürgen Habermas's notion of critique to ascertain how the practice of academic activism ought to be amended. According to Benhabib (1986), Habermas's theory of communicative action is a justifiable form of critique as it re-establishes the relation between self-reflection and autonomy; and it explains autonomy in communicative terms – that is, autonomy is not synonymous with self-legislation or self-actualisation or mimesis, but rather 'the cognitive competence to adopt to a universalist standpoint and the interactive competence to act on such a basis' (Benhabib, 1986: 282). In relation to the notions of self-reflective autonomy and communicative autonomy, we examine what a philosophy of higher education looks like and what the implications of such a form of critique hold for academic activism.

Following on Benhabib's re-articulation of critique, the focus in Chap. 3 is on Michel Foucault (1994) who brought to our attention that any form of critique is important for philosophy (of higher education) because it not only exposes us to philosophical problems about our world but more importantly, it tries to liberate the individual from the 'struggles that question the status of the individual' (1994: 330). For Foucault (1994), on the one hand, the struggle for individuals to assert their right to be different is a legitimate struggle that requires investigation. On the other hand, struggles against individuals are such that 'they attack everything that separates in the individual, breaks his [her] links with others, splits up community life, forces the individual back on himself [herself] and ties him [her] to his [her] own identity in a constraining way' (Foucault, 1994: 330). In this way, Foucault urges us to turn to the subjectivity of the individual again as the struggles reflect an opposition to the effects of power linked with knowledge, competence and qualification – struggles against the privileges of knowledge (Foucault, 1994). By paying particular attention to his conceptions and arguments on power, knowledge, freedom and resistance, we argue that academic activism in the context of a Foucauldian view of the subjectivity of an individual is constituted by at least the following: that individuals are situated in genuine relations of power; that individuals act upon the actions of others; and that individuals' relations of power are constituted by the possibility for agonistic incitement and struggle.

Pulling together the preceding focus on critique and human subjectivity, Chap. 4 turns to the ideas of French philosopher, Jacques Derrida. Derrida (1995) reminds us that critical work in philosophy (and philosophy of higher education) cannot ignore the possibility that any attempt at articulating critique as a foundational discipline would in itself undermine the credentials of such a philosophy to be critical (Derrida, 1995). In other words, critique cannot escape the very limitations, which it seeks to delimit. The mere possibility of critique opens itself up to the possibility of not being emancipatory and self-empowering as there is nothing pure and infallible about treating ways of seeing the world as foundations that can remedy fractured situations. Put differently, following Derrida (1995) it is not enough just to be critical from the inside, but critical agents are also required to act justly towards what lies beyond – that is, to those unforeseen possibilities that cannot be seen in advance as a possibility (Derrida, 1995). What this implies is that when individuals (academics) embark on critique, they reflect on the subjectivities of individuals and evaluate the actions of others in the context of how they view the world. Yet, when individuals are self-reflexive, they still offer reasons and justifications in light of what they consider to be constitutive of emancipatory action itself – that is, they remain critical. Individuals barely look at what lies beyond their actions of critique, which in itself can be a crisis for critique.

In this chapter, we shall look at what drives the critical work of deconstruction in defence of 'the relentless pursuit of the impossible, which means, of things whose possibility is sustained by their impossibility' (Caputo, 1997: 32) concerning what academic activists can do about what lies beyond them and is not immediately apparent. We contend that conceptions of academic responsibility are tied up in relational encounters with texts (reading and writing), as well as teaching and research. As such, academic responsibility cannot be remiss of its potential to cause harm, as in the perpetuation of social injustices. Instead, academic activism as a responsible endeavour centres on giving back and is focused on ensuring beneficial forms of engagement with students, communities, or society. This, we maintain, cultivates a re-conscientisation of the university.

Retaining our reflections on a philosophy of higher education as a discourse for the advancement of academic activism, the attention of Chap. 5 is on another French philosopher, Jacques Rancière. In *Chronicles of Consensual Times* (2010), Rancière invites us to ponder on a 'living philosophy' as a response to 'the consensus governing us … intent upon getting us to believe that 'what is, is all that is' (Rancière, 2010a: viii). What a living philosophy does is to contrast the real experiences of people on earth with their idealised (fictitious) lives in the sky, and then returns by leaving the imaginary position in which people find themselves and are happy to rejoin the reality of their familiar earth-like experiences of perhaps racism, torture and violence. To him, a 'living philosophy' involves a consciousness and a commitment to confronting that which seeks to control how we see and interact with our world; it teaches us 'to take good care of our self and how to live life harmoniously in the everyday' (Rancière, 2010a: viii). We argue that when we apply a living philosophy to stimulate academic activism, we think of encouraging academics to think of how their research – in relation to teaching and scholarship – can stimulate fictitious imaginaries of a society in which people engage in iterations and the free exchange of provocative ideas. Such a society might even be an imaginative one where people live in harmony despite their differences that seem to be irreconcilable. People might even renounce antagonism and encourage the free integration of pluralist ideas of a common humanity. And, when such a living philosophy draws people back to their real experiences, it would contrast life in the idealised world with the perilous societal malaises of hostility, torture and continuous violence

We thought it apt to follow Ranciere's spirited argument for a 'living philosophy' with another impassioned call – Hannah Arendt's (1963) *On Revolution*. Our attraction to Arendt is not so much that we are equating academic activism with the occurrence of a revolution but rather that the spirit of activism cannot ignore a revolutionary spirit. Based on Arendt's (1963) bold analysis of the term 'revolution', we examine what makes such an action what it is and how academic activism can gain a revolutionary drive in the sense of establishing new beginnings in higher education discourse. Thus, we analyse the notion of revolution, in particular how the spirit of a revolution can arouse in academics an activism that embraces irresistibility and novelty (Arendt, 1963).

We are specifically interested in the notion of revolution concerning practices of freedom, equality and novelty – that is, academic activism as 'perplexities of new beginnings' (Arendt, 1963: 208). Despite higher education suggesting a space where people might openly share and express their ideas without hesitancy and fear, we cannot assume that all universities provide open spaces for speech and disagreement, and we cannot assume that all people (academics, students, administrators) participate in this space equally, or, at all. The very pluralism of the public sphere means an array of diverse and conflicting views. It would seem, therefore, that if academic activism were to be revolutionary, it cannot happen without aspiring to make the university a place where freedom holds sway. To think of academic activism as a revolutionary path towards what might be possible, we contend, is to remain open to surprise and strangeness. Conversely, to be open to the unexpected and the strange is to be concerned about what can yet unfold so that higher education institutions should remain open to adapt and respond to ongoing transformations.

Intrigued by Arendt's (1963) deliberations on freedom and equality, we are compelled to take cognisance not only of the phenomenal body of scholarship produced by Paulo Freire, but are reminded by his very embodiment of activism. Although difficult to limit ourselves, our interest in Chap. 7 pertains to the reading of three of Freire's major works, namely *Pedagogy of the Oppressed* (Freire, 1984), *Pedagogy of Freedom* (Freire, 1998a) and *Pedagogy of Hope* (Freire, 2004). One of the world's most celebrated education scholars, Freire did much to advance a critical perspective on (higher) education along the lines of democracy, freedom and liberation. He held that because of the different identities, histories, perspectives and struggles humans bring to the world, it, and hence, humans, is continually changing. Likewise, students and academics are part of the world; their lives unfold in relation to the world. They have certain needs, insecurities, vulnerabilities, fears, beliefs and hopes that live inside of them and cannot be separated from the world. They have to be made aware of human suffering, which too often is viewed from a distance and not seen as a concern of the student's world.

University education cannot be used as means of and for insulated thinking and being; instead, it has to awaken students and academics alike to their interconnectedness, and hence, collective responsibility, to ensure a pursuit of freedom from all manners of oppression. In this chapter, we endeavour to re-read Freire in a post-critical way and to offer some view on how a Freirean notion of courage impacts our thinking of philosophy of higher education and our concern with academic activism. What is important for our own post-critical analysis of Freire's seminal thoughts, is that education is a courageous act in the sense of being open to the world and others; a risk of what is new; and an awareness of our unfinishedness (Freire, 1998a). We follow this with an analysis of Freire's (1994) conceptualisation of critical consciousness or conscientisation as a form of activist representational politics. Here, we pay careful attention to Freire's (1993) articulation of a sensual body, which cannot be disconnected from teaching, learning and, hence, freedom. In this regard, we reflect on the body as a choreographed form of protest and activism. We conclude by arguing that although activism presents itself as forms of resistance and antagonism, the very pursuit to act against that which is oppressive and harmful, is in itself an act of love for humanity and justice.

Our decision to follow a chapter, which leans on and learns from Freire, with one that draws to Judith Butler, resides in their shared exposition of the body as a representational form of activism. Furthermore, our interest in Butler in Chap. 8 emanates from two intertwined reasons: her standing and reformulation of philosophy through a feminist lens and her tireless commitment and activism in ensuring that her writing is made visible in our world. Like so many other scholars, that we have thus far drawn and expanded upon in this book, Butler's work symbolises the kinds of activism university education can no longer do without. This chapter has two points of interest. Firstly, we pay attention to Butler's (1993) contention that 'bodies matter', and specifically, that while certain bodies enjoy legitimacy and value, others do not, and are instead (re)produced as objects. The idea that bodies signify a world beyond themselves, holds particular implications for university spaces and education.

Secondly, we turn to her conversation with Facundo Giuliani (2015), in which Butler offers some remarks about the university and its relationship with philosophy of education. We continue by highlighting some of her main pronouncements about the university and offer some ways to think differently about philosophy of higher education and academic activism. Thereafter, we consider three ways in which the idea of a university of critique intertwined with notions of non-mastery and 'error-living' education might be possible. Firstly, an open and speculative university should cultivate forms of education where making mistakes is considered not only as routine *to* learning, but as a necessary process *for* learning. Secondly, a university grounded in academic freedom is not only pertinent for free, critical and engagement which is unafraid but can play a pivotal role in calling into question existing norms and hegemonies, policies, as well as political structures and discourses. It opens up the possibility of free and critical thought, including intellectual positions. And thirdly, dissent is critical not only as a recognition of alternative or controversial views, but for the very cultivation of academic activism.

As we reach the concluding chapters of this book, we are obligated to pull together and synergise some of the main points, which have thus far been proffered. After covering what we believe is immense and profound theoretical exposition and debates, it becomes necessary to consider academic activism as a form of knowledge production. For this discussion, we turn to Jean-Francois Lyotard's (1979) influential book, *The Postmodern Condition*, which had an enduring effect on the understanding of knowledge in the contemporary world. To Lyotard (1979), knowledge cannot just be subjected to criteria of truth, validity and those of efficiency. Knowledge, he asserts, is also composed in the narratives, opinions, customs, ideologies and myths of humans. To this end, knowledge is also 'embodied in a subject' (Lyotard, 1979: 27). Our decision to focus on Lyotard's seminal ideas in this chapter stems, on the one hand, from his contention that science is obliged to produce 'a discourse of legitimation with respect to its own status, a discourse called philosophy' (1979: xxiii).

On the other hand, we are drawn to some of his main claims about knowledge, performativity and managerialism and how a philosophy of higher education and academic activism in universities could be reconsidered. Lyotard (1979) accentuates the argument in defence of a speculative university by insisting that scientific knowledge should be intertwined with narrative knowledge that will actualise learning possibilities for humanity. In reflecting on higher education in South Africa, we raise concerns about its explicit preoccupations with massification and performativity without due cognisance of the risks of student alienation and a neglect of a responsibility to social justice. The attention seems to be only on graduate production, with scant consideration of the kinds of students being passed through a system. We raise similar concerns about slippages into practices of functionalist technical training, as opposed to immersing students into thinking about what they know so that they might reimagine how things might be otherwise.

We are attracted to Giorgio Agamben's (2012) thoughts and expositions on the Muselmann for various reasons – not only because it offers glimpses into the parallel condition of inhumanity and humanity, but because it provides profound reflections on conceptions of shame, stigma, testimony and responsibility. As our concluding chapter, we take the opportunity to reflect on the kinds of stigma and shame that students and academics can and do experience in higher education – from experiences of discrimination and marginalisation to violence. As troubling as these might sound, higher education has always been a convergence of hope and academic performance, on the one side, coupled with the struggles and tensions created by issues of race, ethnicity, culture, religion and gender, on the other side. It is important, therefore, to take stock of the potential experiences of stigmatisation and shame. Immediately, however, it is equally important to ask who bears testimony to and takes responsibility for the shame and stigma as symbolised through Agamben's (2012) Muselmann?

To us, this is the role of academic activism – the act of bearing witness or testimony resides in a preparedness to do so on behalf of others. To bear testimony, we argue, is to make manifest our humanity and our activism. Academic activism, therefore, does not exist separate to who we are as academics; academic activism resides in our very being. To be an academic activist means to act when we witness shame and stigma; it means to speak out when others will not; and it means to assume responsibility for the 'zones of non-responsibility' (Agamben, 2012: 21) that perpetuate the experiences of higher education.

In concluding, the arguments of this book have fundamentally and predominantly focused on the imperatives and possibilities of academic activism; we have engaged extensively on the role and responsibility of the academic as an individual with autonomous, independent, curious and critical agency. In turn, we have consistently referenced the university as an engaging and rigorous space, unafraid of bold speech and disruptive thought, always pushing and moving beyond that which presents itself, always looking outward, while framed and immersed in a language of autonomous critique and interrogation. Yet, even within our own South African context – a relatively young and eager democracy – we are not remiss of increasing hiccups and impediments as universities strain to detach themselves from infringing threats on their autonomy and academic freedom. We are also aware of the inseparable impact of political tractions on the capacity of universities to stay the course on not implementing its academic programmes, but in sustaining their roles as critical custodians of democracy. We can only assume, as we cast our eyes over other contexts, that higher education in South Africa is not unique in its pressures and struggles, and we can only imagine the additional burdens, constraints, frustrations and fears in contexts, where democracy does not hold sway.

There are necessary questions, therefore, whether academics are indeed capable of fulfilling the kinds of role we have discussed, advanced and advocated for in this book. On the one hand, even when academics are able to play active roles in the public sphere, they might choose not to participate in these; they might opt not to adopt a role of activism. In other words, even with the capacity to do so, academics might decide to impose self-censorship instead. On the other hand, capability does not only pertain to intellect and voice, but to how academics conceive of themselves in relation to their institutions, how they position themselves to their broader political and social contexts. Concomitantly, capability is equally reliant on how universities and broader political contexts conceive of role and responsibilities of academics – that is, the extent to which academics are allowed to adopt positions and articulations of critique. Certainly, as we have touched on in the preface to this book, the risks for academics in certain contexts, are immensely more problematic than not being promoted, or dismissed. At risk are their safety, their livelihood and their lives.

As a continued manifestation of our own activism, we thought it apposite, therefore to include a coda which looks specifically at the possibility of the Muslim university cultivating resistance and dissent through its educational agenda. We argue that such a possibility is perhaps premature considering that autocracy and a reluctance to implement a genuine non-dichotomous view of knowledge seem to work against what it means to be an institution that is reflexive and open. In this way, academic activism might still be an elusive practice at a Muslim university. In response, and in recognising the criticality of cultivating academic activism within Muslim spaces of higher education, we argue for the importance of a pedagogy of resistance and dissent that could enhance the intellectualism so needed in the Muslim university; a willingness to respond to broader social malaises as a fulfilment of education as a human responsibility; an integration with the broader educational aspirations of the democratic state; and a preparedness to being reflectively open to new considerations and fusions of knowledge.

Cape Town, South Africa   Nuraan Davids

Cape Town, South Africa   Yusef Waghid

References

Acar, Y. G. & Canan, C. (2020). Academic activism and its impact on individual level mobilization, sources of learning, and the future of academia in Turkey. *Journal of Community & Applied Social Psychology, 30*, 388–404.

Agamben, G. (2012). *Remnants of Auschwitz: The Witness and the Archive* (D. Heller-Roazen, Trans.). Brooklyn, NY: Zone Books.

Akalu, G. A. (2016). Higher education 'massification' and challenges to the professoriate: Do academics' conceptions of quality matter? *Quality in Higher Education, 22*(3), 260–276.

Arendt, H. (1963). *On revolution.* London: Penguin Books.

Astor, M. (2018). *7 Times in history when students turned to activism.* https://www.nytimes.com/2018/03/05/us/student-protest-movements.html. Accessed 24 Oct 2020.

Badat, S. (2010). *The challenges of transformation in higher education and training institutions in South Africa.* Paper commissioned by the Development Bank of Southern Africa. https://www.ru.ac.za/.../The%20Challenges%20of%20Transformation%20in%20High. Accessed 5 Apr 2020.

Badat, S. (2016). *Deciphering the meanings, and explaining the South African higher education student protests of 2015–16.* https://wiser.wits.ac.za/system/files/documents/Saleem%20Badat%20-%20Deciphering%20the%20Meanings%2C%20and%20Explaining%20the%20South%20African%20Higher%20Education%20Student%20Protests.pdf. Accessed 5 Apr 2020.

Barnett, R. (2016). *Understanding the university: Institution, idea, possibilities.* London: Routledge.

Benhabib, S. (1986). *Critique, norm and utopia: A study of the foundations of critical theory.* New York: Columbia University Press.

Butler, J. (1993). *Bodies that matter: On the discursive limits of sex.* New York: Routledge.

Caputo, J.D. (Ed.) (1997). *Deconstruction in a Nutshell: A Conversation with Jacques Derrida.* New York: Fordham University Press.

Case, J., Marshall, D., & Grayson D. (2013). Mind the gap: Science and engineering education at the secondary–tertiary interface. *South African Journal of Science, 109*(7/8), 1–5.

Case, J.M, Marshall, D., McKenna, S. & Mogashana, D. (2018). *Going to university: The influence of higher education on the lives of young South Africans.* Cape Town, South Africa: African Minds.

Chomsky, N. (1967, February 23). The responsibility of intellectuals. *The New York Review of Books.* https://chomsky.info/19670223/ Accessed 4 Apr 2020.

Cloete, N. (2016). *Free higher education: Another self-destructive policy.* Paper published by the Centre for Higher Education Trust (CHET).

Council on Higher Education (2013). *A proposal for undergraduate curriculum reform in South Africa: The case for a flexible curriculum structure.* Pretoria, South Africa: Council on Higher Education.

Davids, N. (2019, September). The consequences of increasing student alienation in higher education institutions, Council on Higher Education (CHE). *BrieflySpeaking,* No. 9.

Derrida, J. (1995). *Points ... Interviews, 1974–1994* (P. Kamuf et al., Trans.). Stanford, CA: Stanford University Press.

Department of Education (DoE). (1997). *Education White Paper No. 3: A programme on the transformation of higher education transformation.* Pretoria, South Africa: Government Printers.

Republic of South Africa. (1989). *Education act.* Wellington: New Zealand: Government Printer.

Foucault, M. (1994). *Power: Essential works of Foucault 1954–1984 – Volume 3* (J. D. Faubion, Ed.). London: Penguin Books.

Franklin, V. P. (2003). Patterns of student activism at historically black universities in the United States and South Africa, 1960–1977. *The Journal of African American History, 88*(2), 204–217.

Freire, P. (1984). *Pedagogy of the oppressed.* New York: Continuum.

Freire, P. (1998). *Pedagogy of freedom: Ethics, democracy, and courage.* Lanham, MD/Boulder, CO/New York/Oxford, UK: Rowman & Littlefield.

Freire, P. (2004). *Pedagogy of hope.* New York: Continuum.

Giuliano, F. (2015). (Re)thinking education with Judith Butler: A necessary meeting between philosophy and education (interview with Judith Butler). *Encounters in Theory and History of Education, 16*(3), 183–199.

Grey, S. J. (2013). Activist academics: what future? *Policy Futures in Education, 11*(6), 700–711.

Grimm, J. (2018). *Authoritarian Middle East regimes don't like academics – Ask Matthew Hedges*. https://www.opendemocracy.net/en/policing-research-shifting-tides-for-middle-east-studies-after-arab-spring/. Accessed 7 Apr 2020.

Higher Education South Africa (HESA). (2014, March 5). *South African higher education in the 20th year of democracy: Context, achievements and key challenges*. HESA presentation to the Portfolio Committee on higher education and training in Parliament, Cape Town. http://www.hesa.org.za/hesa-presentation-portfolio-committee-higher-education-and-training. Accessed 6 Apr 2020.

Hlengwa, A., McKenna, S. & Njovane, T. (2018). The lenses we use to research student experiences. In P. Ashwin, & J.M. Case, (Eds.), *Higher Education Pathways: South African undergraduate education and the public good* (pp. 149–162). Cape Town, South Africa: African Minds.

Hornsby, D. J., & Osman, R. (2014). Massification in higher education: Large classes and student learning. *Higher Education, 67*(6), 711–719.

Lyotard, J.F. (1979). *The postmodern condition: A report on knowledge* (G. Bennington & B. Massumi, Trans.). Manchester, UK: Manchester University Press.

Mannheim, K. (1991). *Ideology and utopia*. London: Routledge.

Mannheim, K. (1992). The problem of the intelligentsia, An enquiry into its past and present role. In Turner, B.S. (Ed.), *Essays on the sociology of culture* (pp. 91–170). New York: Routledge.

Marginson, S. (2016). The worldwide trend to high participation higher education: Dynamics of social stratification in inclusive systems, *Higher Education, 72*(4), 413–434.

Mohamedbhai, G. (2008). *The effects of massification on higher education in Africa*. Accra: Association of African Universities.

Ng'ethe, N., Subotzky, G., Afeti, G. (2008). *Differentiation and articulation in tertiary education systems: A study of twelve African countries* (World Bank, Paper No. 145). Washington, DC: The World Bank.

Olsen, Johan P. (2005) *The institutional dynamics of the (European) university* (Working Paper). Oslo, Norway: Centre for European Studies.

Rancière, J. (2010). *Chronicles of Consensual Times* (S. Corcoran, Trans.). London: Continuum.

Said, E. (1993). *Representations of the intellectual*. London: Wintage.

Tinto, V. (2003, November 5–7). *Promoting student retention through classroom practice*. Presented at Enhancing Student Retention: Using International Policy and Practice. Staffordshire University.

Tören, T., & Kutun, M. (2018). "Peace Academics" from Turkey: Solidarity until the Peace Comes. *Global Labour Journal, 9*(1), 103–112.

Contents

About the Authors

Nuraan Davids is a professor of philosophy of education in the Department of Education Policy Studies, Stellenbosch University. Her research interests include democratic citizenship education, Islamic philosophy of education and philosophy in higher education. She is the co-editor-in-chief of the *Journal of Education in Muslim Societies*, an associate editor of the *South African Journal of Higher Education* and an editorial board member of *Ethics and Education*. She is a CASBS fellow at Stanford University (2020–2021).

Yusef Waghid holds doctorates in education, policy and philosophy from the University of the Western Cape and Stellenbosch University in South Africa, respectively, and is among Africa's leading philosophers of education today. As a distinguished professor at Stellenbosch University, he has been a prolific author with 380 publications to date of which 43 are academic books and 73 invited contributions to books. His commitment to the advancement of doctoral education including having promoted 31 candidates to completion and examined 78 doctorates culminated in having been honoured by the Association for the Development of Education in Africa in 2015 as a worthy recipient of the prestigious Education Research in Africa Award: Outstanding Mentor of Education Researchers. In recognition of his scholarly works and having published in many of the leading journals in his field, the National Research Foundation in South Africa rated him as an internationally acclaimed scholar who provides exemplary leadership in advancing philosophy of higher education in Africa. He was honoured with the editorships of two prominent academic journals, namely *Citizenship, Teaching and Learning* (since 2018) and *South African Journal of Higher Education* (since 2005) through which he meritoriously supports scholars to publish their seminal works. From 2020 to 2021, he collaborated with renowned international scholars on a leading UNESCO pioneered research project, Education for Flourishing and Flourishing in Education, initiated by the Mahatma Gandhi Institute of Education for Peace and Sustainable Development. His advancement of higher education in Africa is also acknowledged by the Council of Higher Education in South Africa, where he has been a board member since 2019.

Chapter 1
Philosophy of Higher Education and Interpretivism

Abstract This chapter looks at the complexities that underlie the landscape and language of academic activism. While widely understood as a feature of higher education, there is seemingly little consensus of what academic activism implies as lived endeavours, expressions and experiences for academics, as well as management and governance structures. It is, therefore, unsurprising to find that despite understanding the theoretical importance of the role of higher education in actively pursuing and espousing new forms of knowledge, reasoning and judgement, there is disagreement not only on whom and what embodies activism but certainly on whose responsibility it is and what, if any, its parameters are. We explore some philosophical reflections on the notion of academic activism, as espoused through our human experiences, as academics, in relation to the practice of encounters. Concurrently we show how these practices of academic activism connect with a philosophical paradigm of interpretivism that gives activism its rigorous potency. Thereafter, we show how the notion of philosophy of higher education should be reconsidered in line with a more tenable understanding of academic activism.

Keywords Academic freedom · Dissent · Rupturing · Scepticism · Agency

Introduction

We commence this book with an awareness of the complexities that underlie the landscape and language of academic activism. While widely understood as a feature of higher education, there is seemingly little consensus of what academic activism implies as lived endeavours, expressions and experiences for academics, as well as management and governance structures. It is, therefore, unsurprising to find that despite understanding the theoretical importance of the role of higher education in actively pursuing and espousing new forms of knowledge, reasoning and judgement, there is disagreement not only on whom and what embodies activism but certainly on whose responsibility it is and what, if any, its parameters are. In our own political and university contexts, notions of activism are often seeped in historical discourses of protest and resistance, but not necessarily conceived as implicit to

N. Davids, Y. Waghid, *Academic Activism in Higher Education*, Debating
Higher Education: Philosophical Perspectives 5,
https://doi.org/10.1007/978-981-16-0340-2_1

the academia. In taking account of this disparate landscape, we explore some philosophical reflection on the notion of academic activism, as espoused through our human experiences, as academics, in relation to the practice of encounters. Concurrently we show how these practices of academic activism connect with a philosophical paradigm of interpretivism that gives activism its rigorous potency. Thereafter, we show how the notion of philosophy of higher education should be reconsidered in line with a more tenable understanding of academic activism.

Conceiving Academic Activism

Depending on whom one speaks to, the concept of academic activism evokes very different responses. Those who view the academy as somewhat disconnected from society might not necessarily associate the work of academics as a form of activism. A similar view might be shared by those who assign themselves the role of activists – often framed in relation to this or that cause or movement – from animal rights to human rights activists. The implicit question here would be: what makes the work of academic activism? West (1991), for instance, refers to four models of 'intellectual vocation': the oppositional professional intellectual, who uses his or her teaching, writing and research as forms of critique; the establishment of critical groupings or communities of practice within the academy; the professional political intellectual, as engaging directly in civic discourse and public debate; and the intellectual as a critical organic catalyst – one who is perennially attuned to the university within society. Others like Flood, Martin and Dreher (2013: 17) identify four ways in which the academy can be a site for activism: as a means to produce knowledge to inform progressive social change; as a means for conducting research, which itself involves social change; as a site for progressive strategies of teaching and learning; and as an institution whose power relations themselves may be challenged and reconstructed.

   We also know that while ideas of activism are often most easily associated with images and definitions of active protesting and campaigning, activism can also easily adopt forms of muted resistance and retreats – such as silent sit-ins or hunger strikes. In South Africa, activism emanates from waves of relentless resistance against an oppressive apartheid regime, which have often descended into debilitating forces of violence. Universities, in particular, serve as volatile seedbeds for these protests. Neither the volatility of the protests nor the role of the university has abated. Persisting into South Africa's democracy are intersectional collisions between massification, poor academic performance, student debt, high levels of student attrition, exclusion and alienation from dominant institutional cultures as well as educational leadership and democracy (Davids & Waghid, 2020). Flowing from this, therefore, not only do notions of activism and the academy differ concerning whom one speaks to, but they shift in relation to the contexts in which they unfold.

   Maxey (1999: 201), for example, asserts that 'the social world is produced through the acts each of us engages in every day. Everything we do, every thought we have, contributes to the production of the social world'. Teaching, for example, is a relational practice, reliant on human engagement, deliberation as well as debate. Teaching, says Hytten (2017: 387), 'is a form of activism when we ask students to think critically about the world: to unpack their assumptions, to consider alternative viewpoints, to dismantle problematic beliefs, to make careful arguments, and to defend their perspectives'. In order to act on the world, and to be thoughtful democratic citizens, she continues, 'we need to understand how the world operates, which includes the relationships between power, privilege, and knowledge' (Hytten, 2017: 387).

Teaching, therefore, is not simply the sharing and transmission of knowledge; teaching ought to pivot around ensuring that students become critically aware of the world around them and why they hold the views which they do and to act when they witness or encounter any forms of injustice. Teaching has to be preceded by a curiosity to know and a willingness to reflect upon what is already known. Furthermore, if teaching is understood as a relational practice to learning, which takes into account student identities, voices and circumstances, then teaching necessarily leads to the opening and asking of more questions. Teaching, states Griffiths (2013: 221), is not only 'embodied, played out in specific social–cultural contexts', but it is 'changing over the course of a career for reasons beyond the control of any teacher'. Teaching, therefore, like learning, is highly fluid practices, continually shifting in response to the world in which it unfolds.

As teachers of philosophy of education, we are aware, on the one hand, of students' hesitant relationship with our discipline. Students often question the necessity or importance of a philosophy of education, mistakenly thinking that all they need in order to teach is content and pedagogical knowledge of their own specialist subjects. On the other hand, we are especially attuned to the dire need of a philosophical approach and meaning making to teaching and education. We recognise therefore that part of instilling a consciousness into students as why they teach, who they teach and how they teach relies profoundly on what and who we bring into our own teaching. At times this is not an easy endeavour. Our own identities as academics and the roads we have, respectively, travelled in teaching and working at a historically advantaged (white) university are often at odds with the kinds of ideologies presented by students. This forces us into a continuous critical reflection not only of our teaching but of what we bring to our teaching.

In turn, student supervision is a dialogical encounter that requires both the supervisor and the student to give of themselves in terms of intellectual exchange and emotional support – each taking their cue from the other. Previously, we argued that the value of the doctoral encounter, in particular, has the capacity to shift both the supervisor and the student. Inasmuch as the student enters the doctoral journey with particular ideas, which can be transformed dramatically through the writing process, so too, the supervisor (or academic) is often left having to rethink initially held opinions and arguments (Davids & Waghid, 2019a). Student supervision ought to transcend technical hegemony by merely looking at what a text supposedly presents in terms of sentence construction without paying much attention to the epistemological acuteness of students' work. Critique ought to become a necessary practice in supervision so that students produce work, which radically opposes and ruptures undemocratic pasts and parochial self-interests.

Moreover, the pursuit of postgraduate studies should not be limited to the attainment to a qualification. There are ethical responsibilities students ought to be made aware of – responsibilities that extend beyond ethical compliance in terms of conducting research. In this sense, we conceive our postgraduate studies as an extended journey of both conscientiousness, but also consciousness of the knowledge being pursued but, more importantly, of the individual taking shape. In embarking on postgraduate studies, students have to take note of their own agency and responsibility concerning their research and the society in which they find themselves. Educational institutions and societies will remain unjust if they fail 'to reflect or exhibit a lack of appropriate emphatic concern' (Slote, 2007: 95).

Likewise, research is wholly dependent on a willingness by participants to engage with the researcher and to allow the researcher into their ideas, perspectives, lived experiences, observations and practices – particularly in the social sciences. Research is about the establishment and cultivation of that which is yet to be known; it is underscored by a specific curiosity and interest in a particular matter, event or being. It is the desire to know that which motivates both the researcher and the research(ed). And the more the researcher reads, analyses, interprets and delves, the more appealing and rich the research(ed) become. It is in this way that the researcher enters into a philosophy of dialogue with the research and all it encompasses, whether in the form of scientific data, a phenomenon or a human being. The research becomes the experience itself through which the whole is understood. Through the research that which is being researched is given a voice; it is awakened out of its silence and made known through its own voice. While research often departs from preconceived assumptions and hypotheses, research often serves to bring those assumptions into question, yielding unimagined knowledge (Davids & Waghid, 2018). In sum, educational engagement is shaped and dependent on forms of human engagement, whether directly or through observation. The work of the academy has neither a basis nor a purpose without that of human agency and encounter.

To speak about the academy or about activism as if these concepts hold the same implications in all contexts would indicate a neglect of the complexities that reside within each of these concepts. Not only are both concepts (activism and the academy) seeped in deep political, social, civil and economic discourses, but how they respond or fit into these discourses are often determined by the relationship between universities and the state. While some universities co-exist in mutually beneficial relationships with the state and are understood as fulfilling a critical role epistemologically, economically, socially and politically, other universities might find themselves in antagonistic relationships with the state for varying political reasons. As such, what might be taken for granted in one context might be conceived as a risk in another. Constraints and restrictions on academic freedom, for example, can adopt different forms and can, at times, be wholly out of sync with the principles expected from liberal democracies. As noted by Flood et al. (2013: 18), academics who engage in activism may face reprisals, both externally from political opponents and internally from those within the university who perceive their involvement as nonconformist.

In the aftermath of the 'Arab Spring', the façade of condoning critical scholarship in most of the Middle Eastern regimes came to an abrupt halt. Grimm (2018) explains that in most of the countries – Tunisia, Egypt, Syria, Libya, Yemen and Bahrain – that had been disrupted by the 'Arab Spring' in 2011, research on opposition parties, critical civil society, social movements and union became off-limits. In attempts to reclaim and restore their autocratic rule, some countries such as Bahrain, Egypt, the Maghreb, the Gulf States and Turkey, in recognising the disseminating and agitating role of academic communities, deliberately targeted academics (Grimm, 2018). Middle Eastern researchers, states Grimm (2018), routinely suffer from repression by state authorities in the form of intimidation, travel bans or imprisonment on trumped-up charges; others face denial of entry into specific countries. The watchful eye of Arab security services has meant an avoidance by many Middle Eastern academics of intellectual hubs, such as Berlin and London. Grimm (2018) reports that in 2016/2017, the UK-based *Council for At-Risk Academics* recorded the highest demand for external support for academics since the forced exodus of scholars from Nazi-occupied Europe in the 1930s – most of them coming from the Middle East and the surrounding region.

Similar patterns of academic infringement and a 'growing top-down' backlash are evident in Hong Kong (Sharma, 2018). Since the 2014–2015 student-led Umbrella Movement protests, authorities have been intent on trying to limit academic freedom and bring academia under their control. As a result, some pro-democracy academic figures have been removed from their posts, seen promotions blocked or faced extra-legal campaigns to pressure their removal; recruiting or promoting academics with pro-establishment views; and placing arbitrary limits on freedom of speech by declaring certain types of speech 'illegal' (Sharma, 2018). Moreover, reports Sharma (2018), 'state-appointed and politically connected figures have governed universities in a manner divorced from the will of students and faculty'.

Elsewhere in the USA, President Donald Trump signed an executive order protecting freedom of speech on college campuses in March 2019. Surrounded by student activists, Trump said he was taking 'historic action to defend American students and American values that have been under siege' (Svrluga, 2018). While proponents welcomed the executive order against 'fostering an unbalanced, liberal indoctrination of students', others argued that 'freedom of inquiry is a fundamental tenet of higher education, one the government should not be defining' (Svrluga, 2018). The order makes federal funding for universities contingent on assurances of free speech, but it also prompted questions, including who would define and judge free speech and what type of federal funding could be withheld – research dollars, student aid or both (Svrluga, 2018)?

As we proceed with this chapter, we conceive of academic activism as forms of reasoned human agency or actions; encounters, which if couched within the university, should be unconstrained. This understanding takes us to our initial consideration of academic activism as an expression of academic freedom.

Academic Activism as Academic Freedom

In principle, academic freedom infers that both members of staff and students at universities have the right to engage in intellectual engagement and debate, without fear of censorship. As an expression of truth in terms of how an individual might see and experience the world, academic freedom is both a preservation and symbol of intellectual autonomy. With this understanding in mind, it would be reasonable to consider academic freedom as ubiquitous to the life of a university. Notions of the university have long been embedded in matters of inquiry, as being in pursuit of truth, intent upon argumentation, reason and logic – as both a moral responsibility and responsiveness. In the university, says Derrida (2005: 253), 'nothing is beyond question, not even the current and determined figure of democracy, and not even the traditional idea of critique'.

The role of the university, therefore, is to cultivate a culture of questioning and resistance, aimed at ideologies, institutions and social practices (Giroux, 2007: 71). As succinctly expressed by Malik (2015), the university is a space for students to explore new ideas, to expand their knowledge, to interrogate power, to learn how to make an argument, to be shocked and made angry and to accept the challenge of exploring one's own beliefs. Malik (2015: 18) maintains that '[t]o accept that certain things cannot be said is to accept that certain forms of power cannot be challenged'. As such, the university, states Barnett (2016: 47), ought to be a space where ideas are openly traded so that it is of service to society as well as global communities. To Giroux (2007: 5), inquiry ought to be responsive and exercised freely 'in concert with larger concerns over social justice', which includes debased and violent narratives of terror, war, racial injustice, ecological abuse, state violence, etc. (Giroux, 2007: 5).

Following the above enunciations on the role of the university concerning academic freedom, it becomes apparent that in ridding itself of all restrictions and conditionalities, the university should be an unafraid space – as open and free to questioning and responding to modern-day malaises, as it is to bringing into disrepute its own practices. There are profound implications at play here – implications that extend beyond the immediate ambit of the function and purpose of what a university is and what both academics and students ought to be doing. If the function of the university is to push the boundaries continually so that nothing is beyond question, and knowledge remains unbounded, then the work and purpose of the academia cannot be framed by compliance and complacency. Instead, the expectations are those of an active awareness, criticality and reflexivity – as made evident in what academics say, do and write.

Academic freedom, therefore, is not an intangible ideal – something that is aspired to and which is only up for debate when there is some dispute or controversy. Academic freedom exists in all facets and actions of the academy. It exists in how academic appointments are made – in why preference is given to certain groups of people, and not others. It exists in the choice of course material – which texts and authors are prescribed and which perspectives are propagated above others. It exists in how academics teach, how they choose (or not) to engage and deliberate with their students and how they supervise, again, the kinds of texts and theoretical debates to which students are referred. Academic freedom exists in the kinds of scholarship academics embark upon and the kinds of conferences in which they choose to participate. Concomitantly, academic freedom emanates from the outside of the university – in terms of endowments and donations, which are seldom without conditions. Academic freedom (or not) exists on the basis that certain papers (and hence arguments) are accepted for presentation at certain conferences, or not. It is worrying to see the same kinds of arguments being advanced over and over again at a few conferences – with seemingly no room for dissenting voices. All of this, and much more, constitutes the shape and function of a university. And all of this, and much more, demands an active awareness, attention and interrogation.

The academy, therefore, is necessarily an active and vibrant space. By implication, to be an academic does not only mean active participation in the life of the university, and its associated and extended functions, but an active willingness to bring those functions into question. In other words, to be active as an academic demands an attachment to what one does as an academic while being simultaneously equipped and willing to detach oneself for the purposes of self-reflection and critique. In this regard, academic activism manifests in academic freedom. It is through a recognition that a university is without conditionality that academic activism is made visible. As explained by Derrida (2005: 24), the university ought to have 'an *unconditional* freedom to question and to assert, or even, going still further, the right to say publicly all that is required by research, knowledge, and thought concerning the *truth*'. The university, in principle and in conformity with its declared vocation of professing the truth, asserts Derrida (2005: 25–26), should remain an ultimate place of critical resistance.

A university's unconditionality implies a space and ethos in which nothing is beyond question – neither the current and determined figure of democracy nor the traditional idea of critique. The university must always and without reservation be a locus for interrogation, a place where cultural values, intellectual positions and the practices of society are held open to questioning. It is the right and political obligation of the academy within a democracy, argues Derrida (2005: 26), 'to challenge societal convention and to defend speech that allows for creative, contrapuntal, and even subversive forces to exist alongside the cultural mainstream whose social predominance risks delivering a troubling complacency to the unthinking, unreflective consumer'. Hence, it is the activism of academics – their thoughts, arguments, teaching, supervision, mentoring and scholarship – which ensures the active sustainability of academic freedom. Where there are silence, complacency, subdued and uncontroversial scholarship and the acceptance of existing hegemonies, academic activism has ceased, and at risk is not only academic freedom but the very basis of the purpose of a university.

Academic Activism as a Mode of Rupturing

We were in the midst of the country's first ever student uprisings in 1976 – known as the Soweto uprisings – when black students in townships revolted against the compulsory introduction of the Afrikaans language (then considered the language of oppression and discrimination) in schools and some universities. The uprisings were intensified not only by the young age of the protestors but by the tragic death of 14-year-old, Hector Pieterson. Images of his lifeless body, carried by a fellow student, have come to symbolise the brutal dehumanisation of the apartheid regime. Again, in the 1980s, students protested against the inception of a tricameral parliament that would separate the education system in South Africa into exclusive sectors along racial lines: education for 'whites', 'coloured', 'Indians' and 'blacks'. The series of protests during this time saw the emergence of the slogan, 'liberation before education', which saw thousands of protestors forfeit their classes, their academic years and, in many cases, their entire schooling careers, as they struggled against the apartheid state.

Despite the country's transition to a democracy during the early 1990s, the effects of apartheid continue to play a significant role in the daily lives of especially historically disenfranchised and marginalised communities. Moreover, the symbolism of apartheid's racial oppression and exclusion continued through our earlier careers as high school teachers and, now, as university academics. One disturbing illustration of just how deeply racialisation continues to mar the academy, as well as engagements and relationships between academics, is the now-retracted article entitled, *Age- and education-related effects on cognitive functioning in coloured South African women* (Nieuwoudt, Dickie, Coetsee, Engelbrecht, & Terblanche, 2020). These authors, colleagues of ours, maintained that '[c]olored women in South Africa have an increased risk for low cognitive functioning, as they present with low education levels and unhealthy lifestyle behaviors' (Nieuwoudt et al., 2020: 321). The article attracted widespread criticism and outrage, both among academics and civil society. While Jansen (2019) labelled it as 'racist nonsense', Boswell (2019) campaigned for the successful retraction of the article because of its racist ideological underpinnings, its flawed methodology and its reproduction of harmful stereotypes of 'coloured' women. In response, the university's senate adopted a motion, which reads: 'We believe the university should become a key site for developing a critique of race in science and research, and establishing related institutional practices and processes'. Four proposals were referred for further consideration and action:

1. That 'consideration be given to instituting a campus-wide mechanism dedicated to transforming research and science' – referred to the Vice-Rector: Research, Innovation and Postgraduate Studies
2. That 'consideration be given to offering a module on anti-racism, democracy and critical citizenship to all first-year students' – referred to Senate's Academic Planning Committee

3. That 'a suite of short courses be offered by the Research Office for all staff members' on topics such as 'the use of human categories in research and science' – referred to the Vice-Rector: Research, Innovation and Postgraduate Studies
4. That departments such as Gender and Critical Race Studies be institutionalised at SU – referred to the Senate's Academic Planning Committee (Stellenbosch University, 2019)

Regardless of whether any of these proposals will be implemented, if universities wish for students to be critically aware, responsible and responsive to the world they are in, then universities have to be unconditionally open to critiquing any form of injustice. Universities, therefore, as the epistemological and ethical spaces of students, have to be just in how they conceive of themselves and how they interact with students and staff, and they have to be seen as acting in the face of injustice.

Our own activism against racial exclusion, illiberal educational practices and structures and a racial symbolism that continues to reify whiteness and privilege has been incessant. We remain as vigilant about it as we did before the onset of democracy. The interesting realisation about apartheid is that its blatant ideological racism confirms a kind of brutal honesty, which otherwise might be disguised by other forms of discrimination or marginalisation. Apartheid has allowed us insights into the human condition and its propensity for undignified conduct. While agonisingly unfair, apartheid has sensitised us, on the one hand, to the human capacity for inhumane action and, on the other hand, to the sheer resilience of what it means to be human. Activism for us as academics evolved as forms of dissent and resistance against those practices that undermine the emancipatory discourses of decoloniality and democratisation.

For us, firstly, dissent means those modes of human action that trigger upheavals of thought along the lines of discomfort and controversy. To show dissent, one has to be prepared to act controversially such as to counteract in a belligerent fashion what seems to be quite demeaning and unjust. And, when one voices, in a dissenting way, one's objection against that which discriminates and marginalises, the response from the other can adopt a semblance of provocation. Showing dissent does not simply mean to disagree but rather to take matters of public concern into belligerent controversy. That is, one does not have to be apologetic and too hospitable or friendly to proffer one's truth claims against forms of human injustice, in particular, discrimination and marginalisation.

Exclusion of students, for example, takes on many different forms – some quite blatant, but mostly subtly, and disguised through other practices of marginalisation. The issue of language at our institution is an especially volatile one. There has been exceptional resistance from both inside and outside the university against the institution's shift away from Afrikaans as its sole medium of instruction. Against the background of what is a deep ideological struggle for the preservation of not only a language but the Afrikaner identity, ('black') students who cannot speak Afrikaans often find themselves in rather disconcerting environments either when certain academics persist in wanting to teach only in Afrikaans or when they dismiss a student's writing as 'not good enough' on the basis of language barriers. The alienating experiences of students as they enter educational spaces from which they have historically been excluded hold tremendous consequences for their academic performance. In contexts such as these – where the potential for discrimination and exclusion is rife – the voicing of dissent should not adopt a non-belligerent tone. Often, when students or academics tread lightly and attempt to deal with what is blatant discrimination diplomatically or politely, the discrimination simply persists because perceivably the impression is that the discrimination is protected within deeper hegemonic structures and cultures. As a result, being provocative in one's vehement objection against a language that discriminates and marginalises others – in this instance, a black minority group of students – would be a much more assertive and eloquent way in which to address such a contentious matter.

Now, of course, such action requires a measure of risk-taking, particularly in the case of students, but this is what activism demands – an exertion of human agency that might, at times, be out of character so that the impact of that which is protested against is brought to the fore.

Dissent is meant to provoke clarity of thought and to encourage others who perpetrate an injustice to be moved by one's articulations. What makes the articulation of belligerent and distressful reasons a manifestation of dissent is that such reasons are meant to rupture patterns of hegemony and exclusion. Only when humans are provoked to think for themselves and to restrain unjust human action, then there would be a real possibility for understanding and possibly a reversal of repressive action. We doubt that that apartheid would have ended in the way that it finally did without the human resolve to act decisively and belligerently and without the human resolve to sacrifice opportunities for education or safety to dismantle an unjust ideology. As expressed by Eamonn Callan (1997), real change is only possible when dissent takes the forms of belligerent and distressful actions. Dissent, states Callan (1997: 210), 'sustains our personal investment in the truths that really matter and reminds us of their full significance by showing us vividly what it means to speak and live against them'.

The point we are making is that liberation is only possible when educational matters are addressed through belligerent and distressful acts of dissent. Disagreement and ethical confrontation are constitutive of educational encounters that are perceived tolerantly and require judgement and discernment in order to ensure 'a more circumscribed and disciplined kind of deliberation that will respect the limit of reasonable disagreement when questions of political coercion are at stake' (Callan, 1997: 218). Concomitantly, as educational spaces, neither universities nor academics can choose to avoid belligerence, since as Callan (1997: 220) argues, 'ethical avoidance is a blindly and regressive social tendency that pulls us away from the dialogical conditions that would enable us collectively to distinguish the pluralism that deserves our respect from the pluralism that does not'. We cannot imagine universities retaining their spaces for disagreement and disruption of thought without provocative acts of belligerence and distress – that is, without dissent there is no real possibility for disruptive institutional discourses. It is dissent that makes it possible to enact academic activism.

Secondly, academic activism also involves showing dissent towards curricular matters that seem to constrain emancipatory action. Academics like ourselves raise doubts about curricular content matter and then proceed to change such matters according to a discourse of deliberative democratic education. Put differently, academic activism does involve not only changing curricular content but, more importantly, endeavours to bring it in line with notions of democratic education that draw upon forms of iterative human engagement. The point about raising doubts and bringing thoughts and practices about curriculum into controversy is a matter of acting with scepticism. By implication, showing dissent as an instance of academic activism involves becoming sceptical towards curricular matters that affect ourselves and students. It is Stanley Cavell (1979) who reminds us that acting sceptically involves treating matters of moral concern with suspicion – that is, with some radical doubt – as such matters do prejudice not only others but also ourselves.

When we started to rethink and rewrite the philosophy of education courses in our department, we wanted to insert some alternative perspectives into our courses that would invite students to think differently about education. The previous courses presented the philosophy of education as some objective lens through which educational matters had to be looked at neutrally and without questioning. In other words, epistemological inquiry seemed to have been biased towards the search for objective truths and a passive adherence to an idealistic vision of knowledge. As part of our own academic activism, these philosophy of education courses were reconceptualised and rewritten along the lines of a politics of struggle and contestation, especially how the newly found curricular content addresses the notion of otherness in non-prejudicial ways. In fact, our own academic activism at the institution we practise philosophy of education takes on the form of sceptically raising doubts about curricular matters that seem to undermine otherness and difference – a matter of engaging in radical pedagogical rupturing.

Significantly, over the years that we have been teaching this course, we have witnessed how curricular changes evoke different forms of engagement from the students. Not only do we see wider participation from historically silent pockets of students, but we see more meaningful attempts at making sense of the nature and aims of education, as students show a greater preparedness to step outside of their own perceptions and perspectives. In this regard, we agree with Hytten (2017: 388) that in conceiving teaching as activism, it is insufficient only to raise students' critical consciousness. It is not enough for students only to be able to think differently. Students, as Hytten (2017: 388) asserts, also 'need tools to act differently in the world: to speak back to power'. To Hytten (2017: 388), teaching is activism 'when we cultivate in students the habits necessary for a life of participatory and engaged citizenship, laying the foundation for actions they may take in their lives outside of the classroom, without presuming or dictating what those actions should be'.

Thirdly, academic activism cannot just be confined to the walls of university classrooms or the fences of institutional buildings. The very idea of an academic activist is synonymous with that of a change agent. In other words, it is one thing to recognise human vulnerability and political hegemony and exclusion, but it is something else to commit yourself to bringing about substantive change in one's sphere of human existence. Whenever the opportunity arises, we articulate our opposition to spheres of human and educational injustice. When one recognises a vulnerability in society, it behoves one to not only rethink the vulnerability but actually to commit oneself arduously about changing an injustice. Here we are specifically reminded of the activist actions of academics who do not hold back when it comes to articulating our objection to understandings of education and curricular practices that seem to constrain rather than emancipate human action.

For instance, academic activism does not only reside in recognising the injustice associated with curtailing free speech, but through their writings, academics endeavour to show their dissatisfaction in constraining freedom of human expression – that is, academic expression should always be free, and any attempt to constrain such speech is to undermine activism in itself. In light of such a view of becoming change agents through academic activism, in particular raising our objection vociferously against curtailing freedom of speech, we disagree with Amy Gutmann's (2003) view. Her argument for inhibiting free speech on the grounds that such speech seems to be injurious to others and, therefore, has to be constrained is perhaps too apologetic in denying free speech. Who decides what is harmful and objectionable for others? If white supremacists are not allowed to articulate their spurious claims at university campuses, there is little opportunity for critics to actually show dissent and raise their radical doubts about any kind of discriminatory or dubious claims. In our previous work, we argued in defence of free speech and openness and that regulating any form of speech would be debilitating for iterative democratic action itself (Davids & Waghid, 2019b).

In sum, we have argued that academic activism is a form of rupturing that brings into play notions of dissent, scepticism and change agency. Next, we analyse how such a view of academic activism can contribute to reconceptualising philosophy of higher education with a specific emphasis on interpretivism.

Towards a Renewed Understanding of Philosophy of Higher Education

Academic activism can be considered as a form of dissent that enables academics and students in particular to raise doubts about educational matters of public concern. They then endeavour to change undesirable and unreflective perspectives pertaining to higher education with the intent that such actions would be subjected to opposition and disagreement, suspicion and doubt and the possibility that things can be altered otherwise. We now examine how such a notion of academic activism reconstitutes an understanding of philosophy of higher education in reference to the seminal thoughts of Stanley Cavell (1979).

Firstly, seeking disagreement and oppositional thinking is what makes a philosophy of higher education what it is. The point about such a philosophy of education that is guided by disagreement and oppositional thinking is that one can never know with certainty that which we subject to scrutiny. As aptly put by Cavell (1979: 45), concerning an interpretation of arguments, 'we do not know with certainty of the existence of the external world (or of other minds) … Our relation to the world as a whole, or to others in general, is not one of knowing, where knowing construes itself as being certain'. The importance here of doing philosophy of higher education is to repudiate or disagree with that with which we are confronted to at least gain some reasonable sense of what is at stake. This expression of disagreement, as Cavell (1979) puts it, will at least give us meanings that seem to underscore human action in particular contexts – a matter of uncovering truths of disagreement. And, for us, an important task of an academic activist is to search for such truths in which disagreement and repudiation manifest. As alluded to earlier in this chapter, the insistence upon pursuing truth, following Derrida (2005), resides in a university's commitment to being unconditionally open and resistant to attempts of constraint and closing down. The university, according to Derrida (2004: 97), 'is there to tell the truth, to judge, to criticise in the most rigorous sense of the terms, namely to discern and decide between the true and the false…'. The concern here, however, is not to arrive at one truth, but to recognise that there is no one truth, that there are always multiple perspectives of how we engage with and interpret the world around us. In engaging with these multiple perspectives, or truths, we do so to create spaces for deliberation as well as disagreement.

Secondly, using scepticism as a repudiation of truth claims will contextualise a philosophy of higher education as a discourse that 'undercuts the validity [authenticity] of our criteria' (Cavell, 1979: 46). In doing philosophy of higher education, our concern should no longer be for a search for validity as accuracies do not exist in practices that involve human beings because people are fallibility. This implies that doing philosophy of higher education should be about how humans analyse the actions of others without the assumption that they can accurately perceive others' feelings and emotions – that is, as aptly stated by Cavell (1979: 46), 'we cannot … have their sentience, say literally have a pain of theirs'. Put differently, when humans analyse the actions of others, they do so in the context of how others present themselves and not by what we presume others are doing. This is not to say that truth does not exist but, rather, that truth is always influenced and framed by the perspective from which it is being narrated. In a philosophy of higher education, scepticism serves as a helpful lens and approach against infringements and propagations of dogma. Scepticism is a reminder that rigidity of thought and argumentation is out of place in universities and that uncertainty is what drives the academy to always look beyond that which is said and claimed.

Thirdly, becoming a change agent stimulates a philosophy of higher education towards establishing a social contract of 'answerability for or toward others' (Cavell, 1979: 438). When academic activism guides a philosophy of higher education towards answerability, then such a discourse becomes concerned with discharging one's responsibility towards others (Cavell, 1979: 456). Moreover, following Cavell (1979: 465), doing philosophy of higher education implicates us 'to *humanize* this creation'. This means accepting responsibility for ourselves in enacting our answerability towards other humans and non-humans. In this regard, change only becomes visible and meaningful when enacted in relation to another. A teacher witnesses the effects of her teaching only when those effects are shown in the knowledge or actions of those she teaches. As academics, our agency becomes evident in what we teach and how we teach, as it does in what we write – these are the effects of the change which we have the potential to bring.

According to Cavell (1979: 438), '[i]n respect of my fellow citizens, it tells me why I am answerable for what happens to them …'. Of course, while humans enact their responsibility towards others, there is always the possibility that they might act 'inhumanly' (Cavell, 1979: 438). It is possible for a teacher to act responsively, responsibly and humanely, but encounter responses that are neither reciprocal nor desirable. But, of course, teaching, like academic activism, cannot be dependent on responses or reciprocity. If all encounters were smooth and mutually satisfying, there would be no need for the exertion of human agency or activism. When faced with non-reciprocity, or antagonism, a teacher's response cannot follow suit. Here Cavell (1979: 494) correctly cautions responsible humans not to slander, torment and vilify others or to perpetuate human injustice and suffering. The idea of answerability to others infers a moral responsibility, which aligns with change agency as an enactment of academic activism.

Concluding Thoughts

Academic activism does not only offer ways in which humans can become better beings of analysis and thinking but also how humans can enact their humanity towards others more profoundly and justifiably. Another, says Cavell (1979: 435), 'may be owed acknowledgement simply on the ground of his [her] humanity, acknowledgement as a human being, for which nothing will do but my revealing myself to him [her] as a human being, unrestrictedly, as his or her sheer other, his or her fellow, his or her *semblable*'. Academic activism, therefore, as forms of human agency, is always relational, responsive, oppositional and aimed at bringing about change – whether political, social and economic – and is always educational.

As we conclude this chapter in which we have tried to make sense of what academic activism is and how it is interpreted and lived through a lens of a philosophy of higher education, it is apt to focus on the importance of reflection as a form of activism. In the busy-ness of teaching, reading, writing, conferencing, supervising, mentoring, connecting and responding to the myriad demands from both within and outside of the university, it is easy to keep on moving. Yet, academic activism demands a pause and being still long enough for some reflection on what academics do and what it is the university is or not doing. Being able to act responsibly and responsively, and being able to sustain relationships with colleagues and students, demands a stillness, even ambivalence for the necessity of absorption and reflection.

Reflection allows for a stepping out of the institutionalisation and formalisation of the academy; it allows for the suspension of action and acting so that new understandings and learnings might be realised. Human agency does not necessarily have to manifest as action; human agency resides equally in our capacity to be still, to listen, to ponder and to dwell on this or that for the purposes of possibly arriving at deeper understandings. The capacity to reflect, as Maxey (1999: 201) reminds us, is itself a form of activism; '[b]y actively and critically reflecting on the world and our place within it, we are more able to act in creative, constructive ways that challenge oppressive power relations rather than reinforce them'. Through reflection, academic activism can adopt subtleties of humility, sensitivity and compassion, which otherwise might not have been present – thereby ensuring an openness of uncertainty.

References

Barnett, R. (2016). *Understanding the university: Institution, idea, possibilities*. London: Routledge.

Boswell, B. (2019). Letter to the Editorial Board of Aging, Neuropsychology and Cognition. http://www.agi.ac.za/agi/news/petition. Accessed 30 Apr 2020.

Callan, E. (1997). *Creating citizens: Political education and liberal democracy*. Oxford, UK: Oxford University Press.

Cavell, S. (1979). *The claims of reason: Wittgenstein, skepticism, morality, and tragedy*. Oxford, UK: Oxford University Press.

Davids, N., & Waghid, Y. (2018). Prioritising higher education: Why research is all that matters. *South African Journal of Higher Education, 32*(2), 1–7.

Davids, N., & Waghid, Y. (2019a). *Teaching and learning as a pedagogic pilgrimage: Cultivating faith, hope and imagination*. New York/London: Routledge.

Davids, N., & Waghid, Y. (2019b). *Universities, pedagogical encounters, openness, and free speech*. Lanham, MD/Boulder, CO/New York/London: Lexington Books.

Davids, N., & Waghid, Y. (2020). Higher education transformation, inequality and education leadership-in-becoming. In I. Rhensburg, S. Motala, & M. Cross (Eds.), *Transforming universities in South Africa: Pathways to higher education reform*. Leiden, the Netherlands: Brill Sense.

Derrida, J. (2004). *Eyes of the university*. Stanford, CA: Stanford University Press.

Derrida, J. (2005). The future of the profession or the unconditional university (Thanks to the "humanities," what could take place tomorrow). In P. P. Trifonas & M. A. Peters (Eds.), *Deconstructing Derrida*. New York: Palgrave Macmillan.

Flood, M., Martin, B., & Dreher, T. (2013). Combining academia and activism. *Australian Universities' Review, 55*(1), 17–26.

Giroux, H. A. (2007). *The university in chains*. Boulder, CO: Paradigm Publishers.

Griffiths, M. (2013). Critically adaptive pedagogical relations: The relevance for educational policy and practice. *Educational Theory, 63*(3), 221–236.

Grimm, J. (2018). Authoritarian Middle East regimes don't like academics – Ask Matthew Hedges. https://www.opendemocracy.net/en/policing-research-shifting-tides-for-middle-east-studies-after-arab-spring/. 13 April 2020.

Gutmann, A. (2003). *Identity in democracy*. Princeton, NJ: Princeton University Press.

Hytten, K. (2017). Teaching as and for activism: Challenges and possibilities. *Philosophy of Education, 2014*, 385–394.

Jansen, J. D. (2019). Racist medical myths persist with SA's diseased apartheid mentality. https://www.timeslive.co.za/ideas/2019-04-25-racist-medical-myths-persist-with-sas-diseased-apartheid-mentality/. Accessed 1 May 2020.

Malik, K. (2015). Diverse societies should not curtail free speech. https://www.news.uct.ac.za/images/archive/dailynews/lectures/tbdavie/TBDavieLecture2015.pdf. Accessed 16 Apr 2020.

Maxey, I. (1999). Beyond boundaries? Activism, academia, reflexivity and research. *The Royal Geographical Society, 31*(3), 199–208.

Nieuwoudt, S., Dickie, K. E., Coetsee, C., Engelbrecht, L., & Terblanche, E. (2020). Age- and education-related effects on cognitive functioning in colored South African women. *Aging, Neuropsychology, and Cognition, 27*(3), 321–337.

Sharma, Y. (2018). Academic freedom is facing 'growing threats' – Report. https://www.universityworldnews.com/post.php?story=20180126115034644. 24 April 2020.

Slote, M. (2007). *The ethics of care and empathy*. London: Routledge.

Stellenbosch University (2019). Senate adopts motion on transforming research and science at SU. https://www.sun.ac.za/english/Lists/news/DispForm.aspx?ID=6455. 24 April 2020.

Svrluga, S. (2018). Trump signs executive order on free speech on college campuses. https://www.washingtonpost.com/education/2019/03/21/trump-expected-sign-executive-order-free-speech/. 30 April 2020.

West, C. (1991). Theory, pragmatism and politics. In J. Arac & B. Johnson (Eds.), *Consequences of theory* (pp. 22–38). Baltimore: Johns Hopkins University Press.

Chapter 2
Criticality and Higher Education

Abstract In this chapter, we are interested in how a critical-social educational theory can most appropriately advance human existence. To this end, we draw on Seyla Benhabib's (Critique, norm and utopia: a study of the foundations of critical theory. Columbia University Press, New York, 1986) re-articulation of Jürgen Habermas's notion of critique to ascertain how the practice of academic activism ought to be amended. According to Benhabib (Critique, norm and utopia: a study of the foundations of critical theory. Columbia University Press, New York, 1986: 279), Habermas's theory of communicative action is a justifiable form of critique as it re-establishes the relation between self-reflection and autonomy and it explains autonomy in communicative terms, that is, autonomy is not synonymous with self-legislation or self-actualisation or mimesis, but rather 'the cognitive competence to adopt to a universalist standpoint and the interactive competence to act on such a basis' (Benhabib, Critique, norm and utopia: a study of the foundations of critical theory. Columbia University Press, New York, 1986: 282). In relation to the notions of self-reflective autonomy and communicative autonomy, we examine what a philosophy of higher education looks like and what the implications of such a form of critique hold for academic activism.

Keywords Critique · Self-reflection · Communicative autonomy

Introduction

In the previous chapter, we conceived of academic activism as forms of reasoned human agency, actions or encounters – intent upon shaping and producing better humans and humane engagement and focused upon social justice. It seems apt to follow this conception with how a theory of critique – more specifically critical-social educational theory – can most appropriately advance human existence. To us, the matter of critique is a crucial one, especially so when it is seemingly omitted from the cultures and discourses of (South African) universities. While much attention has been given to the necessity of deliberative engagement and the cultivation

© The Author(s), under exclusive license to Springer Nature Singapore
Pte Ltd. 2021
N. Davids, Y. Waghid, *Academic Activism in Higher Education*, Debating
Higher Education: Philosophical Perspectives 5,
https://doi.org/10.1007/978-981-16-0340-2_2

of decolonised pedagogical knowledge spaces, very little, if any, such concern has centred on critique, bringing into question notions of a thinking university.

Remaining with the interpretivist paradigm, established in Chap. 1, in this chapter, we turn to Seyla Benhabib's theory of critique. Standing in the traditions of Kant and Habermas, Benhabib (1986) articulates an understanding of critique that makes a necessary connection between rationality and autonomy. That is, any form of analysis of the social world is an act of philosophy (of higher education) and that such an analysis is dependent upon 'its commitment to the dignity and autonomy of the rational subject' (Benhabib, 1986: 15). According to Benhabib (1986: 279), Habermas's theory of communicative action is a justifiable form of critique as it re-establishes the relation between self-reflection and autonomy. It also explains autonomy in communicative terms – that is, autonomy is not synonymous with self-legislation or self-actualisation or mimesis, but rather 'the cognitive competence to adopt to a universalist standpoint and the interactive competence to act on such a basis' (Benhabib, 1986: 282). In relation to the notions of self-reflective autonomy and communicative autonomy, we examine what a philosophy of higher education looks like and what the implications of such a form of critique hold for academic activism.

Critique

Benhabib (1986) articulates an understanding of critique that stands in the traditions of Kant and Habermas: firstly, by making a necessary connection between rationality and autonomy in the sense that any form of analysis of the social world is an act of philosophy (of higher education) and secondly, that such an analysis is dependent upon 'its commitment to the dignity and autonomy of the rational subject' (Benhabib, 1986: 15). The mode in which social life appears, contends Benhabib (1986: 4), 'is an indication of the extent to which individuals are alienated from their social praxis'. Certain groups of students at South African universities, for example, might have gained external access to institutions from which they have been historically excluded, but the manner (or mode) in which they experience these institutions might place them at a distance, rather than evoking a sense of belonging. Their direct experiences of their encounters with the space and discourse of the institution serve only to remind them that their physical presence is not an indicator of internal inclusion and recognition. That they continue to stand on the peripheries of their university experience – whether in lecture theatres or the social spaces of student residences – confirms that their historically reduced identities have yet to find resonance and a place of belonging within their educational spaces.

When they protest against this displacement and alienation – as a manifestation of critique – their actions, following Benhabib (1986: 4), do not 'merely disclose the dependence of thought upon social being, of consciousness upon material praxis'. Rather, their actions also criticise 'this dependence from the standpoint of the struggle for the future'. The students recognise that their silence will serve not only as the further entrenchment of their exclusion but will legitimise these practices as a permissible norm. Too often, students and academics alike resort to a language of 'this is how things have always been' as a justification for questionable behaviour.

Consider, for example, the widespread practices of initiation, often defined and accepted as the bedrock of universities residences. In 2001, the Minister of Education requested an inquiry into cultural initiations, following a number of deaths at schools and university. One of these cases involved that of a second-year student, who had been forced to participate in an initiation ritual at the university where we are based. After having his hair shaven off, being stripped naked and having his body painted, the student was dropped off outside of town and forced to walk back to the university hostel. While walking back, he was hit and killed by a car (SAHRC, 2001). The inquiry by the South African Human Rights Commission (2001: 16) found that although university administrators argued in support of the maintenance of initiation practices, 'as part of the tradition and culture of the university', such views were not articulated by student groupings and some staff members who spoke to the SAHRC outside of the meetings with the administration (SAHRC, 2001: 16). These student groupings and staff members favoured the abolishment of initiation practices. They described these processes as 'human rights abuses and in conflict with a democratic culture, and as having more negative aspects to them than positive' (SAHRC, 2001: 16).

At another South African university, an initiation ritual involved female and male students from residences devising a song and 'serenading' each other. While the initial intention was to enable students to get to each other, 'song lyrics became increasingly suggestive, and sexy dance moves crept in, along with questionable dress requirements' (De Klerk, 2013: 91). In a letter to the Dean of Students and the Vice-Chancellor, a student described 'serenading' as follows:

[L]ong compulsory evening practices demanding increasing levels of frenzy and excitement from performers; being sent out in pyjamas to watch boys dressed in T-shirts and boxers sing to them, accompanied by 'pelvis rolling and crass lyrics'; being instructed to serenade a men's res in return ('we roll our butts like strippers, the boys cheer. We push our breasts out, shake our hips, and gyrate our pelvis. All in accordance with the routine we have been taught. And the boys yell, 'Yeah!' as their eyes pop'). ... an 'icebreaker' session involving women's room keys being anonymously handed to the boys.... (De Klerk, 2013: 91)

What initiation rituals serve to do is to clarify and establish the 'rules' of a particular residence or university; it serves to dictate the conditions for student acceptance, inclusion and belonging. What it entrenches is a divide between those students who participate, and are, therefore, included, and those who refuse, thereby confirming their 'outsider' status. Not only is it a highly exclusionary practice, but it sets into motion certain norms regarding how students are to be treated going into the future. When students, parents as well as academics and administrators protest against initiation practices, which, in many instances, are long-standing and considered as part of the traditions of the university, the resistance is not only against a present-day dilemma but against what the implications are for future generations of students, higher education as well as social and societal norms.

Firstly, to Benhabib (1986), critique aims to grasp the present as a contradictory totality in which different normative ideals lend ideological justification to a social objectivity that oppresses human beings and frustrates their human potential; the goal of critique is to further the autonomy of the subject. The autonomy of the subject cannot be furthered or extended without 'the philosophical task of clarifying and reconstructing the norms to which criticism appeals' (Benhabib, Butler, Cornell & Fraser, 1995: 64). As such, for social critique to be valid, and for relativism to be avoided, critique must appeal to some normative criteria that exist outside the critic's own context. Critique, therefore, allows for the individuals to enact their autonomy and agency by bringing into question certain norms, certain taken-for-granted practices – such as institutional traditions or modes of engagement, as encountered in initiation rituals, for example. This is not necessarily an antagonistic process, as the purpose of bringing into question can sometimes be limited to simply making the other aware of a presumed practice, which has not been subjected to scrutiny before.

The student who wrote to the Dean of Students and the Vice-Chancellor to raise her concerns about 'serenading' did not enter into any disagreement or conflict with other students or the university administration. Instead, her point 'was made forcefully' by making the institution aware that 'by turning a blind eye to sexist behavior which is heterosexually normative, the institution could be accused of condonement, if not encouragement, of such behavior' (De Klerk, 2013: 92). As Marriott (2018) clarifies, '[c]ritique legislates the judicious use of reason by separating it from any metaphysical or dogmatic origin, so that any risk of being carried away by the fictitious or merely pleasing is curtailed by the rule of philosophical judgement'. It is only when philosophy becomes critique, he continues, that it is then able properly to articulate reason and what is essential to it. In this sense, critique is constituted as a defence against or a victory won over that of unreason: a victory that, conversely, shows critique to be always shadowed or at risk from the various lapses that would founder it.

For example, public schools in South Africa are given leeway in terms of defining their admission criteria for learners. Despite constitutional guidelines prohibiting any form or grounds for exclusion, a number of historically advantaged schools continue to employ criteria, which include granting preference to learners, who have historical ties with the respective school. In other words, applicants are explicitly asked as to whether previous generations of their family had attended the school. On the face of it, this seems like a rather mundane question, but in the context of South Africa's segregated schooling history, this question has direct implications for learners, whose parents and grandparents would have been disallowed from attending these schools. When one critiques what the school might couch as one of its traditions, it is often startling to realise how the schools do not necessarily see this criterion as a potential means of exclusion. Instead, there is a vociferous defence of long-held traditions and customs, even when these are blatantly discriminatory and socially unjust. Attempts to question and reframe schools as cohesive and inclusive spaces are interpreted as disruptive actions or as 'take-over' measures to nullify historical codes and ways of being.

Similar expressions of critique can be levelled at initiation practices of certain universities, which are consciously tied to the preservation of traditions, which might hold unintended consequences of alienation or estrangement among students, who enter these spaces from different historical and social backgrounds. Only once the practice is explained from the perspective of those who do not have generational ties does the school or the university possibly begin to see the harmful effects. Of course, being made aware of something does not necessarily result in that practice being reconsidered or ceased, but what critique facilitates and brings to the fore is not only different perspectives and perceptions but the confirmation of multiple truths and lived experiences. In this regard, critique can be used and understood as a form of awareness, as a means of getting individuals to engage from the perspective of the other – hopefully with a purpose of detachment so that new forms of understanding might emanate.

Critique, when understood in this way, adopts an activist premise in that it is aimed at questioning for the sake of awareness and reconsideration; it is an active process not concerned with labelling something as right or wrong, but in bringing something into contestation for the purpose of reconceptualisation. Following the above, we would venture that the goal of critique is not only to further the autonomy of the subject, as contended by Benhabib (1986), but also to extend the perspectives and meaning-making of contexts – thereby broadening the scope for both participation and disagreement. When individuals or groups critique an ideology, or an institution and its practices, it invites or forces the institution to critically reflect on that which is being critiqued – with the possibility that new outcomes might be attained and that more voices might be taken into account.

Secondly, critique also aligns itself with 'the struggles of those [people] for whom the hope of a better future provides the courage to live in the present' (Benhabib, 1986: 15). In this way, critique is concerned with re-establishing the link between autonomous rationality and emancipation, that is, 'of making good the unfulfilled promise of justice and freedom' (Benhabib, 1986: 329). Her description provides an apt background to how those who are oppressed or discriminated against persevere – only because of a hope that their condition will change. There is a certain resignation of tolerating a particular struggle, but with the belief that the future will be different. By implication, what critique brings to a philosophy of higher education is a moral imperative that accompanies human interactions such as those grounded in a sense of community where human responsibility, care and solidarity are no longer just confined to the private sphere of intimacy but extended to the public sphere of needs and solidarity.

In the recent #FeesMustFall protests, a number of students expressed their resistance and opposition to exorbitant university fees by not attending classes, not submitting assignments and not writing tests, as well as examinations. They knew that their actions would hinder their academic progress and, in some cases, compromise their registration in particular programmes. Yet, they persisted in their protests, recognising that unless the issue of fees was adequately addressed by the state and universities, future generations of students would be subjected to the same or greater financial burdens. These students understood that when students are turned away or drop out of universities because of an incapacity to pay fees, they are facing similar kinds of exclusion experienced during apartheid. Although framed differently – as in not being tied to race and rather to finances – the effect and implications of exclusion are the same. The same category of students, who were historically excluded because they were 'black', are also being excluded in a democracy because they do not have the economic capital to access or to remain in higher education.

Yet, the reason for a lack of economic capital is directly connected to apartheid's dispensation of racial inequality and inequity. It is for this reason that students experience anger and frustration – they see the democratic government as discounting the debilitating and residual effects of apartheid. These students are prepared to place their own studies at risk – not only for themselves but for all others, who might stand to benefit from a reduction in university fees. To them, the cause is greater than individual needs, and they see their opposition as a continuing narrative against the kinds of injustices perpetuated during apartheid. What this viewpoint confirms is that inasmuch as activism can be tied to self-interests, it can just as easily represent actions on behalf of others. There are broader social, political and moral issues at play.

Thirdly, for Benhabib (1986: 342), critique brings a communicative ethic to human relations based on 'the belief that the exercise of human reason is essential to the attainment of moral autonomy and fulfillment, public justice and progress' (Benhabib, 1986: 344). As she sums up her advocacy for critique, the ideal community of communication allows 'the unfolding of the relation to the *concrete other* on the basis of autonomous action. Only then can we say that justice without solidarity is blind, and freedom that is incompatible with happiness, empty' (Benhabib, 1986: 342). Put differently, critique is concerned with the creation of a 'new self- and other-relations that lie beyond the logic of capital, and of administrative-bureaucratic and technical rationality' (Benhabib, 1986: 343). By implication, critique relooks at emancipation in such a way that it is no longer just concerned with the 'democratization of administrative decision-making processes but [also] the formation of communities of need and solidarity in the interstices of our societies' (Benhabib, 1986: 353). In short, critique is concerned with both the cultivation of a self-reflective and communicative autonomy – as is evident in the actions of students who oppose exorbitant university fees and who are intent upon realising and living in a socially just democracy.

On Self-Reflective and Communicative Autonomy

Mainstream conceptions of autonomy, explains Friedman (2003: 87), share a common core understanding: first, reflection of some sort on relevant aspects of the self's own motivational structure and available choices and second, procedural requirements having to do with the nature and quality of that reflection (as in being sufficiently rational and uncoerced). While Benhabib centralises the concept of autonomy in her writings, she emphasises that the subject is constituted through social relations, as such, is embedded in a concrete lifeworld. Autonomy is not autocracy, she asserts, 'but rather the ability to distance oneself from one's social roles, traditions, history, and even deepest commitments and to take a universalistic attitude of hypothetical questioning toward them' (Benhabib, 1999: 353–354).

To Benhabib (1985: 91), 'autonomy is not only self-determination in accordance with just norms but the capacity to assume the standpoint of the concrete other as well'. She maintains that an individual's autonomy does not simply exist. Rather, 'the subjects of reason are finite, embodied, and fragile creatures, not disembodied cogitos or abstract "unities of transcendental apperception"' (1994: 174). To Benhabib (1994: 174), it is only by learning to interact in a human community that the human infant becomes a self, a being capable of speech and action. The identity of the self, explains Benhabib (1994: 174), is constituted by a narrative unity that integrates what 'I' can do, have done and will accomplish with what you expect of 'me'.

Autonomy, therefore, following Benhabib, emerges from and takes shape through a dialogical engagement with others. The human infant, she explains, 'becomes a person through contingent processes of socialization, acquires language and reason, develops a sense of justice and autonomy, and becomes capable of projecting a narrative of which she is not only the author but the actor as well' (Benhabib, 1994: 174). Students, for example, do not simply embark on protests; there is a particular context of socialisation, of recognition and, more often, of misrecognition, which pushes them towards resistance. What the context is or how students arrive at a decision to voice their resistance is not necessarily a shared understanding. In fact, very often, that or those being protested against do not necessarily understand the reasons for the resistance due to a myriad of reasons. Sometimes, there is simply a schism between the lived experiences of the individual and the concrete other. While the #FeesMustFall and #RhodesMustFall campaigns took place at all universities in South Africa, the intensity of these campaigns varied in relation to the particular historical identities, as well as the presence of a critical base of 'black' students. The majority of 'white' students could not relate to the demands for the removal of the statue of Cecil John Rhodes from the University of Cape Town. In turn, many privileged students have little understanding of food insecurity experienced by a significant number of students. The general perception is that when students receive financial support, they have enough funding to cover all their needs. Funding, however, has specific designations and limitations, and students are most vulnerable at the commencement of the academic year when they are waiting for funds to be released and at the end of the academic year, as funds are depleted.

At the time of writing, students at a few universities demanded the delay of the online academic programme, which has been forced upon universities due to the COVID-19 national lockdown. At first glance, and if one is unaware of the concrete others, one might think that any attempt to further delay an academic year, which is already at risk of not being completed, is an uninformed and frivolous call. But, upon careful consideration, the demand might not be that misplaced in light of the high number of students, who have access to neither digital devices nor the Internet.

How, therefore, can teaching and learning proceed when the educational field is so unequal? Other times it has to do with a deliberate oppression of the other, where there is a genuine belief of superiority, based on race, religion, class or culture, and hence a deliberate refusal of acknowledgement or equal recognition. Then, of course, there are indeed actions, which might not be considered as reasonable or justifiable, such as students embarking on wanton practices of violence and vandalism, as forms of protest.

However distorted and imperfect human reasons may be, such reasons constitute the basis of self-autonomous actions. In a way, reasonable analyses are not just literary criticism, aphorism or poetry but are enlightened or practical reasons proffered in justifying the legitimacy of social actions (Benhabib, 1986: 329). In other words, reasons have been thought through concerning social and historical contexts in which they manifest. In the case of students' resort to violence, justifications stem from similar actions used to overthrow the apartheid government. And while the ideological context might have changed to that of a democracy, the experiences of apartheid remain present in the continuing unequal and, at times, hopeless lives of the majority of black people. Those who engage in the philosophical activity of claiming reasons on the basis of discourses of argumentation, disputation, debate and adjudication have actually used their self-autonomous agency to do so.

Following her take on such a Habermasian notion of self-reflective autonomy, Benhabib (1986: 305) contends:

> Every agent capable of speech and action can participate in discourses ... Everyone may problematize any assertion ... Everyone may introduce every assertion into a discourse ... Everyone may express his [her] attitudes, wishes, and needs ... No one may be prevented from enjoying her above-outlined rights in virtue of constraints that may dominate within or without discourses.

Individuals, therefore, firstly, must have an equal chance to initiate and to continue communication; secondly, they must have an equal chance to make assertions, recommendations and explanations and to challenge justifications; thirdly, they must have equal chances as actors to express their wishes, feelings and intentions; and fourthly, they must act as if in contexts of action there is an equal distribution of chances to order and resist orders (Benhabib, 1985: 87). She explains that while the symmetry stipulation – captured in the first two actions – of the ideal speech situation 'refers to speech acts alone and to conditions governing their employment, the reciprocity condition refers to existing social interactions and requires a suspension of situations of untruthfulness and duplicity on the one hand, and of inequality and subordination on the other' (Benhabib, 1985: 87).

In the case of a university engaging with students regarding gender-based violence, for example, the primary concern of the university cannot be about protecting the reputation of the institution, or about reformulating policies, when the issue at hand is the actual safety and security of students. Moreover, it does not help to engage with students in this regard as if the university has more information or has a better direct experience of the debilitating impacts of gender-based violence. If the scourge of gender-based violence is to be addressed, then there has to be an institutional preparedness to reconceive it as a social justice issue, which impacts on the rights of individuals (not limited to women), to engage freely and without fear in the public sphere. In our opinion, what this understanding implies is that questions need to be asked about how the university's public sphere and institutional culture are used to perpetuate sexist or exclusionary dogmas. What needs to be disrupted, therefore, are not only acts and perpetuations of gender-based violence but the systemic structures that allow gender-based violence to unfold, in the first instance.

Benhabib's (1985: 87) third and fourth conditions of the ideal speech situation, namely, that individuals must have equal chances as actors to express their wishes, feelings and intentions and they must act as if in contexts of action there is an equal distribution of chances to order and resist orders, are especially pertinent for academic activism as a manifestation of academic freedom. Not only does her assertion that all individuals ought to be included, or afforded the opportunity for speech, but that this chance be availed equally. Despite its foundational centrality within universities, academic freedom remains a highly contested matter – with disagreements easily descending into disturbing patterns of 'disinvitation' of speakers or academics, or forms of disruption, involving heckling and ridiculing, which ought to have no place in a university. Moreover, it is often the case, by virtue of institutional hegemonies, that some individuals have more rights and, hence, more voice than others.

These hegemonies are as prevalent in the public sphere of a university, as they are in lecture theatres, or within the supervision process between an academic and his or her student. Students from minority groups often struggle to assert themselves among their peers, or they fear asking questions in case the question might be deemed as stupid. In turn, we are aware that 'black' students, and in particular 'black' students at our institution, who come from other parts of the African continent, might not enjoy the same levels of support as other students. Their presence at the university is not only constitutive of a minority group but is heavily laden with historical and contemporary politics, which make their navigation on campus and through the academic programme especially cumbersome. A number of African students are not only at our institution because they wish to pursue a degree at a South African university, but they are also there because of civil unrest, ethnic conflict and political upheaval, which make it near to impossible for them to consider higher education in their own countries.

What Benhabib (1985), however, is proposing in terms of countering any inherent inequalities is a presumption of equality – specifically phrased by her as: 'the speakers must act *as if* in contexts of action there is an equal distribution of chances'. It is an argument similarly propagated by Rancière (1999: 19) when he describes equality as 'empty freedom' that everyone possesses. Rancière (2002) conceives of equality as a quality of the individual, rather than society. As such, the individual has the political agency and autonomy not only to counter inequality (without having to wait on society) but also to lay claim to equality, when this right is being deprived. As such, it should not matter that students come from different backgrounds, which historically might have been constructed along racial and racist categories, or that black African students might be treated differently to other foreign students. What matters is that individuals conceive of themselves as equal to all others and presume that the context in which they find themselves will see and engage with them as equals.

Relooking Academic Activism According to Critique

Integrating an ethics of critique, academic activism embraces a 'politics of empowerment' that seeks to combine 'the logic of justice with that of friendship' (Benhabib, 1986: 352). Here, we specifically think of doing 'academic' things together – reading, writing and talking – for the sake of not only producing justly spirited scholarly works, for instance, a co-authored text or edited collections, but also creating anew a community of friendship and solidarity that would allow such a newly found community to fulfil its emancipatory potential more prudently. Of course, academic activism does not assume only a politics of intersubjectivity as if anything and everything should be done in the interest of the community. Rather, such activism also assumes what Benhabib (1986: 351) refers to as 'the politics of collective singularity'. In this sense, critique endorses both intersubjective and combined singular human actions that can empower and emancipate humans. Academic activism seen in such a light confirms not only people's humanity but also their human individualities. When academic activists look at the claims of the 'concrete other', they 'view each and every rational being as an individual with a concrete history, identity, and affective-emotional constitution … [through which] we abstract from what constitutes our commonality and seek to understand the distinctiveness of the other … [and] seek to comprehend the needs of the other, their motivations, what they search for, and what they desire' (Benhabib, 1986: 341).

Often we find ourselves working with multiple contributors to a book, and through our activist stances, we seek to support contributors through which others feel recognised and confirmed as concrete individual beings with specific needs, talents and capacities. In a way, our differences in joint academic work complement rather than exclude one another. The norms of our engagement are constituted by solidarity, friendship, love and care. In turn, much of our work revolves around our encounters with our students – whether in lecture theatres in a teaching-learning scenario or as supervisors of master's or doctoral studies. While teaching and learning involve its own set of processes and dialogical encounters, the supervision process has its own rhythm. While separate and distinct in terms of qualification and socialisation, both processes (teaching and supervision) speak to the emancipation of students. Both teaching and supervision are aimed at the evolution of something and someone new.

In the case of the Postgraduate Certificate of Education (PGCE) students completing the philosophy of education module, the intention is to invite them into a space of reflection, deliberation and hopefully disruption, as they detach from seeing the world in a singular fashion. Our activism as teachers is made visible to the extent to which students feel empowered through engaging in their learning; it lives in pedagogies of simultaneous disruption and comfort as students feel safe in engaging with that which is unfamiliar and unknown. We have found that even in large classes, it is possible to create spaces of deliberation, friendship and emancipation, not only between ourselves and students. We find that when we venture into that which is less topical or makes students uncomfortable (such as the prevalence of racism, homophobia or xenophobia), students who ordinarily would not engage with each other often end up in debates. In engaging with and from different perspectives, they inadvertently emancipate themselves from particular perspectives, which might have narrowed their worlds, rather than broadening them. To Hytten (2017: 386), classrooms are activist spaces – it is where knowledge is contested, habits are developed and communities are created – even if teachers are not critically conscious of the impacts of their pedagogical choices, efforts and relationships.

Hytten (2017: 386) raises concerns, however, about the risks of indoctrination – when teaching becomes so partisan that it slips into the propagation of particular views and beliefs as if these are the only truths. When does activism cease and become indoctrination? While it might be good for academics to feel strongly about this or that issue, and while they might want their students to develop similar views and stances about these issues, there is a legitimate risk of an infringement of a particular worldview onto students. Indoctrination, states Merry (2018: 165), works contrary to education – 'not only because it entails the inculcation of unshakable beliefs or commitments, but also because it involves the inculcation of unwarranted beliefs and commitments – that is, those unsupported by reasons and evidence'.

Quite differently, however, academic activism should not infer the inculcation of unwarranted beliefs. As forms of reasoned human agency, actions or encounters, it is continuously aimed at cultivating autonomous agents. Autonomy, as Callan (1997: 118) argues, 'enables us to choose intrinsically good lives; autonomy confers that ability without creating a bias against any particular ways of life that might have intrinsic value'. The challenge for activist teachers, as Hytten (2017: 386) asserts, is to adopt moral stances, to frame curricula and to design pedagogical activities around social justice values and commitments, but without stifling students' genuine inquiry. Students should feel neither compelled to buy into the particular views of an academic nor intimidated or afraid to disagree with an academic. In other words, academic activism should not fulfil the purpose of swaying students to this or that position. Instead, academic activism should make students alert to broad possibilities and perspectives and should be unconstrained and unregulated in terms of the positions or opinions they wish to adopt.

Depending on the kind of relationship between a supervisor and student, the supervision process can allow for more intimacy in terms of contact and time and, hence, a better sense of the other. The one-on-one construction of supervision lends itself to the potential formation of a particular kind of relationship, which can exceed the mere advising and promotion of this or that thesis. Of course, it is entirely possible for this encounter to be wholly mechanical – dependent on designated consultation slots, drafts, comments, revisions and more drafts. A supervision encounter, as a form of academic activism, foregrounds the relationship between the supervisor and the student. On one level, the encounter suggests an implicit relationality, which necessarily hinges on responsibility and responsiveness from both the supervisor and the student. The student's thesis writing requires supervision. As such, he or she is in need of a supervisor who will act responsibly in relation to the student by responding to the student's writing.

In turn, in order to supervise, the supervisor is in need of a student who will act responsibly by first producing the text, and then responding to the feedback and guidance, as provided by the supervisor. The relationship does not only centre on getting to know each other through the exchange of texts, but developing a friendship in the Derridian sense. To Derrida (1997: 204), friendship is 'a sort of trust without contract'; it consists *of* loving, rather than *being* loved or expecting to be loved (Derrida, 1997: 235). Friendship is constituted by extending oneself to another, without any expectation of reciprocity and without being befriended in return. To Derrida (1997: 62), friendship demands a 'certain esteem of the other without genuine intimacy'; genuine friends are independent, autonomous and self-sufficient – that is, they 'keep an infinite distance' (Derrida, 1997: 63). In sum, friendship is neither relational nor mutually contingent. In extending friendship to the student, the supervisor actively works towards not only supporting and guiding the academic success of the student but also inviting and mentoring the student into an academic discourse and scholarship.

Accompanying this mentoring is a willingness to engage with students on matters beyond the academic project, to support in ways that speak to the personal circumstances of students, which make the supervision process more complex, but also potentially more rewarding. When academics or supervisors endeavour towards cultivating relationships with students, they do so on the basis of trust and a professional commitment to eliciting a relationship, or friendship, which will ensure the best options for students – whether in terms of academic achievement or human worth.

In the interest of our academic efforts of the community for the sake of need and solidarity, we do not encourage one another to abandon our self-autonomy to question the interpretive assumptions of work. Through reflexive questioning, we not only articulate our needs as individuals but also engage with others about their needs. In this way, our self-reflection (autonomy) does not take us away from looking critically at our own work but rather invites us to communicate and engage in deliberation with other authors about their work. In this regard, Benhabib (1986: 333) posits '[t]he linguistic access to inner nature [of our academic work] is both a distancing and coming together ... that we can name and drives what motivates us, we are closer to freeing ourselves of its power over us; and in the very process of being able to say what we mean, we come one step closer to the harmony of friendship of the soul with itself' (Benhabib, 1986: 333–334). Thus, for us, academic activism in scholarly writing is at play when our communication of that which interests us is open and reflexive in relation to our needs and cultural persuasions so that our autonomy as persons is for once influenced also by the standpoints of the concrete others in our academic projects.

As Benhabib (1986: 335) argues, '[a]lthough all finite agents describe their own well-being, each defines this well-being in a different way'. This implies that academic activism not only takes different forms and expressions, but the expectation is always there that these different perspectives of academic activism might come into disagreement and conflict. In this sense, while one academic or student might feel strongly about academic freedom as an unconstrained tenet of a university, others might feel equally strongly that this tenet always is conditioned and curtailed by the potential harm of such speech. In a recent example, it became apparent that an invited speaker at a university gathering intended to speak on the harmful effects of academic freedom. An activist group – comprising students and academics – wrote to the invited speaker, insisting that he reconsider the argument of his presentation. Oddly enough, the activist group did not conceive of their request as an infringement of academic freedom or as a constraint of the speaker's autonomy. Ironically, in writing the letter out of concern for what the activist group interpreted as the speaker's undermining of academic freedom, the group slipped into their own argument by insisting that the speaker aligns his argument with their views. The moment an individual's autonomy is narrowed or limited, the concrete other is suppressed, which means that new ideas and arguments can neither unfold nor be challenged. Such an understanding or action is as contrary to academic freedom as it is to academic activism.

References

Benhabib, S. (1985). The utopian dimension in communicative ethics. *New German Critique, 35*(Special Issue on Jurgen Habermas), 83–96.

Benhabib, S. (1986). *Critique, norm and utopia: A study of the foundations of critical theory.* New York: Columbia University Press.

Benhabib, S. (1994). In defense of universalism – Yet again! A response to critics of situating the self. *New German Critique, 62*(Spring), 173–189.

Benhabib, S. (1999). Sexual difference and collective identities: The new global constellation. *Signs, 24*(2), 335–361.

Benhabib, S., Butler, J., Cornell, D., & Fraser, N. (1995). *Feminist contentions: A philosophical exchange.* New York: Routledge.

Callan, E. (1997). *Creating citizens.* Oxford, UK: Oxford University Press.

De Klerk, V. (2013). Initiation, hazing or orientation? A case study at a South African University. *International Research in Education, 1*(1), 86–100.

Derrida, J. (1997). *Politics of friendship* (G. Collins, Trans.). London/New York: Verso.

Friedman, M. (2003). *Autonomy, gender, politics.* Oxford, UK: Oxford University Press.

Hytten, K. (2017). Teaching as and for activism: Challenges and possibilities. *Philosophy of Education, 2014*, 385–394.

Marriott, D. (2018). The becoming-black of the world? On Achille Mbembe's *Critique of Black Reason.* https://www.radicalphilosophy.com/article/the-becoming-black-of-the-world. 4 May 2020.

Merry, M. (2018). Indoctrination, Islamic schools, and the broader scope of harm. *Theory and Research in Education, 16*(2), 162–178.

Rancière, J. (1999). *Disagreement: Politics and philosophy* (J. Rose, Trans.). Minneapolis, MN: University of Minnesota Press.

Rancière, J. (2002). *Afterword. The philosopher and his poor* (A. Parker, C. Oster, & J. Drury, Trans.). Durham, NC: Duke University Press.
South African Human Rights Commission (SAHRC). (2001). Report into initiation practices at educational institutions and a preliminary report on cultural initiations. https://www.sahrc.org.za/home/21/files/Reports/REPORT%20INTO%20INITIATION%20PRACTICES.pdf2001.pdf. 6 May 2020.

Chapter 3
Turning to the Subjectivity of the Individual

Abstract In this chapter, we pay particular attention to Michel Foucault's (Power: essential works of Foucault 1954–1984 – Volume 3. Faubion JD (ed). Penguin Books, London, 1994) conceptions and arguments on power, knowledge, freedom and resistance. Foucault (Power: essential works of Foucault 1954–1984 – Volume 3. Faubion JD (ed). Penguin Books, London, 1994) urges us to turn to the subjectivity of the individual again as the struggles reflect opposition to the effects of power linked with knowledge, competence and qualification – struggles against the privileges of knowledge. We argue that academic activism in the context of a Foucauldian view of the subjectivity of an individual is constituted by at least the following: that individuals are situated in genuine relations of power; that individuals act upon the actions of others; and that individuals' relations of power are constituted by the possibility for agonistic incitement and struggle.

Keywords Michel Foucault · Subjectivity · Individual · Power · Resistance · Freedom

Introduction

It is the French philosopher, Michel Foucault (1994), who brought to our attention that any form of critique is important for philosophy (of higher education) because it not only exposes us to philosophical problems about our world but, more importantly, it tries to liberate the individual from the 'struggles that question the status of the individual' (1994: 330). For Foucault (1994: 330), on the one hand, the struggle for individuals to assert their right to be different is a legitimate struggle that requires investigation. On the other hand, struggles against individuals are such that 'they attack everything that separates in the individual, breaks his [her] links with others, splits up community life, forces the individual back on himself [herself] and ties him [her] to his [her] own identity in a constraining way' (Foucault, 1994: 330). In this way, Foucault urges us to turn to the subjectivity of the individual again as the struggles reflect opposition to the effects of power linked with knowledge,

© The Author(s), under exclusive license to Springer Nature Singapore
Pte Ltd. 2021
N. Davids, Y. Waghid, *Academic Activism in Higher Education*, Debating
Higher Education: Philosophical Perspectives 5,
https://doi.org/10.1007/978-981-16-0340-2_3

competence and qualification – struggles against the privileges of knowledge (Foucault, 1994: 330).

What follows from such a Foucauldian understanding of struggles is that the main objective of academic activism is to liberate individuals from forms of domination, exploitation and subjectivity. By paying particular attention to his conceptions and arguments on power, knowledge, freedom and resistance, we argue that academic activism in the context of a Foucauldian view of the subjectivity of an individual is constituted by at least the following: that individuals are situated in genuine relations of power; that individuals act upon the actions of others; and that individuals' relations of power are constituted by the possibility for agonistic incitement and struggle. Foucault's positioning holds particular resonance for us as black academics employed at a historically white university. As 'blacks', our status presents an a priori struggle. South Africa's democracy has certainly not dispelled the racist categorisation of 'black'; there are imbedded and residual connotations of presumptive incompetence and disqualification. For us, the tension does not emanate necessarily from a desire to be different; we are already different by virtue of our racial categorisation. Consequently, we do not enter the institution or its culture as academic or individual equals. Instead, we are left with an unending struggle to prove and re-prove ourselves, thereby actively asserting our activism by being who we are.

Power, Resistance and the Subject of the Individual

Power, states Foucault (1997: 292), has immediate connotations of a political structure, a government and a dominant social class – a hierarchical construction between a master and a slave. Instead, therefore, he prefers 'relations of power', which he describes as 'human relationships, whether they involve verbal communication such as we are engaged in at this moment, or amorous, institutional, or economic relationships' (Foucault, 1997: 292). Power relations, Foucault (1997) maintains, are always present, at different levels; they are not fixed; they are relational and can be modified. Power relations, however, are contingent on the freedom of subjects to resist. Where one subject is at the disposal of the other and is unable to resist, the relations of power no longer exist (Foucault, 1997). To Foucault (1980: 89), power is relational to freedom. By implication, power denotes, firstly, a dependency between one and others (Foucault, 2000: 340) and, secondly, a network of persons or associations that function in an atmosphere of freedom (Foucault, 1980: 90).

Students, for example, enter an institutional structure and discourse where relations of power exist at multiple points: from access, participation and inclusion in academic, residential and social settings; classroom engagement and academic assessment; to qualification and graduation. For academics, like ourselves, who come from historically marginalised and maligned racial and ethnic identities and histories, there are similar obstacles of power in terms of access, participation, inclusion and recognition. Yet, students and academics alike have the freedom to question, disagree and resist what they are taught and how they engage with institutional practices – this confirms their autonomous subjectivity to act. Concomitantly, they have the same freedom to choose not to act – which might not necessarily infer an acceptance of what they encounter, but either an indifference or an unwillingness to try to engage and to disrupt what hegemonies are on display. Whatever the motivation, individuals (academics and students) have the freedom to act, or not.

According to Foucault (1994: 331), the subjectivity of an individual can be construed in two ways: first, the individual is a 'subject to someone else by control and dependence' and, second, the individual subject is 'tied to his[/her] own identity by a conscience or self-knowledge where both meanings suggest a form of power that subjugates and makes subject to' (Foucault, 1994: 331). Now when individuals struggle against forms of power relations such as forms of ethnic, social and religious domination; forms of exploitation that separate individuals from what they produce; and forms of subjectivity and submission that tie the individual to herself and submit her to others, they offer forms of resistance (Foucault, 1994: 329). In other words, individuals use their resistance 'to bring to light power relations, locate their position, find out their point of application and the methods used' (Foucault, 1994: 329). Here Foucault refers to the subjectivity of the self as resisting power relations by analysing what power relations dominate and control individual humans.

Forms of resistance against different forms of power, contends Foucault (1980: 97), imply that power happens within the freedom of the individual who resists what he or she encounters. Resistance to power, explains Foucault (1991: 75), is about 'detaching the power of truth from the forms of hegemony, social, economic, and cultural, within which it operates at the present time'. Students are imbued with the power to contest and critically scrutinise what they learn, and, in a Foucauldian sense, this means even resisting what thoughts teachers expect them to make their own. Here we again think of indoctrination – whereby students are not permitted to question what they are taught and how they are taught or to engage with the possibility of other texts and ideas. New ideas or considerations are frowned upon and dismissed as being without merit, even when their merits are barely considered. Indoctrination, of course, is not limited to interactions (or a lack thereof) between academics and students. They are as prevalent among academics as they are between academics and their respective institutions. It might be the case, in both instances, that only certain orthodoxies or pedagogies are propagated – 'the ways in which things have always been done' – an argument which serves as both justification and reason. Indoctrination is not limited to the uncritical inculcation of a set of beliefs or viewpoints; it also refers to the internalisation of particular ways of thinking, which is counterintuitive to any ideas of free thinking or critique.

The Foucauldian question that arises is, how does power manifest itself and, what is the role of individual subjects in power relations? In the first place, Foucault (1994: 337) designates power as relational in the sense that 'it brings into play relations between individuals (or between groups)'. When certain individuals exercise power over others, they 'induce others and follow from one another' (Foucault, 1994: 337). In this way, power relations are exercised. If we take the example of performance appraisal in an academic environment, such action to appraise the work performance of others is a relational act. It requires one academic to appraise others.

Moreover, while the expectation might be that professionalism dictates due process and protocol, the reality is that who individuals are and the existing relationships between individuals often determine the content of the appraisal. And, because power is relational, the individual upon whom is acted can respond in particular ways. It could be that an appraised academic might be dissatisfied with her performance score and then set out to find other reasons, why she might have achieved a poor appraisal. In our faculty, the annual performance process is fraught with endless prior departmental and faculty-based discussions and debates, as certain academics attempt to bring the process into disrepute. Endless hours are spent on discussing weighting allocations for teaching, research and community engagement. And despite agreements being reached, how the appraisal tool is used within departments shifts in relation to who does the appraisal and who is being appraised. The result is more deliberation and adjustment when the faculty executive convenes to finalise the appraisal scores.

Secondly, a power relationship, according to Foucault (1994: 340), is 'a mode of action that does not act directly or immediately on others. Instead, it acts upon their actions'. This implies that when one acts upon another, there is always the possibility that the other can resist; otherwise, there is no point, following Foucault, to speak about a power relationship. In his words:

> A power relationship … can only be articulated based on two elements that are indispensable if it is really to be a power relationship: that the other (the one over whom power is exercised) is recognized and maintained to the very end as a subject who acts: and that, faced with a relationship of power, a whole field of responses, reactions, results, and possible inventions open up. (Foucault, 1994: 340)

By implication establishing a power relationship 'is always a way of acting upon one or more acting subjects by virtue of their acting or being capable of action' (Foucault, 1994: 341).

Thirdly, Foucault (1994: 342) also explains a power relationship as an act of governmentality in the sense that power is only exercised over 'free subjects'. In his words, '[a]t the very heart of the power relationship, and constantly provoking it, are the recalcitrance of the will and the intransigence of freedom' (Foucault, 1994: 342). In this way, a power relationship becomes one of 'agonism' in which mutual incitement and struggle exist at the same time (Foucault, 1994: 342).

The problem with performance appraisal as it manifests in a university environment is that it cannot always be 'measured' according to prescribed criteria of appraisal in relation to a Likert scale of performance scores. The only aspect that really concerns evaluators, so it seems, is the actual scores academics have achieved according to the institution's criteria of the appraisal. These scores are used to determine salary increases; they are also used when the academic seeks promotion or applies for a research sabbatical. Often the final scores assigned to academic do not take into account the immense workload involved in teaching, student supervision and involvement on various committees. The performance appraisal has an unintended consequence of cultivating competitive work environments, as well as forcing academics to focus on research, rather than on any administrative responsibilities. This brings into further disrepute the function of the appraisal system as being directed at enhancing academic performance. In this regard, what academic activism requires is that an academic's freedom to submit to the appraisal system should be made known to the university authorities. If academics cannot actively pursue their freedom, they would in fact not be in a power relationship with those who appraise them, but rather in a relationship of subordination and servitude in which their activism has been stunted.

In brief, academic activism, in the context of a Foucauldian view of the subjectivity of an individual, is constituted by at least the following: that individuals are situated in genuine relations of power; that individuals act upon the actions of others; and that individuals' relations of power are constituted by the possibility for agonistic incitement and struggle.

Academic activism, following Foucault, resides in his conceptualisation of resistance, which is to 'incite, seduce, … and push actions to the extreme …' (Foucault, 2000: 341) and to resist 'regimes of truth'. To Foucault (1997: 129), 'regimes of truth' are produced by virtue of multiple constraints, which, in turn, 'induces regulated effects of power'. In this regard, 'truth isn't outside power, or deprived of power' (Foucault, 1997: 129). Each university, as made evident through its discourse and types of knowledge, establishes its parameters between that which matters and that which does not and between that which will be accounted as truth and that which will be discounted as untrue. How these parameters of truth are established is determined through relations of power and its corresponding field of knowledge. Power, as Foucault (1991: 194) informs us, 'produces domains of objects and rituals of truth'.

Despite 26 years of democracy, a number of South African universities continue to exist and operate in cultures and discourses of colonialism. Colonialism has a pervading presence in the architecture, institutional culture, language and curriculum. Of course, South Africa is not unique in this regard. Although most writings on the African university begin by acknowledging a list of premodern institutions as precursors to the modern African university, explains Mamdani (2016: 69), neither the institutional form nor the curricular content of the modern African university is derived from precolonial institutions. Instead, their inspiration is the colonial modern.

Similarly, Teferra and Altbach (2004: 23) assert that the African continent is dominated by academic institutions shaped by colonialism and organised according to the European model. They maintain that higher education in Africa is an artefact of colonial policies, which has been shaped and influenced by a multitude of European colonisers, including Belgium, Germany, the Netherlands, Italy, Portugal and Spain. Britain and France, they continue, have left the greatest and lasting impact, not only in terms of the organisation of academe and the continuing links to the metropole but, most importantly, in the language of instruction and communication (Teferra & Altbach, 2004: 23). There is an obvious tension here: on the one hand, South Africa has presumably rid itself from both colonialism and apartheid;

on the other hand, however, it continues to be mired in the same legacies and regimes of truth, which ensured its oppression.

Following the above, how can universities embark on emancipation through education, when their institutional cultures and curricula (regimes of truth) continue to be framed in ethics of oppression? To Foucault (1991: 75), the only way to resist the regimes of truth is by 'detaching the power of truth from the forms of hegemony, social, economic, and cultural, within which it operates at the present time'. Each individual, or student, following Foucault (1980), has the power and freedom to resist. To Foucault, the choice is quite explicit in that either the individuals exert their power against what they experience as oppressive or othering or they remain trapped in subjugation. In this regard, students and academics alike, by virtue of their own freedom and power to act, have the capacity to liberate themselves by foregrounding their own regimes of truth. In the South African context, calls for the decolonisation of universities are not limited to ending the domination of colonialist epistemological traditions. Conceptions of decolonisation emanate from deeper crises and dystopias of power, misrecognition and exclusion. The calls for decolonisation, therefore, have to do with a recognition of other regimes of truth, other ways of being and thinking, which continue to be excluded and disregarded. In this regard, for decolonisation as emancipation to be realised, students and academics exert their power through their voices and begin to tell their own stories, so that histories and knowledge, which have, thus far, remained untold and unrecorded, might emerge.

Significantly, the realisation of a decolonised university space and curriculum is not necessary only for the liberation of historically disadvantaged ('black') students; it is as pertinent for historically advantaged ('white') students. The invisibility of 'whiteness' and its embedded hegemonies of power continue to prevent most 'white' students and academics from, on the one hand, taking stock of their own privilege and, on the other hand, recognising that the public sphere (and private sphere in terms of socio-economic deprivation) offers entirely different pathways and experiences for 'black' individuals. The employment of 'black' academics at the institution where we are based is a relatively recent phenomenon – with this only happening a few years after the onset of democracy in 1994. Most 'white' academics have never worked with 'black' academics or taught 'black' students prior to the demise of apartheid. For some 'white' academics, the idea of having 'black' colleagues, or acknowledging that their 'black' peers could have the same knowledge and competence as they do, presents some uncomfortable truths, which causes a few of them to question their own racialised understanding of the world.

While not a first in South Africa, the experiences of Professor Mamokgethi Phakeng, the current Vice-Chancellor of the University of Cape Town, provide a disturbing illustration of what can happen in the academy when qualification and competence are blindly associated only with whiteness. Nine months after being appointed in her former position as the Deputy Vice-Chancellor for Research and Internalisation in 2017, Phakeng was subjected to a malicious smear campaign, which alleged that her qualifications are fake. Emails were sent to a list of mainly 40 'white' people, which included as former Vice-Chancellor, members of the UCT council, senior professors and alumni. In addition to being accused of not having the requisite qualifications, Phakeng was accused of not having achieved intellectually, of being dishonest and of not having the necessary gravitas for the position of Vice-Chancellor (Staff reporter, 2017). In labelling the campaign as racism, Phakeng argued that 'white' professors are not subjected to similar scrutiny and, moreover, that there are many 'white' academics, who are given professorships, despite not having any doctoral qualifications.

Decolonisation, therefore, should not only be conceived and called for concerning the emancipation of those who have been subjected to colonisation. It should also be called for and by 'white' people, so that they, too, might be emancipated and recognise that the world does not respond to all people in the same way.

Power, Knowledge and Freedom

As students and academics resist taken-for-granted regimes for truth, they push to the fore new regimes of truth and new knowledge. In exerting their power to resist, they produce knowledge, which otherwise might not have been known. In turn, in making new knowledge known, and thereby confirming the existence of other truths, students and academics reveal their own power. To Foucault (1972: 182–183), knowledge is a 'group of elements, formed regularly by discursive practice'; it is the 'the field of coordination and subordination of statements in which concepts appear, and are defined and transformed'. Moreover, knowledge, says Foucault (1972: 183), is 'that of which one can speak in a discursive practice, and which is specified by that fact', emphasising that 'knowledge is not the sum of what is thought to be true, but rather the whole set of practices that are distinctive of a particular domain'. In turn, academics are in positions to play significant roles in inviting students into conversations and deliberations through which knowledge might be transformed. Here, we think of storytelling as a means of entering the lives of academics or teachers and students. By nature, state Connelly and Clandinin (1990), people lead storied lives and tell stories of those lives. Teachers and students, they continue, are storytellers and characters in their own and other's stories.

These stories, as Fay (1996) reminds us, are not self-contained – that is, no life can be a story in itself, which means that new stories and new forms of knowledge can and will emerge. As academics and students listen to each other, there are opportunities and spaces to engage with that which might have been untold and unrelated, and hence, perhaps, for initial perceptions and biases to be adjusted and re-storied. These kinds of encounters confirm the existence of new truths, knowledge and power, which can only emerge through practices of listening to others. In listening to the stories and voices of others, power shifts from one to the other. This is not to say that listening is a passive process, but rather that power exists in taking ownership of a particular story and truth; power exists in having a voice.

Foucault conceives of knowledge and power as co-existing in a dyadic relationship. To him, 'It is not the activity of the subject of knowledge that produces a corpus of knowledge, useful or resistant to power, but power/knowledge, the processes and struggles that transverse it and of which it is made up, that determines the forms and possible domains of knowledge' (Foucault, 1998: 27). To Foucault (1998), power/knowledge can be either positive or negative; it can be either productive or restrictive. It is produced when it advances new ideas, debates and disagreements, when it offers opportunities for new ways of thinking, for new considerations and the taking into account of previously unconsidered ways of being.

Contrastingly, power/knowledge, following Foucault, can be negative when it is restrictive and propagates one truth or one form of knowledge as the only one worth knowing. This kind of knowledge limits deliberation and dissensus and restricts the potential of students or individuals to step beyond the predetermined boundaries of what is permissible and what is not. Indigenous knowledge, for example, is often frowned upon and dismissed as backwards – the indictment being that it is 'non-Western' and, hence, of no value. So, too, indigenous languages occupy uncomfortable spaces within educational institutions. Students quickly learn that their indigenous tongues will not find acceptance in university classrooms. They quickly learn that if they wish to access the institutional space of higher learning, and if they wish to succeed, then that depends on the mastery of the English language.

It is no surprise, therefore, to find that the emergence of the concept of 'indigeneity', in relation to the practice of African philosophy, is a relatively recent discipline on the academic front and has constructed the formation of African philosophy as a separate intellectual endeavour (Masolo, 2003: 25). In this sense, Foucault's (1998) power/knowledge is not only restrictive in terms of an inward focus, but it is as restrictive when it subjugates and suppresses. Apartheid South Africa holds profound examples of these kinds of actions – with the most notable one being the propagation of Afrikaans as the only medium of instruction when it was abundantly clear that the majority of black learners could neither speak nor understand the language.

So, too, power/knowledge is negative when academics use their positions of presumed power to reduce the voices and contributions of either students or other academics. It might be, for example, that students are invited to participate, yet no due consideration is given to what they have to say. Their participation matters only insofar as it provides a demonstration of something, but the content and substance of the contribution itself are of no matter. These stifled encounters are not limited to teaching and are as prevalent in student supervision. Students are not only introduced to the same theorists year after year, but they are initiated into rigid research paradigms, whereby a study is either quantitative or qualitative. There are no spaces for stepping out the conceptual, theoretical and methodological boxes, as prescribed by the supervisor. Other times, students are repeatedly directed to the same kind of research question. While this kind of approach might certainly lessen the load on the supervisor, in not being required to engage with new theoretical frameworks and research questions, students are left poorer. Their initiation into the academy is one of reduced thinking and academic compliance.

Similar encounters are surprisingly common among academics, whereby more senior professors might conceive of themselves as custodians of the types of knowledge, which other academics ought to follow and read. New theories and approaches, while listened to initially, are considered flawed or weak. In this way, the types of knowledge foregrounded in an academic department or faculty remain the same. Programme content and pedagogies remain unchanged – despite immense contextual political, social and economic shifts. Newly appointed academics are expected to adhere to pre-existing theoretical approaches; they are mentored into existing hegemonic structures, where the predominant ethos is that of collegial amenability. Similar discourses are evident in the structures of the university executive, where dissent is considered akin to antagonistic non-collegiality and, as such, should be squashed rather than encouraged. There are obvious concerns with desiring to perpetuate a climate of agreement and silence within any university setting. Silence certainly does not necessarily imply acceptance of whatever views are being espoused; silence can also suggest either apathy or a fear of speaking out. This means even when a matter is being mismanaged, few, if any, academics would be willing to use their voice, thereby not only feeding into existing power structures but allowing mismanagement to transpire.

Power/knowledge adopts the formation of academic activism when it is intent upon opening and broadening new truths and knowledge, rather than dismissing and shutting these down. Power/knowledge is reliant on the voices, as well as a boldness of academics and students. It recognises that universities cannot be embedded in languages and practices of compliance and complacency and that knowledge is entirely dependent on a courage to state and write that which has not been articulated before.

Despite Foucault's (1991) differentiation between power/knowledge as either positive or negative, he is opposed to conceiving the effects of power as only negative. He cautions against describing the effects of power as that which it 'excludes', 'censors', 'masks' or 'conceals' (Foucault, 1991: 194). Instead, he argues, 'power produces; it produces reality; it produces domains of objects and rituals of truth. The individual and the knowledge that may be gained of him belong to this production' (Foucault, 1991: 194). Power, says Foucault (1980: 93), is everywhere – 'not because it embraces everything but because it comes from everything', including all individuals. The individual – the student or academic – has the power and the freedom to act, to comply, to accept or to question and resist. For Foucault (1997: 284), freedom 'is the ontological condition of ethics'. In this sense, freedom is a practice, which must be practised ethically.

Stated differently, the essential condition for the practice of ethics is freedom – that is, to have the ability to opt for one action, and not another. Knowing how to act ethically, maintains Foucault (1997: 286), requires hard work: 'Extensive work by the self on the self is required for this practice of freedom to take shape in an *ethos* that is good, beautiful, honorable, estimable, memorable, and exemplary'. This brings to the fore a critical element of academic work and academic activism. While universities attach great importance to the adherence of ethical conduct during research, similar attention is not necessarily given to the ethical conduct of academics in their interactions and engagements with students. Stated differently, the focus on ethical requirements seems to be more centred on research methodologies than it is on human encounters. How do academics conceive of themselves? How do they understand what it means to act ethically concerning teaching, supervision as well as assessment or examination? How should academics engage with their students? When are ethical considerations and boundaries compromised? Here, our concerns are not only about how academics teach, supervise and assess students' work. We are as concerned about the type of relationships academics construct and enter into with their students (Davids & Waghid, 2020).

We have repeatedly emphasised the importance of friendship and humane engagement between teachers (academics) and students. We have argued that when teachers endeavour toward cultivating relationships with students, they do so on the basis of trust and a professional commitment to eliciting a relationship, or friendship, which will ensure the best options for students – whether in terms of academic achievement or human worth. Following Derrida (1997: 306), we argue that democratic community is often evident in certain classrooms, where concerted efforts are made by teachers to cultivate spaces of unconstrained engagement and where students experience inclusion, recognition and belonging to the extent that they feel free to voice their opinions and arguments. Where teachers foreground and insist upon respectful and humane engagement, students tend to follow suit, because they recognise such engagement as valuable to themselves and others (Davids & Waghid, 2020). In this way, if academics wish to cultivate classrooms and, indeed, influence and shape students to be respectful and dignified in the way they engage with others, then both the persona and pedagogical practices of the academic have to be in sync with these principles. Practices of humiliation, discrimination, marginalisation and exclusion have no place in either a democratic classroom or what it means to teach and act as a moral subject.

To Foucault (1997: 286–287), there are four ways in which an individual might understand him- or herself as the moral subject of his or her actions. The first part concerns that part of the individual, which acts as the focus of moral conduct; the second part centres on what makes an individual recognise his or her moral obligations. The third is concerned with how an individual might transform and work on him- or herself. And the fourth focuses on the type of person an individual desires to be. Teachers and, by implication, academics, by virtue of their positions, are presumed to hold themselves to a standard of ethics. Few would disagree with the contention that not only is teaching a thoroughly relational activity but should also be couched in ethical conduct. It is common for educational institutions to prescribe these ethics in a professional code or framework, which, at times, are framed by broader and national codes, typically found in higher education. These codes or frameworks are not without criticisms – predominantly centring on why academics would need to be regulated in their conduct in the first place. However, other concerns, such as those raised by Levinson (2015), speak to contexts in which ethics are expected to operate. People, she argues, 'make decisions in contexts rather than vacuums, embedded in webs of relationships, sensitive (perhaps overly so) to particularities and nuances, adopting roles and perspectives that are situational rather than universal' (Levinson, 2015: 220).

Most academics would comfortably describe themselves as ethical beings; they would not conceive of themselves as acting in ways that might be considered as unacceptable or undesirable. However, these concerns, while important, are not Foucault's (1997) only focus. He is as concerned with the transformation of individuals in terms of how they desire themselves to be. The importance of this discussion resides in the idea of academic activism as a liberatory action – liberatory not only in terms of academic freedom but liberatory in relation in how academics are able to transform themselves in relation to the 'webs of relationships' (Levinson, 2015), in which they might find themselves. While teaching and student supervision are relational practices, they are not predictable, as might be typically suggested by predetermined learning outcomes. Pedagogy, explains Todd (2001: 436), demands that its subjects 'learn to become' – a phrase she borrows from Castoriadis (1997). According to Todd (2001: 433):

> 'Learning to become' depicts well the ontological stakes in processes of learning, both with respect to the benefits of change and the high prices to be paid in terms of the coercive nature of subject formation. It echoes the comments students often make when they begin to think and experience their own lives differently through new ideas, concepts, and relationships to other people. It is not uncommon, for example, to hear even adult students say, 'I have never thought of myself this way before reading this book', or, 'My life has changed as a result of taking this class'. My own educational history speaks to such moments of elation. These declarations of change, however, are often accompanied by statements of struggle in making a relationship to a knowledge 'outside' the subject; students wrestle with the otherness and difference presented to them through the curriculum and through the bodies of teachers and students they encounter.

In light of these struggles which students encounter, says Todd (2001: 436), 'in practice there is a great deal of uncertainty and unpredictability to the pedagogical enterprise. People [academics and students] bring a host of idiosyncrasies and unconscious associations that enable them to resist, transform and create symbolic attachments which pedagogy cannot predict or control'. At times, the resistance between teachers and students arises from their respective identities. Students struggle to connect with who their teachers are, in the same way that teachers might either not care or not know how to connect with the identities and lifeworlds of students. Instead, teachers embark on the pedagogical project with scant regard for the importance of establishing relations of care and trust. It matters who teachers are, and it matters who students are. If the pedagogical encounter is to succeed in transforming and liberating both students and teachers, then each has to be known to the other. Activist teachers do not only have a clear sense of their responsibilities to their students; they have an equally clear understanding of the necessity of being responsive to the needs and idiosyncrasies of students. Moreover, activist teachers and teaching recognise the fluidity and unpredictability of the pedagogical encounter by not trying to frame teaching and learning with pre-judgements.

One of the biggest challenges in higher education in South Africa is how to straddle the historical, socio-economic divide between students. As far as schooling experiences, students follow vastly different pathways – pathways that continue into how they navigate and experience university environments. The majority of students, who have come from historically disadvantaged backgrounds, encounter immense financial challenges and pressures, even when they are recipients of state-aided funding. It is not unusual for students to have financial obligations concerning extended family members. Often funding, meant for books and other learning resources, are used for the purchasing of much-needed food and other basic amenities – not only for themselves but for siblings and other family members. This in itself presents a range of ethical questions, and without negating these, we cannot lay claim to fully understanding these without due cognisance of having to deal with the trauma and pain of hungry family members.

Inevitably these divergent pathways and idiosyncrasies impact upon the academic performance of students, and academics are continually faced with having to make judgements on whether or not to penalise students for late submissions or failing them for poor performance on a test, or not allowing a thesis to pass. Of course, it would be ethical to adopt an approach, which insists on treating all students fairly and equally and, hence, expecting the same calibre of academic performance of all students regardless of their circumstances. But, would it be unethical for an academic to exercise his or her judgement concerning students as individuals, and hence recognise that students are, in fact, not equal in circumstances, and it would, in fact, be unfair to expect the same standard?

We do not necessarily have the answers to these questions. We are, however, confronted with them on a fairly regular basis. Following on Foucault (1997) as well as Todd (2001), it is helpful to consider these ethical dilemmas in relation to the transformation, and, hence, freedom, of both the academic and the student. If students are in a state of becoming, as posited by Todd (2001), then by implication, because of the relationality of the teaching-learning encounter, so too are academics and teachers. In this regard, academic activism looks at what it is that academics desire from their students and meeting that desire with their own desires for their students.

Activism takes shape when academics connect with the desires of their students. That is, they meet students in terms of where they are at and then work with them towards attaining that which is desired. In this way, both students and the academic stand to transform and gain from the encounter. Students reach the desire of academic success by attaining knowledge and its accompanying power and freedom. In turn, the success of the student is that of the academic's as well – in that the academic recognises his or her role and responsibility concerning the student and, as such, acts in the best interests of students. Each time the academic undergoes this process by virtue of educational encounters, the academic shifts and has the potential to transform how he or she chooses to engage with students. What makes this understanding and approach of academic activism valuable is that it holds an equal potential to liberate both students and academics from their own subjectivity.

References

Castoriadis, C. (Ed.) (1997). Psychoanalysis and politics. In *World in fragments: Writings on politics, society, psychoanalysis, and the imagination* (D. A. Curtis, Trans.) (pp. 125–136). Stanford, CA: Stanford University Press.

Connelly, M., & Clandinin, D. J. (1990). Stories of experience and narrative inquiry. *Educational Researcher, 19*(5), 2–14.

Davids, N. & Waghid, Y. (2020). *Teaching, friendship and humanity*. Singapore: Springer.

Derrida, J. (1997). *Politics of friendship* (G. Collins, Trans.). London: Verso.

Fay, B. (1996). *Contemporary philosophy of social science: A multicultural approach*. Oxford, UK: Blackwell Publishers.

Foucault, M. (1972). *The archaeology of knowledge* (New York: Pantheon Books). Translation from the French. L'Archeologie du Savoir (Paris: Gallimard, 1969).

Foucault, M. (1980). Power and strategies. In C. Gordon (Ed.), *Power/knowledge* (pp. 134–145). New York: Pantheon.

Foucault, M. (1991). *Discipline and punish: The birth of a prison*. London: Penguin.

Foucault, M. (1994). *Power: Essential Works of Foucault 1954–1984 – Volume 3*. J. D. Faubion (Ed.). London: Penguin Books.

Foucault, M. (1997). *Ethics: Subjectivity and truth*. P. Rabinow (Ed.) (R. Hurley & others, Trans.). London: Allen Lane, The Penguin Press.

Foucault, M. (1998). *The history of sexuality: The will to knowledge*. London: Penguin.

Foucault, M. (2000). Omnes et Singulatem': Towards a critique of political reason. In D. J. Faubion (Ed.), *Power: Essential works of Foucault, 1954–1984, Vol 3*. London: Penguin.

Levinson, M. (2015). Moral injury and the ethics of educational injustice. *Harvard Educational Review, 85*(2), 203–228.

Mamdani, M. (2016). Between the public intellectual and the scholar: Decolonization and some post-independence initiatives in African higher education. *Inter-Asia Cultural Studies, 7*(1), 68–83.

Masolo, D. A. (2003). Philosophy and indigenous knowledge: An African perspective. *Africa Today, 50*(2), 21–38.

Staff Reporter. (2017). UCT, Professor Mamokgethi Phakeng and accusations of fake qualifications. https://mg.co.za/article/2017-10-11-uct-professor-mamokgethi-phakeng-and-accusations-of-fake-qualifications/. 30 May 2020.

Teferra, D., & Altbach, P. G. (2004). African higher education: Challenges for the 21st century. *Higher Education, 47*, 21–50.

Todd, S. (2001). Bringing more than I contain': Ethics, curriculum and the pedagogical demand for altered egos. *Journal of Curriculum Studies, 33*(4), 431–450.

Chapter 4
Deconstruction Through Writing

Abstract This chapter turns to the ideas of French philosopher, Jacques Derrida. We look at what drives the critical work of deconstruction in defence of 'the relentless pursuit of the impossible, which means, of things whose possibility is sustained by their impossibility' (Caputo, Deconstruction in a nutshell: a conversation with Jacques Derrida. Fordham University Press, New York, 1997: 32). Specifically, we look at what academic activists can do regarding what lies beyond them and is not immediately apparent. We contend that conceptions of academic responsibility are tied to relational encounters with texts (reading and writing), as well as teaching and research. As such, academic responsibility cannot be remiss of its potential to cause harm, as in the perpetuation of social injustices. Instead, academic activism as a responsible endeavour centres on giving back and is focused on ensuring beneficial forms of engagement with students, communities or society. This, we maintain, cultivates a re-conscientisation of the university.

Keywords Jacques Derrida · Deconstruction · Reading · Writing · Academic responsibility · Re-conscientisation

Introduction

When individuals embark on critique, they reflect on the subjectivities of individuals and evaluate the actions of others in the context of how they view the world. However, when individuals are self-reflexive, they still offer reasons and justifications in light of what they consider to be constitutive of emancipatory action itself – that is, they remain critical. Individuals barely look at what lies beyond their actions of critique, which in itself can be a crisis for critique. French philosopher, Jacques Derrida (1995), reminds us that critical work in philosophy (and philosophy of higher education) cannot ignore the possibility that any attempt at articulating critique as a foundational discipline would in itself undermine the credentials of such a philosophy to be critical (Derrida, 1995). In other words, critique cannot escape the very limitations it seeks to delimit. The mere possibility of critique opens itself

© The Author(s), under exclusive license to Springer Nature Singapore Pte Ltd. 2021
N. Davids, Y. Waghid, *Academic Activism in Higher Education*, Debating Higher Education: Philosophical Perspectives 5,
https://doi.org/10.1007/978-981-16-0340-2_4

up to the possibility of not being emancipatory and self-empowering as there is nothing pure and infallible about treating ways of seeing the world as foundations that can remedy fractured situations.

Put differently, following Derrida (1995), it is not enough just to be critical from the inside, but critical agents are also required to act justly towards what lies beyond – that is, to those unforeseen possibilities that cannot be seen in advance as a possibility (Derrida, 1995). To us, it is certainly not enough to merely critique what we observe and experience as academics; it cannot be our task only to highlight certain issues and injustices. There has to be a preparedness to change that which requires change, to participate as is required and, more importantly, to hold ourselves to the same scrutiny to which we subject others and the world around us. This means recognising that inasmuch as we might think we are alert and attuned to our contexts and any potential pitfalls, we do not enter or occupy these contexts without our blinkers and biases. There are matters and questions which lie beyond that which is immediately or abundantly evident to us.

In this chapter, we look at what drives the critical work of deconstruction in defence of 'the relentless pursuit of the impossible, which means, of things whose possibility is sustained by their impossibility' (Caputo, 1997: 32) in relation to what academic activists can do towards what lies outside of them. We contend that conceptions of academic responsibility are tied up in relational encounters with texts (reading and writing), as well as teaching and research. As such, academic responsibility cannot be remiss of its potential to cause harm, as in the perpetuation of social injustices. Instead, academic activism as a responsible endeavour centres on giving back and is focused on ensuring beneficial forms of engagement with students, communities or society. This, we maintain, cultivates a re-conscientisation of the university.

On Deconstruction, Reading, Writing and Activism

Derrida's (1995) conception of deconstruction occupies a significant position in the tradition of critical (educational) philosophy. For him, deconstruction 'always aims at the trust confided in the critical, critical theoretical agency, that is, the deciding agency ...' (Derrida, 1995: 54). In Derridian terms, deconstruction has a critical-theoretical orientation. Although Derrida does not directly claim deconstruction as a way to enact critical theory, he does not disconnect deconstruction from the critical agency of such a theoretical position. Likewise, deconstruction for Derrida is 'deconstruction of critical dogmatism'. This suggests that Derrida recognises the possibility in critical (educational) theory of becoming dogmatic, such as reifying critical theory to the level of the unquestionable (dogmatic). As such, he encourages critical agents to become even critical of critical theory itself. For instance, to think that critical theory has resulted in the empowerment and emancipation of humans without remaining cognisant of the possibility that critical theory can actually disempower humans as well is to remain unaware of such a possibility even though, following Derrida (1995), it might seem to be an impossibility.

Derrida is adamant that deconstruction is not a method in philosophy (of higher education) and cannot be transformed into one but, instead, insists that it (deconstruction) can be understood as a form of questioning interested in a 'constitutive outside' (Derrida, 1982). Hence, when meanings are analysed and afforded explanations, a deconstructive reading of meanings would be about what lies beyond an understanding of meanings as they unfold; it is interested in the traces of meaning represented by the text. Put differently, deconstruction is interested in meanings that are excluded and perhaps not thought of – that is, meanings of what is different and other. Deconstruction, states Norris (1987: 19), is meticulously seeking out aporias, blind spots or moments of self-contradiction in the text that involuntarily betray the tension between rhetoric and logic, what the text says and what it is intended to mean. Of course, what the text means lives with the one who engages with it; interpretations of the text reside with individuals and the lived experiences they bring to that text. What this means is that depending on who readers are, and the contexts they bring, the text will adopt different meanings. By implication, therefore, the critical potential of deconstruction unfolds when it tries to be open to that which might not have been thought of – that is, deconstruction is concerned with 'an openness towards the unforeseeable incoming' of the other and otherness (Caputo, 1997: 47). In this sense, deconstruction questions the very possibility of what appears to be impossible.

For instance, if one has to explain deconstruction concerning asking questions about what lies outside, then to read a text in a deconstructive manner implies that one does not limit one's questioning to what one is confronted with in the text. Instead, one's critical questioning is extended beyond meanings inside of the text to meanings that lie within or beyond the margins of a text. In this way, one is open to what is not there and perhaps what is still to come – and often what is still to come is a condition of impossibility with which deconstruction is concerned. As aptly articulated by Gert Biesta (2009: 93), deconstruction can be seen as offering yet another conception of criticality in that it envisages to go beyond the present and the given, another way, in short, for 'outside' judgment to become possible. Again, Biesta (2009: 93) posits, 'the aim of deconstruction ... is not to destroy but to affirm and do justice to the impossible, to what cannot be foreseen as a possibility'.

What follows from the aforementioned understanding (if this is possible) of deconstruction is that academic activism cannot strictly be about knowing the 'inside' of university classrooms, spaces or politics. That in itself would be a critical concern with what is constitutive of what makes university dynamics possible. Here, we specifically think of doing a critical analysis of classroom pragmatics, in particular how students interact with university teachers in the realm of argumentation and rational justifications. However, in light of a deconstructive analysis of classroom pragmatics, academic activists (university teachers) would at once be concerned with conceptions of pedagogical engagements between students and teachers that lie beyond their current thinking and how such actions critically (from the outside) influence their sense of community. In other words, deconstruction would be concerned not just with what meanings come through in questioning pedagogical interactions, but how new meanings pertaining to the in-coming of the other from outside might manifest. For instance, by now deliberative engagement between university teachers and students are mostly influenced by iterations and reflexive scrutiny on what people have to say. As soon as something else that lies beyond our thinking perhaps is brought into the realm of discussion, then the possibility of a seeming impossibility would have been achieved. So, instead of focusing on meanings constitutive of critical pedagogical actions, the deconstructive activist would be concerned with bringing the impossible from the outside. It is in this sense that we understand Derrida (1995) when he posits that educational relations ought to prepare students for the incalculable – that is, educational practices have to look out for that other and otherness that 'is not ... possible'.

We now specifically look at Derrida's (1977) use of deconstruction in his major work, *Limited Inc*, considered as the clearest exposition of the notion of deconstruction. Derrida (1977) explains deconstruction in the context of writing. For him, writing can only be seen as a means of communication – that is, 'an especially potent means of communication extending enormously ... the domain of oral or gestural communication' (Derrida, 1977: 3). He goes on to assert that writing is about communicating 'something to those who are absent' where absence is 'a continuous modification and progressive extenuation of presence' (Derrida, 1977: 5). Thus, for Derrida (1977: 7), written communication retains its function as writing – that is, its readability despite the disappearance of any receiver – if it remains iterable in the absence of such and such a person. He posits, '[t]o be what it is, all writing must, therefore, be capable of functioning in the radical absence of every empirically determined receiver ... [a]nd this absence ... is a rupture in presence, the "death" or the possibility of the "death" of the receiver' (Derrida, 1977: 8).

Now, what can be inferred from Derrida's deconstructive analysis of writing is that not only is writing a form of communication of presences but also an iteration in the absence and beyond the presence of empirically determined subjects (Derrida, 1977). Thus, when academic activism assumes the form of writing, such a form of communication cannot just be about disseminating thoughts through the images and words in texts, but also to provoke those receivers intent on engaging with the writing to rupture the sender's (writer's) thoughts in her absence. Put more succinctly, deconstructive writing, as a form of academic activism, has to provoke readers (academics and students) to 'recognize other possibilities in it [writing] by inscribing it or grafting it onto other chains' (Derrida, 1977: 9). By the latter, Derrida implies that the thoughts of the writer (sender) should give rise to new codes that open up the 'iterability (repetition/alterity)' of writing. By implication, writing invites people to deconstruct meanings beyond their present understandings to the extent that meanings are construed beyond what might perhaps be implied.

In our own supervision of doctoral students and, by implication, our own writing, we insist that they look beyond the taken-for-granted and to (re)construct and deconstruct meanings iteratively in the absence of authors. Somehow, in this regard, our academic activism extends to provoking students to come up with meanings of concepts and practices in iterative fashions that might even subvert and/or extend previous understandings. In this way, the scholarly work of students might just be more rigorously theoretical than just focusing on pedantic narrations through arcane literature reviews. Like Derrida, we caution students not to cite authors' theoretical positions too extensively without clarification and meaning. By this it meant that we actually discourage students to cite works by merely duplicating what has already been said without engaging deconstructively with texts to ascertain what has not been said or what might be in the margins of theorists' work – that is, what lies beyond their presences in texts. Doing so would be to remain disengaged from a 'desire-to-say-what-one-means' (Derrida, 1977: 12) and thus failing to make sense of citationality itself.

Some students find the approach of being encouraged to question and disrupt dominant debates and theories especially problematic – mainly because they have been subjected to many years of educational processes and structures, in which they were not asked to engage and think critically. They approach theory as an unshakable truth – one which they should not question or undermine and, thus, prefer to work with that which is already known and to repeat what has already been said. Much of the anxiety around doctoral supervision centres on mentoring and assisting students in finding their own voice. For this reason, both of us are in strong support of retaining the *viva voce* (oral or verbal examination) as a necessary part of the doctoral examination process. Very few universities in South Africa have held on to this practice and, instead, rely on a textual examination of the thesis.

Often, we find that despite being made aware that the examination process of a doctoral thesis includes the component of a *viva voce*, external examiners (academics) often find reasons not to participate. While some see the *viva voce* as unnecessary by virtue of the fact it is not an examination requirement at their own universities, others see it as a waste of their time and prefer to send a list of questions, rather than taking the time to engage with students directly. We hold that even when students are able to construct a particular argument and produce a thesis, they are not necessarily adept at speaking on their research. That is, they have yet to develop their academic voice. What the *viva voce* does is to invite students into a space with examiners, where they are able to present their research, address any questions as well as talk-back to examiners, thereby deliberating on their work with experts in the field. The importance of this process is not limited to academic engagement on theoretical and conceptual matters; of equal importance is the initiation into an academic discourse of rigorous but respectful deliberation and debate.

A New Type of University Responsibility

Reading Derrida in the context of education 'calls for an engagement of his form of reasoning and analyzing with educational issues' (Biesta & Egéa, 2011: 4). It needs time, patience and attention. Furthermore, reading infers 'at the least, the taking of a position, in work itself, toward the politico-institutional structures that constitute and regulate our practice, our competences, and our performances' (Derrida, 1992a:

23). Derrida devoted a great deal of attention to his own teaching, approaching it, as Naas (2015: 3) explains, 'with a very clear pedagogical purpose'. According to Naas (2015: 3), Derrida led his students to read texts closely and patiently in their letter and then taught them how to read them in relation to other texts, themes and questions from the history of philosophy and literature. In addition to teaching his students about various philosophical and literary themes, figures and problems, he taught them 'how to read, how to question, and, thus, how to teach in turn' (Naas, 2015: 1). When we reflect on how Derrida conceived and approached his teaching, his seminars and his engagements with his students, it becomes apparent that the focus is more on the processes of attentiveness and thoughtfulness.

Certainly, in engaging with Derrida's texts, as we attempt to do in this chapter, we are able to gain insights into education – its dilemmas and challenges, but, in a Derridian sense, not necessarily find solutions. Solutions imply clarification, answers and closure. Derrida, of course, calls on us to question, relentlessly (Egéa, 2018). Indeed, says Egéa (2018: 120), 'any attempt to summarize complex concepts, to recall them more or less exactly, more or less precisely in order to be able to try and draw some specific "implications" to be "applied" to education would not carry much meaning, and would amount to misreading this author [Derrida]'.

What, therefore, might be the purpose and point of deconstruction? Significantly, Derrida (1995: 324) conceives of this question in relation to responsibility, and not knowledge. In order to elicit decisions and events, he explains, 'responsibilities are at stake', which 'must not follow knowledge, nor proceed from knowledge like consequences or effects' (Derrida, 1995; 324). These responsibilities, continues Derrida (1995: 324), 'which will determine as you say "where it is heading" are heterogeneous to the order of formalizable knowledge, and probably or no doubt to all the concepts upon which was built...'.

Individuals (academics and students) are faced with circumstances where responsibility has to be assumed for whatever action is taken and where it becomes pertinent to take a stand on this or that. This can be difficult, as Derrida acknowledges. It is even impossible, he asserts, 'to conceive of a responsibility that consists in being responsible *for* two laws, or that consists of responding *to* two contradictory injunctions. No doubt. However, there is no responsibility that is not the experience and experiment of the impossible' (Derrida, 1992b: 44–45). These contradictory injunctions or aporias – that is, the possibility of argument for two inconsistent positions – are what constitutes responsibility. Dilemmas, according to Derrida, are inherent in the concept of responsibility and are, in fact, the very condition of its possibility (Egéa, 2018: 122). Had these dilemmas not existed, or had these decisions been made easy to make, and could follow a set of rules or programme, explains Egéa (2018: 122). There is, in fact, no decision to be made: therefore, no responsibility to be taken.

Consider the example of the #FeesMustFall campaign in which students at South African universities protested against exorbitant tuition fees and demanded free higher education. Many students found themselves in a dilemma and were conflicted as to whether to participate in the protests, with the hope of achieving a goal of free higher education, or whether to continue going to lectures and write examinations – thereby prioritising their education and, in some cases, completing their degrees. Indeed, as this conflict of interest became evident amidst tensions among students, the argument from protesting students was that they were protesting not only for themselves but for others, like those who were continuing with their studies and generations to come. This kind of debate presents a certain moral dilemma – which forces students to take responsibility for one of two decisions – either remain focused on studying and not waste an academic year, thereby preventing the possibility of incurring a greater financial burden, or participate in the protests, with the possibility of attaining financial relief for all students, thereby achieving a goal greater than the individual.

While the preceding discussion focused on an aporia, which students might encounter, universities face similar aporias in terms of how it conceives of its responsibility in relation to its society. In addition to conceiving of responsibility as dualistic and contradictory, Derrida (2004: 91) equates responsibility with 'a summons requiring a response'. This infers that when a university is summoned or called upon to act in response to a particular situation – whether it is climate change, food security, water scarcity or poor literacy levels – it does so by acting responsibly. At times, however, universities find themselves conflicted between their responsibility and their response.

The example of the University of Fort Hare, which was established in 1916, provides a fascinating and critical story for engaging on (academic) activism in a South African context. The university is built on the site and retains the name of a British military stronghold. Originally known as the South African Native College, Fort Hare had its origins in the liberal missionary tradition, 'with all its ambiguities, and … its products included homeland leaders as well as nationalist politicians, and the functionaries of segregationist and colonial states as well as assertively African political and cultural leaders' (Morrow & Gxabalashe, 2000: 482). The university was the only institution in Eastern, Central and Southern Africa to provide higher education to Africans. Alumni include the likes of Robert Mugabe, Oliver Tambo, Nelson Mandela, Govan Mbeki, Mangosuthu Buthelezi and Robert Sobukwe. The institution is regularly celebrated for its immense contributions to the struggle against apartheid – as exemplified through its prolific history on student activism – as well as its contributions to the leadership of South Africa and Africa. However, a number of students, such as Oliver Tambo and Mangosuthu Buthelezi, were expelled for being activists against oppression and could not complete their studies at Fort Hare. Hence, while the institution may celebrate its anti-apartheid legacy, the paradox is that universities, such as Fort Hare, at times, militated against its own student activists.

When Derrida (2004: 148) describes the university as 'the responsibility of a community of thinking', he has in mind both its reason (to be) and its justification (for being). In other words, the university is as much a part of the community in which it finds itself as it stands outside of it in as far as such a university needs to justify its existence through noble intentions. In this sense, the university has the choice to respond or not and how to respond – that is, acting with 'freedom of judgement' (Derrida, 2004: 97). By finding a reason to respond or act, the university acts with justification, but, by so doing, takes a risk because the university cannot know what is yet to come (Derrida, 2004: 155).

When one reflects on the decision by Fort Hare to expel certain activists or agitators, as they were called, then it becomes necessary to unpack notions of responsibility, as well as community. Certainly, the specific history of Fort Hare speaks to its exclusive catering to 'black' students. Alongside the African National Congress (ANC) Youth League, Fort Hare served as an incubator of 'black' intellectuals and future 'black' political leaders (Badat, 1999: 83). Despite this foundational premise, its apartheid context compelled the university to act against the very students, who had acted against apartheid. In other words, because of the hegemony of the apartheid state, an oppressed university had to act against its own equally oppressed students when they did the right thing by opposing the state. Fort Hare could not enact its responsibility of defending them and their actions. The university could not act in the interests of its own community, but, instead, had to comply with the laws of an apartheid regime. In order for the university to continue to be, it has to be seen as acting in line with the dominant, oppressive discourse.

In continuing, a university should be prepared to find 'new ways of taking responsibility' – of embarking on what it does not have and what is not yet (Derrida, 2004: 148). These new responsibilities, he maintains, 'cannot be purely academic'. 'If they remain extremely difficult to assume, extremely precarious and threatened, it is because they must at once keep alive the memory of a tradition and make an opening beyond any program, that is, toward what is called the future' (Derrida, 1983: 16). This is what Derrida understands as a university's 'reason to be' [*raison d'être*]. To Derrida (1992a: 10–11) 'a new type of university responsibility' is one which would no longer appeal to 'a pure ethico-juridical agency, to a pure practical reason, to a pure idea of the law', but would instead be based on a deconstruction, which is 'limited neither to a methodological reform that would reassure the given organisation, nor, inversely, to [a] parade of irresponsible or irresponsibilizing destruction, whose surest effect would be to leave everything as it is, consolidating the most immobile forces of the university' (Derrida, 1992a: 23). He explains that '[t]o have a *raison d'être*, a reason for being, is to have a justification for existence, to have a meaning, an intended purpose, a destination; but also, to have a cause, to be explainable according to the "principle of reason" or the "law of sufficient reason"' (Derrida, 1983: 3). In the case of Fort Hare, it became necessary to expel student activists or agitators to remain free from state agitation.

To Derrida it is not a matter of simply asking questions for the sake of arriving at reasons, but also of 'preparing oneself thereby to transform the modes of writing, approaches to pedagogy, the procedures of academic exchange, the relation to languages, to other disciplines, to the institution in general, to its inside and its outside' (Derrida, 1983: 17). In this regard, academics and students alike may 'assume within the university, along with its memory and tradition, the imperative of professional rigor and competence … the most serious tradition of the university even while going as far as possible, theoretically and practically, in the most directly underground thinking about the abyss beneath the university' (Derrida, 1983: 17). In assuming 'new ways of taking responsibility', the university has to question and to interrogate and according to Derrida (1983: 17) 'cannot fail to be accompanied at least by a movement of suspicion, even of rejection with respect to the profession-alization of the university in these two senses, and especially in the first, which regulates university life according to the supply and demand of the marketplace and according to a purely technical ideal of competence'.

Instead, assuming new ways of taking responsibility means adopting a public responsibility so that the university can extend and enlarge the rights of humans, thereby resisting human rights violations (Derrida, 2005). On the one hand, Derrida (2004: 153) purports the responsibility of such a university is to ensure that the rights of those who make up the university (teachers and students) are to open up one risk against another – always risking the 'worst'. On the other hand, the public responsibility of a university is to engage in provocative reflection to imagine a moral future that is not yet (Derrida, 2004). In the above sense, the responsibility of a university ought to be twofold: to take risks and to be provocative-reflective – referred to by Derrida (2004: 151) as '[t]he new responsibility of the thinking [uni-versity]'. Such an understanding of a university would extend the responsibility of the university beyond reason, critique and technical and instrumentalist thinking and towards a university of activism. The conception of responsibility for which we are arguing here is strongly connected to a moral action that is informed by a sense of fairness and justice. To Derrida (2004), justice comes in the form of responsibil-ity to the other as difference – that every individual has a responsibility to live with the other and to treat the otherness of the other justly. It also means that, in order to live responsibly, we have to live with others and be mindful of how we treat each other. In not acting responsibly, one does not enact one's humanity in relation to the other and, by so doing, fails to recognise that one's humanity is so because of a relational co-belonging (Waghid & Davids, 2013).

Academic Responsibility as Activism

Following the above, what are the implications for a university, its teaching, its research and, hence, its teachers and students when it advances 'new ways of taking responsibility'? It seems apposite to address the latter question by turning to the ideas of Gayatri Chakravorty Spivak – not only because she describes herself as his friend and ally but because she had translated his much-acclaimed *Of Grammatology*, at a time when she did not know who he was or what informed his thinking. Most profoundly, as she reflects upon undertaking this translation, she describes it as deconstruction – as a 'critical intimacy, not critical distance', because 'you actually speak from inside... Because you are doing it from the inside, with real intimacy. You are kind of turning it around. It's that kind of critique' (Paulson, 2016). Spivak captures her initial encounter with Derrida as follows:

> Yes, we became friends. We were allies. You see, one of the things he understood, perhaps more than I did at that point, was the meaning of this Asian girl who really didn't have much French, launching this book into the world in her own way, so far out of the European coterie

of high philosophy. He and I would go out to eat – and he was a swarthy man, a Sephardic Jew from Algeria – and people would take him to be Indian, and I'm Indian and my cultural inscription is strong and sometimes I wear a sari, so it was a joke and he would say, "Yes, I'm Indian." He understood the beauty of the situation of this young person who was neither a French PhD nor a native French speaker or native English speaker for that matter, and she was offering his text, not because she was worshipful toward him, because she hadn't even known who he was. She was offering his text to the rest of the world, and they were picking it up. There was something very attractive for him about that situation. (Paulson, 2016)

Significantly, her account echoes our earlier description that deconstructive writing as a form of academic activism has to provoke readers (students) to 'recognize other possibilities in it [writing] by inscribing it or grafting it onto other chains' (Derrida, 1977: 9). To Derrida (1977), the writer should give rise to new codes that open up the 'iterability (repetition/alterity)' of writing. By implication, writing invites people to deconstruct meanings beyond their present understandings to the extent that meanings are construed beyond what might perhaps be implied. In Spivak's case, her translation of *Of Grammatology* (1976) is preceded by a monograph-length introduction – 'almost a book in itself' (Paulson, 2016). This, then, provides insights into the textual and contextual connection between Derrida and Spivak and, hence, the stark influence of Derrida on Spivak's works.

Responsibility, states Spivak (1994: 19), 'annuls the call to which it seeks to respond'. For Spivak, just asking what the responsibility of academics could be 'is perhaps already to betray the ideal of academic responsibility in which one was trained'. To formalise responsibility, explains Spivak (1994: 22), infers that 'all action is undertaken in response to a call (or something that seems to us to resemble a call) that cannot be grasped as such'. In this context, response does not only mean to 'respond to', as in '*give* an answer to', but also the related situations of 'answering to', as in 'being responsible for a name … of being answerable for'. When we ponder on responsibility as actions of giving back and answering to, what emerges are implicit suggestions of returning and reverting – a sense of being indebted to. What this infers is that academic activism does not wait for assignments of responsibility; activism implies being already alert to what is needed. By virtue of having certain capacities, and having access to certain resources as well as knowledge, academics are already in positions in which they ought to act responsibly – that is, their positions dictate that they have to give back. This pertains to not only acting responsibly in relation to teaching, or supervising, but acting responsibly in terms of what academics do with their positions in relation to society. Hence, when there are societal wrongs and dystopias, such as corruption, oppression, violence, poverty and hunger, academics ought to have a presumptive responsibility to speak out and act against these. To remain silent or passive is, following Spivak (1994), a form of betrayal of academic responsibility.

Often, academics are aware of a wrong – whether in relation to students or their colleagues, yet they remain quiet, preferring not to get involved, for fear of reprisal or being unpopular. Over the last few years, our faculty has been subjected to serious criticisms from students regarding the professionalism of at least three academics, who were accused of not being punctual for class or not arriving at all, not providing course frameworks, being unprepared for teaching and providing inadequate assessment feedback on assignments. Especially problematic about the students' complaints was that they had been posted on various social media complaints. Many academics in the faculty were very annoyed by the students' actions, claiming that that the students had not followed protocol pertaining to student grievance procedures. It soon became apparent, however, that the students had indeed lodged numerous complaints, but that nothing had come of these. Not only were a number of academics, including members from the faculty executive, aware of the complaints, but they agreed with the students' complaints. What was disturbing was that none of these academics felt responsible for insisting that the students' complaints be addressed or that the faculty initiate an inquiry into why the same academics are repeatedly accused of unprofessional conduct. Instead, academics opted to discuss the issues among themselves in small groups, after meetings or in corridors, but were not willing to act in ensuring that unprofessional conduct ceases. Reasons proffered in defence of their silence included 'maintaining collegiality' or 'it's the responsibility of the chair of the department, or Dean'. The problem with these justifications, however, is that they feed into continuing patterns of unprofessional conduct; they undermine teaching and learning in a faculty which is responsible for producing and shaping teachers, and they bring the entire faculty into disrepute. In this sense, we would agree with Spivak's (1994) contention that to remain silent or passive is a form of betrayal of academic responsibility.

Universities exist in realms of epistemological production and reproduction, via its teaching, reading, writing and students – at least, as one understanding. On the one hand, therefore, conceptions of academic responsibility are tied to relational encounters with texts (reading and writing), as well as teaching and research. These are necessarily ethical – where engagements and interactions are perpetually harnessed by hope, trust and confidence in the other – that is, between academics and students. On the other hand, academic responsibility cannot be remiss of its potential to cause harm, as in the perpetuation of social injustices. Giving back and answering to are not limited to ensuring beneficial forms of engagement with students, communities or society. 'To give back' or 'to answer to' is to awaken to 'new ways of taking responsibility' – that is, a re-conscientisation of the university. At the heart of this – certainly for us as academics in a particular context of repeated calls for the decolonisation of universities – re-conscientisation involves a (re)turn to mutual and reciprocal recognition and belonging. This recognition is not limited to encounters between humans (or academics and students). It necessarily includes different forms of knowledge and the capacity of different people to bring forth these kinds of knowledge – much in the way that Derrida, according to Spivak, 'understood the beauty of the situation of this young person who was neither a French PhD nor a native French speaker or native English speaker for that matter, and she was offering his text, not because she was worshipful toward him, because she hadn't even known who he was' (Paulson, 2016).

For a university to 'give back' and to give of itself as a sort of debt confirms two imperatives. One pertains to Derrida's (2004: 147) conception of the university as 'the responsibility of a community of thinking', which alludes to both its reason (to be) and its justification (for being). Its very being implies that it has to do or contribute something. The university, therefore, has to assume responsibility for its being and for what it does – that is, informed by reason. The community refers to that which constitutes the university – students, academics, administrators and leaders – as well as those it serves. There are seemingly no boundaries implicit within Derrida's (2004) concept of 'the responsibility of a community of thinking'.

Moreover, in being able to 'perform its mysterious work' (Derrida, 2004: 156), it has to remain in a state of 'becoming' (Derrida, 2004: 155), which brings us to the second imperative. To Spivak (1994: 23), the notion of responsibility is 'seen as an intermediary stage, caught between an ungraspable call and a setting-to-work' – suggesting that responsibility extends into that which is yet to unfold and be understood – that which is 'mysterious' (Derrida, 2004: 156). In this regard, academic activism as 'new ways of taking responsibility' resides in a recognition that responsibility is without end. Academics cannot know all there is to know; they cannot know what is yet to unfold through their teaching and writing. In the same way, academics cannot know how students interpret what they are taught and how they learn, or how much of their learning resides in what they directly encounter in relation to an academic, or how much of their learning derives from the margins of these encounters. Yet, the responsibility of the academic and the university remains – internalised not only in what is taught and researched but in the silences of not yet knowing.

References

Badat, M. S. (1999). *Black student politics, higher education and apartheid from SASO to SANSCO, 1968–1990*. Pretoria, South Africa: Human Sciences Research Council.

Biesta, G. (2009). From critique to deconstruction: Derrida as a critical philosopher. In: M. A. Peters & G. Biesta (Eds.), *Derrida, deconstruction, and the politics of pedagogy* (pp. 81–96). New York: Peter Lang.

Biesta, G. J. J., & Egéa-Kuehne, D. (Eds.). (2011). *Derrida & education*. New York: Routledge.

Caputo, J. D. (Ed.). (1997). *Deconstruction in a nutshell: A conversation with Jacques Derrida*. New York: Fordham University Press.

Derrida, J. (1977). *Limited Inc*. Evanston, IL: Northwestern University Press.

Derrida, J. (1982). *Margins of philosophy*. Chicago: University of Chicago Press.

Derrida, J. (1983). The principle of reason: The university in the eyes of its pupils. *Diacritics, 13*(3), 2–20.

Derrida, J. (1992a). Mochlos; or, the conflict of the faculties. In R. Rand (Ed.), *Logomachia: The conflict of the faculties* (pp. 1–34). Lincoln, NB: The University of Nebraska Press.

Derrida, J. (1992b). *The other heading reflections on today's Europe* (P.-A. Brault & M. B. Naas, Trans.). Bloomington, IN/Indianapolis, IN: Indiana University Press.

Derrida, J. (1995). *Points … Interviews, 1974–1994*, E. Weber (Ed.) (P. Kamuf & others, Trans.). Stanford, CA: Stanford University Press.

Derrida, J. (2004). *Eyes of the university: Right to philosophy 2*. (J. Plug, Trans.). Stanford, CA: Stanford University Press.

Derrida, J. (2005). The future of the profession or the unconditional university (thanks to the 'humanities', what could take place tomorrow). In P. P. Trifonas & M. A. Peters (Eds.),

Deconstructing Derrida: Tasks for the new humanities (pp. 11–24). New York: Palgrave Macmillan.

Egéa, D. (2018). Derrida's archive and legacy to education: Between past and future. In P. Smeyers (Ed.), *International handbook of philosophy of education* (pp. 115–134). Dordrecht, the Netherlands: Springer.

Morrow, S., & Gxabalashe, K. (2000). The records of the University of Fort Hare. *History in Africa, 27*, 481–497.

Naas, M. (2015). *The end of the world and other teachable moments: Jacques Derrida final seminar*. New York: Fordham University Press.

Norris, C. (1987). *Derrida*. London: Fontana Press.

Paulson, S. (2016). Critical intimacy: An interview with Gayatri Chakravorty Spivak. https://lareviewofbooks.org/article/critical-intimacy-interview-gayatri-chakravorty-spivak/#! 14 May 2020.

Spivak, G. C. (1994). Responsibility. *Boundary 2, 21*(3), 19–64.

Waghid, Y., & Davids, N. (2013). *Citizenship education and violence in schools: On disrupted potentialities and becoming*. Rotterdam, the Netherlands: Sense Publishers.

Chapter 5
The Pursuit of a Living Philosophy

Abstract In this chapter, we argue that when we apply Jacques Rancière's (Chronicles of consensual times (trans: Corcoran S). Continuum, London, 2010a; Dissensus: on politics and aesthetics (trans: Corcoran S). Continuum, London, 2010b) living philosophy to stimulate academic activism, we think of encouraging academics to think of how their research – in relation to teaching and scholarship – can stimulate fictitious imaginaries of a society in which people engage in iterations and the free exchange of provocative ideas. Such a society might even be an imaginative one where people live in harmony despite their differences that seem to be irreconcilable. People might even renounce antagonism and encourage the free integration of pluralist ideas of a common humanity. And, when such a living philosophy draws people back to their real experiences, it would contrast life in the idealised world with the perilous societal malaises of hostility, torture and continuous violence.

Keywords Jacques Rancière · Living philosophy · Consensus · Aesthetics · Violence · Imaginaries

Introduction

Retaining our reflections on a philosophy of higher education as a discourse for the advancement of academic activism, the attention of this chapter is on another French philosopher, Jacques Rancière. In *Chronicles of Consensual Times* (2010a), Rancière invites us to ponder on a 'living philosophy' as a response to 'the consensus governing us … intent upon getting us to believe that "what is, is all that is"' (Rancière, 2010a: viii). What a living philosophy does is to contrast the real experiences of people on earth with their idealised (fictitious) lives in the sky and then returns by leaving the imaginary position in which people find themselves and are happy to rejoin the reality of their familiar earth-like experiences of perhaps racism, torture and violence. To him, a 'living philosophy' involves a consciousness and a commitment to confronting that which seeks to control how we see and interact

N. Davids, Y. Waghid, *Academic Activism in Higher Education*, Debating Higher Education: Philosophical Perspectives 5, https://doi.org/10.1007/978-981-16-0340-2_5

with our world; it teaches us 'to take good care of our self and how to live life harmoniously in the everyday'.

Often, when we complete promotion applications or are asked to speak on our teaching or research, we are asked about our specific teaching or writing philosophies. It is a question, we believe, often not afforded enough recognition or thought. To us, it means asking of ourselves how we conceive of ourselves in relation to teaching and writing and, in turn, what we hope to achieve by these actions. These are not uncomplicated questions; it forces us back to the origin of why we do what we do and what we hope to gain from it. It is easier to speak about teaching and its philosophical imperatives, for example, than it is to critically reflect on our teaching as a living philosophy.

In response, we argue that when we apply a living philosophy to stimulate academic activism, we think of encouraging academics to think of how their research – in relation to teaching and scholarship – can stimulate fictitious imaginaries of a society in which people engage in iterations and the free exchange of provocative ideas. Such a society might even be an imaginative one where people live in harmony despite their differences that seem to be irreconcilable. People might even renounce antagonism and encourage the free integration of pluralist ideas of a common humanity. And, when such a living philosophy draws people back to their real experiences, it would contrast life in the idealised world with the perilous societal malaises of hostility, torture and continuous violence.

'What Is, Is All That Is'

The chronicles addressed in his book, states Rancière (2010a: vii), 'is not a way of responding to the events of passing time'. Instead, he explains:

> To speak of a chronicle is to speak of a type of reign: not the career of a king, but the scansion of a time and the tracing of a territory, a specific configuration of that which happens, a mode of perception of what is notable, a regime of interpretation of the old and the new, of the important and the ancillary, of the possible and impossible. (Rancière, 2010a: vii)

For Rancière (2010a), consensus provides the most appropriate way through which to sum up what reigning means. Consensus is 'not people's agreement amongst themselves but the matching of sense of sense: the accord made between a sensory regime of the presentation of things and a mode of interpretation of their meaning' (Rancière, 2010a: viii). The consensus governing us, contends Rancière (2010a: viii), 'is a machine of power insofar as it a machine of vision and interpretation that must ceaselessly set appearances right'; it is the primary political operator in the systems of power of 'Western democracies'. Consensus claims to observe merely that which we can all see in aligning two propositions about the state of the world; 'it asserts a reality that is unique and incontrovertible' (2010a: ix).

Yet, this is not the case. While it tries to convince us that 'what is, is all that is' (2010a: viii), this machine of power, maintains Rancière (2010a: viii), bends our reality and, in fact, seriously constrains our ability to imagine and plan for a different future. Consensus, following Rancière, has nothing to do with peace; its essence is not peaceful discussion and reasonable agreement as opposed to conflict or violence (Rancière, 2010b: 42). On the contrary, it is the perfect ideological ground from which to continuously wage war with those societies, which are not 'Western democracies' and which are unable to participate in the consensual unison promoted by the dominant 'machine of vision and interpretation'. To this end, Rancière does not conceive of consensus as another manner of exercising democracy – as shared in an interview with Davide Panagia (2000: 125). To Rancière, consensus is 'the negation of the democratic basis for politics: it desires to have well-identifiable groups with specific interests, aspirations, values, and "culture"' (Panagia, 2000: 125).

Depending on the context, consensus adopts many forms and hegemonies, putting into effect ripples of disenfranchisement, violence and silence. In his *Chronicles*, Rancière refers to an array of political atrocities – made possible through consensus. He refers to ethnic cleansing, 'humanitarian wars' and 'wars on terror', which he describes as being at the core of consensual times (Rancière, 2010a: viii).

It is easy to track similarities between Rancière's (2010a) consensus and colonialism – both conceptually and methodologically. As concepts, both consensus and colonialism speak to a 'machine of power', which relies on subjugated others so that hegemonies might reign. Likewise, it is possible to employ consensus as a methodological lens that ensures the proliferation of particular ideologies, such as colonialism. Both consensus and colonialism wage wars against the (subjugated) other and their way of life; it has nothing to do with peaceful engagement or agreement. Despite its geopolitical disparities, there are deep commonalities, for example, between the colonialism inflicted upon South Africa by the Dutch and the British and the attempts by 'Western democracies' to enforce democracy onto the people of Iraq, as one example. The consensus, asserts Rancière (2010a: ix), says that 'there is but a single reality whose signs must be depleted; that there is but a single space, while reserving the right to redraw its borders; that one unique time exists, while allowing itself to multiply its figures'.

Colonialism, says Maldonado-Torres (2007: 243), 'denotes a political and economic relation in which the sovereignty of a nation or a people rests on the power of another nation, which makes such nation an empire'. As such, colonialism is about the assertion of absolute power and must be understood in relation to the loss of freedom of indigenous peoples in every aspect of their existence (De Oliveira Andreotti, Stein, & Ahenakew, 2015). Colonialism refers to deliberate practices of domination and power through the subjugation and exploitation of one people over another. This domination extends not only into political and economic control but centres on very particular constructions and practices of dehumanising the other, which allows the coloniser to justify or legitimise its actions. The actions of colonialism are made visible in administrative and architectural structures, inasmuch as it manifests in military occupation, the marauding of resources, the dispossession of land and, of course, the control of education (Davids, 2019: 107).

Although most writings on the African university begin by acknowledging a list of premodern institutions, as precursors to the modern African university, states Mamdani (2016: 69), neither the institutional form nor the curricular content of the modern African university is derived from precolonial institutions. Instead, the African continent is dominated by academic institutions shaped by colonialism and organised according to the European model (Teferra & Altbach, 2004). To Teferra and Altbach (2004), higher education in Africa is an artefact of colonial policies, which has been shaped and influenced by a multitude of European colonisers, including Belgium, Germany, the Netherlands, Italy, Portugal and Spain. Britain and France, they continue, have left the greatest and lasting impact, not only in terms of the organisation of academe and the continuing links to the metropole but, most importantly, in the language of instruction and communication (Teferra & Altbach, 2004).

Long after the departure of colonialism, coloniality remains deeply entrenched in legacies of privileged networks, wealth, land and language often remain, as has been the case in South African universities. South Africa, explains Cross (2020), is a unique case in which official political discourse created the perception that colonialism had ended with the establishment of the Republic of South Africa in 1961 and its acceptance into the United Nations, with only the problem of apartheid remaining:

> This perception was challenged by [Joe] Slovo's (1976) concept of 'internal colonialism' or 'colonialism of a special type'. Slovo characterised South Africa as a system of internal colonialism in that there was no spatial separation between the colonising power (the white minority state) and the colonised black people; nevertheless, the situation displayed all the features of classic colonialism in terms of economic and social relations between the black majority and the white minority. (Wolpe, 1975 in Cross, 2020: 104)

Within this framework, explains Cross (2020: 104), in 1977, the African National Congress adopted the position that apartheid South Africa was a case of colonialism of a special type, a stance re-stated at the 2017 Consultative Policy Conference.

To Maldonado-Torres (2007), coloniality survives colonialism; it embodies long-standing patterns of power that define culture, labour, intersubjectivity relations and knowledge production well beyond the strict limits of colonial administrations. (South) African universities emerged as colonial projects. It is unsurprising, therefore, the curricula at South African universities are largely Eurocentric and continue to reinforce white and Western dominance and privilege while at the same time being full of stereotypes, prejudices and patronising views about Africa and its people (Heleta, 2016). To Cross (2020), the call for decolonisation foregrounds the long and deeply entrenched colonial and apartheid experience of the majority of South Africans – 'It offers powerful epistemologies that enable us to probe old and new problems and to rethink our conceptions of social justice (including cognitive and epistemic justice)' (Cross, 2020: 104).

Perhaps 'What Is, Is [Not] All That Is'?

Now, while consensus might infer a disposition and inclination that 'what is, is all that is' (Rancière, 2010a: viii), human agency and academic activism, however, suggest that nothing is what it is. In this regard, Rancière offers us the idea of dissensus, which, unlike consensus, he describes as being based on a logic of equality, and is interested in disrupting the 'machine of vision and interpretation' (Rancière, 2010a: viii). Dissensus is as concerned with the arbitrariness of political participation, as it is in highlighting the inherent differences within societies. If consensus is 'the negation of the democratic basis for politics' (Panagia, 2000: 125), then the essence of politics, according to Rancière (2010b), is dissensus. Dissensus, he clarifies, 'is not a confrontation between interests or opinions. It is the demonstration (manifestation) of a gap in the sensible itself' (Rancière, 2010b: 38). To him, '[p]olitical demonstration [academic activism] makes visible that which had no reason to be seen; it places one world in another'. Through protests and activism, students, for example, take their challenges and frustrations with alienating institutional cultures and excessive tuition fees, for example, into the public sphere.

What is ordinarily a private encounter between students and university administration moves into another realm where the constraints of speech are erased. What happens next is not only the merging of two worlds – that of the university and a public sphere – but the positioning of high university tuition fees and unaccommodating and unrepresentative institutional cultures as matters of public concern. As students move through streets in protests, and as they take to the generative activist spaces of social media, sharing their plight across global contexts, they demonstrate the imperative of their argument while also sketching 'the frame of reference enabling them to see it [their argument] as one' (Rancière, 2010b: 38). Political argumentation, says (Rancière, 2010b: 38), 'is at one and the same time the demonstration of a possible world in which the argument could count as an argument, one that is addressed by a subject qualified to argue, over an identified object, to an addressee who is required to see the object and to hear the argument that he "normally" has no reason either to see or to hear. It is the construction of a paradoxical world that puts together two separate worlds'. Universities, like the public sphere, are constituted by a surplus of subjects (academics, students, administrators), who introduce a surplus of objects and ideas.

These subjects, explains Rancière (Panagia, 2000: 124), do not have the consistency of coherent social groups united by common property or a common birth. Rather, '[t]hey exist entirely within the act, and their actions are the manifestation of a dissensus; that is, the making contentious of the givens of a particular situation' (Panagia, 2000: 124). In South Africa, the public might be as unaware of high tuition fees, as they are with concerns about curricula, which continue to disregard indigenous knowledge and experiences. So, too, they might be unaware of the increasing rates of gender-based violence, which continue to be a scourge on university campuses, but, seemingly, do not receive the urgent attention it warrants. Yet, exorbitant fees, university curricula and epistemologies and, certainly, gender-based violence are indeed public concerns. Activism or political demonstration or argumentation, therefore, 'make visible that which is not perceivable' (Panagia, 2000: 124–125).

According to Sanborn and Thyne (2011), one result that academic scholarship can attest to is that students have long played roles in some of the more momentous uprisings over the course of modern history. History is replete with examples of student activism against immense odds – from the student sit-ins to abolish legalised racial segregation in the USA in 1960; pro-democracy protests in Tiananmen Square in 1989 and again in 2019; the student uprisings across Africa and the Middle East, commonly referred to as the Arab Spring, in 2010; and, of course, because of the context of this book, in South Africa, where student activism was critical in the political struggle against apartheid and which, significantly, has not abated since the country transitioned to democracy.

By virtue of its characterisation as an activism practised by students, and not academics, the tendency is to differentiate between these two types of activism – the one belonging to academics and the other as the domain of students. Yet, other than the different subjects (academics and students), what differentiates student activism from academic activism? As previously discussed in the first chapter of this book, activism is commonly associated with political, social and economic campaigns; it can manifest in research, teaching and writing. By all accounts, student activism is almost always tied to political, economic and social contestations. In South Africa, it is impossible to conceive of the struggle against apartheid without taking stock of the massive role of students, as they embarked on protests, placing their liberation before their education. For many, their actions resulted in detention by the apartheid government, while for some, it ended in their deaths. Student activism – political demonstration and argumentation – has certainly not abated in South Africa's democracy. Often described as the continuation of an ongoing narrative, we would be inclined to think that the context of a democracy indeed presents a contextual difference – a difference that ought to shift the way the state engages with the dissensus of students.

Students' contestation with the apartheid state was necessarily couched in anger and frustration. Their argumentation, while framed as student protests, was not limited to university-based dilemmas or dystopias – although inferior infrastructure and unequal academic programmes and support were certainly enough reasons for the protests. Instead, their protests merged the two worlds of higher education and citizenship, which, in this case, could not be described as 'a paradoxical world' (Rancière, 2010b: 38). The necessity of this merger has not ceased now that democracy has been attained. If anything, the intensification of student activism should be perceived and experienced as a welcome manifestation of democracy. Student protests, calling for decolonised university spaces and curricula, have as much to do with a recognition of indigenous epistemologies as it has to do with the recognition and restoration of the oppressed people in South Africa. The imperatives of higher education cannot be dislodged from the imperatives of democracy. Student activism, states Altbach (1992), is inherent in the nature of the academic community; where student activism is accepted as a legitimate element of the political system, it is more likely to have an impact on society.

Towards a Living Philosophy and Academic Activism

Politics, states Vihalem (2018: 2–3), is not conceptualised; it is visualised:

From street banners to television advertisements, it must be showed-off and staged, it must be realized in the sensible. Politics is not so much a matter of discussing and doing, as it is a matter of fantasizing, promising, representing and reproducing – on a deeper level it is sensed rather than thought. Far from being kept apart from politics, aisthesis seems to be the very medium of politics: politics is what is sensed and what is felt. Politics is the texture of aesthesis. The inherently utopian, platonic imperative to distinguish and keep apart aesthetics from politics is doomed to disappear.

One of the discerning features and attractions of Rancière's writing is that he has always drawn parallels between politics and aesthetics. We find, therefore, that as of approximately 1995, he chose to focus on artistic productions that either epitomise or contest the notion of consensus, as promoted by a 'machine of power' (Rancière, 2010a: viii). To him, both of these (politics and aesthetics) provide absorbing media and perspectives on how individuals conceive of themselves in relation to their environments, society and others. Aesthetic acts, says Rancière (2004: 4), 'are configurations of experience that create new modes of sense perception and induce novel forms of political subjectivity'. To him, the aesthetic is implicit in politics. This is because politics involves both perception and participation; moreover, politics are aesthetic because it decides what is seen and revealed, and what is not, as well as what is said and how it is meant to be interpreted.

In the world of politics, much is shrouded in smokescreens of speeches, which should seldom be understood in terms of what is being said; there is a persistent engineering of perceptions that are often quite removed from fact and truth. So, too, illusions are created about notions of participation, consultation and collective decision-making. This double meaning of perception and participation, of partition and sharing, explains Vihalem (2018), is what intimately links politics to aesthetics in Rancière's thinking. It follows, therefore, according to Vihalem (2018: 6), 'that aesthetics is not a wise and informed discourse on arts, reflecting on the nature and legitimacy of its procedures and distancing itself from the sensible... Instead, aesthetics means primarily how we (the collective is to be privileged over the individual) sense or see, hear, touch and so forth'.

These double meanings serve to create an unwise and uninformed discourse, which, no doubt, create great uncertainty and unhappiness among people, communities and societies. A state's purpose, argues Rancière (2004: 196), 'is not merely to provide a living but to make a life that is good. Otherwise it might be made up of slaves or animals other than man, and that is impossible, because slaves and animals do not participate in happiness, nor in a life that involves choice'. Happiness, as Vihalem (2018) points out, is not everyone's inalienable right; instead, it is perceived as a privilege that is not part of the commonly sensible. As a counter, Rancière (2010a) proposes a living philosophy. A living philosophy involves a consciousness and a commitment to confronting this 'machine of power insofar as it is a machine of vision and interpretation' (Rancière, 2010a: viii), so that people might take better care of themselves – '[t]o transform one's life and make it philosophical by making philosophy become life meant learning to flee as quickly as possible, as far as possible'. To change one's life is 'to live life harmoniously in the everyday ... [and] simultaneously to enjoy the thrill of travelling in the Platonic chariot across the radiant heaven of Ideas and to have the half-hearted comfort of thought and body in the smallest things in life' (Rancière, 2010a: 81).

In depicting this living philosophy concerning the cinematographic work of Amélie Poulain, Rancière (2010a: 81) offers the following account: firstly, as a real person, Amélie is 'the little fairy who changes the lives of those around with her simple decision, assuaging their inconsolable hearts, unifying solitary souls, punishing the wicked, rewarding the good and moving the sedentary' (Rancière, 2010a: 81) – a matter of escaping the greyness of reality into the ideal. She carefully recreates her world by orchestrating the lives of people around her – intent upon finding happiness. In this regard, a living philosophy means that one casts a look at what seems ideal or imaginary from the vantage point of one's real-life experiences. Secondly, as put by Rancière (2010a, 2010b: 81), 'it would be all mere illusion if the one who projected her ideal sky into the lives of others did not also take care of herself and know how to cash in on her dreams for an occasion that has offered itself in prosaic reality' – a matter of returning from the ideal sky back into reality. What a living philosophy does is to contrast the real experiences of people on earth with their idealised (fictitious) lives in the sky and then returns by leaving the imaginary position in which people find themselves and are happy to rejoin the reality of their familiar earth-like experiences of perhaps racism, torture and violence. This leads (Rancière, 2010a, 2010b: 81) to claim, '[f]iction is more beautiful than reality. Reality is more beautiful than any fiction'.

When we apply a living philosophy to stimulate academic activism, we think of encouraging academics to think of how their research (in relation to teaching and scholarship) can encourage fictitious imaginaries of a society in which people engage in iterations and the free exchange of provocative ideas. Such a society might even be an imaginative one where people live in harmony despite their differences that seem to be irreconcilable. People might even renounce antagonism and encourage the free integration of pluralist ideas of a common humanity. Moreover, when such a living philosophy draws people back to their real experiences, it would contrast life in the idealised world with the perilous societal malaises of hostility, torture and continuous violence. Considering that such a living philosophy is mostly concerned with changing the lives of those who dedicate themselves to it, it might just be that ordinary people would begin experimenting more on how to take better care of themselves and to change undesirable situations in their societies. In other words, amateurs who practise a living philosophy might turn the debilitating real-life experiences into an art of good living.

Here, we think about the unpredictable outcomes of research, teaching and writing – those moments of learning, which might not have occurred otherwise. Conceptualising research leans on the capacity of academics to imagine how things might be different from what is. It requires a hopeful desire that believes in the unpredictability and serendipity of human connectedness. When academics, as researchers, engage with participants or respondents, we invite them into predefined schedules of questions, focus group discussions or conversations – without always knowing what might emerge. Together, through the medium of research, there is an open space for new and unconsidered possibilities.

Research, writing as well as teaching require imagination and wonder; all of these practices rely on a willingness to shift between the two worlds of what *is* and what *might be*. In the end, what a living philosophy requires is to remove theoretical sophistication and to encourage everyone to take 'everyday care of the self' (Rancière, 2010a, 2010b: 80). Until the onset of South Africa's democracy, education, and, specifically, the Bantu Education Act (Act no. 47 of 1953), was primarily used to enforce racially segregated educational spaces and policies. In turn, the Extension of University Education Act (Act no. 45 of 1959) put an end to black students attending white universities, which, at the time, were mainly the universities of Cape Town and Witwatersrand. In segregating higher education institutions in terms of racially constructed categories, the Extension of University Education Act saw the establishment of separate 'tribal colleges' for black university students – which included the universities of Fort Hare, Vista, Venda and the Western Cape. Not only were the educational spaces segregated, but the types of education on offer at different schools and higher education sites differed immensely concerning their respective racial and ethnic categorisations.

In the words of Hendrik Verwoerd – who carries the dubious honour of being described as the architect of apartheid – 'There is no place for [the Bantu] in the European community above the level of certain forms of labour … What is the use of teaching the Bantu child mathematics when it cannot use it in practice?' (Clark & Worger, 2004: 49). Education, as Giroux (2017) reminds us, can all too easily 'become a form of symbolic and intellectual violence that assaults rather than educates'. He continues, the violence inflicted through education 'amount[s] to pedagogies of repression and serve[s] primarily to numb the mind and produce what might be called dead zones of the imagination'. The kinds of student, academic and civil activism which led to the eventual erasure of education as forms of epistemic violence emanated from beliefs in a reimagined society of how things ought to be and can be. Education, asserts Giroux (2017), 'is vital to the creation of individuals capable of becoming critical social agents willing to struggle against injustices and develop the institutions that are crucial to the functioning of a substantive democracy'.

Next, we examine how living philosophy can take care of new fictions of evil and criminal democracy.

Living Philosophy Is a Matter of Opposing 'New Fictions of Evil'?

While it is apparent in this chapter, we consider Rancière's (2010a) conception of a living philosophy worthwhile and attractive in relation to a reimagined world, which, of course, should not be confused with escapism but with finding reconceived ways of being and living. Yet, as we conclude this chapter, we do so, by taking issue with Rancière's (2010a) position on new fictions of evil. In his analysis of three films (*Elephant*, *Dogville* and *Mystic River*) that speak to us of evil in general, law is radically absent (*Elephant*); the accomplice of evil designates the victim to suffer and leaves the care of punishing the torturers to the bandits (*Dogville*); and the accomplice of evil leaves unpunished the crime of the honest family father/gangster/righter of wrongs (*Mystic River*) (Rancière, 2010a). These fictitious films come to the same conclusion, namely, 'that doing good in a bad world is impossible and so violence is necessary' (Rancière, 2010a).

Now, if Rancière is right in the sense that evil 'cannot be righted except at the expense of another evil which remains irreducible' (Rancière, 2010a, 2010b: 115), then his position on evil seems somewhat tenuous. Instead, we would like to use his conception of a living philosophy to show that there should always be a possibility to combat evil non-violently or without the use of more evil. And, for him to argue that '[t]here is good and bad violence ... violence which oppresses and violence which liberates' (Rancière, 2010a, 2010b: 114) is, in fact, a recipe for continuous evil. In this sense, we find it problematic to conceive of violence as *not* causing harm or affliction, and as such, the idea of violence being good presents a particular contradiction that can only yield to more justifications of violence.

If our real-life experiences are permeated by misery, revolts, exploitation, humiliation, perversity, monstrous trauma, savagery, massacres and crime, as Rancière (2010a, 2010b) describes in his analysis of evil, then using his living philosophy will enable us to think in an idealised way about what human experiences would look like without being marred by evil. Surely a living philosophy would stimulate one to think of contentment, pleasure, honour, healing, gentleness and non-transgression. And, if we can recast such idealised fictitious onto our real-life experiences, there might be a minute possibility that evil can be thwarted without violence. As academic activists wanting to use a living philosophy to rethink student violence on South African university campuses, we cannot help thinking that condoning student violence in the form of burning down lecture halls and libraries will only breed more violence. Already we witness, over and over again, how the equally heavy-handed and violent responses by the police and the army have served only to mar the cessation of student violence. While it might be possible to constrain student upheavals through forceful actions by the authorities temporarily, such actions have never shown to remediate or redirect the actions of students. Instead, police violence or brutality has only played into a cycle of more student violence. Where, therefore, is the harmonious life, which ought to be cultivated through Rancière's living philosophy, if such actions by students are not condemned as violence and, hence, rendered as despicable and out of place in a democracy?

The problem we have with a Rancièrean take on violence is that violence can never be good and bad as in both cases, violence domesticates and exacerbates more violence. In this way, we disagree with Rancière (2010a: 114) when he claims 'there is violence which oppresses and violence which liberates'. In South Africa, as it is elsewhere, this is a familiar argument – that the use of violence was necessary to overthrow the evil and violence of apartheid. But there is a price to pay – not only by innocent bystanders who are absorbed into the violence but by those who have to live with the knowledge that they are indeed capable of such atrocities. This is the effect of violence – it changes who we are and whom we might become. This is as true for perpetrators, as it is for victims.

In August 2012, both of us were attending the International Network of Philosophers of Education in Addis Ababa. While standing in the foyer of our hotel, after a long day of conferencing, we became aware of despicable displays of violence on the nearby television screens. Our interest peaked immediately, as we became aware that the images were in South Africa. At first, we thought it was a documentary on protests against apartheid. It soon became apparent that it, in fact, was a report on the day's events – a day which would become known as the Marikana massacre. With horror and shame, we stood in that foyer, watching members of the South African police service empty their guns into miners, who had been striking for higher salaries, leaving 34 miners dead and another 78 injured.

The massacre marks the most brutal and inhumane display of force by the police authorities – since last witnessed during apartheid. The parallels between the Marikana massacre and the Sharpeville massacre of 1960, which also involved police and protestors (this time against apartheid), were not only inevitable but especially distressing. While the two massacres were both characterised by inhumane actions by the police and deaths of protesters, there are also two key differences. The Sharpeville protests were against an oppressive state; protesters were killed by police who represented this state. The Marikana protesters were asking for higher salaries so as to improve their living conditions – after a series of failed negotiations with the state; 34 of them were killed by police, who represent a democratic state. Such monstrous evil cannot be considered as liberatory, and in this sense, Rancière would be wrong to assume that violence actually liberates. Similarly, we cannot imagine that police brutality against students, who set university buildings, libraries and artworks alight, would be tantamount to liberating the institutions from student protestations and violence. The point is that violence breeds more violence, and unless we find idealised ways to rethink our non-violent responses to violence, violence will continue unabated.

Much has been written about the violence used by students in their struggle against apartheid. Could we have imagined a post-apartheid South Africa in which violence is not considered an option to curb political oppression and exclusion? The answer would be affirmative, and significantly, we believe that had violence not been such a notable feature of the struggle against apartheid, South Africa's democracy might indeed be less violent. Fanon (2004) appropriately reminds us that when the colonised are determined to put their faith only in violent methods, they confirm the message which they have learnt from the colonist – which is that the only language the colonist understands is that of force. There is a worrying concern, therefore, that while students embark on protests and calls for decolonisation, they do so through violent means – from damage to statues and artworks and confrontations with security staff and police to the burning of the buildings and brutal clashes between student factions (Hall 2016).

These kinds of actions are decidedly contrary to a language of decolonisation, which is directed at healing and rehumanising by engaging with others and spaces with dignity and respect. This language is evident in the actions of activists such as Martin Luther King Jr. and Mahatma Gandhi, who are well-known for their strategies of provoking violent responses through their non-violent protests. Both would deliberately lead peaceful protests into what they knew to be hostile communities and where they knew they would be met with violent responses from authorities. Yet, these confrontations played powerful roles in garnering support and sympathy for the protestors.

Similarly, we cannot imagine a university system in which coercion and exclusion are used to bring about freedom and equality for all students. This in itself would be a way of undermining autonomous university education, to say the least. It is hard to unlearn the actions and practices of history, but until we do, we will not find a reality which is 'more beautiful than any action' (Rancière, 2010a: 81).

References

Altbach, P. G. (1992). Politics of students and faculty. In B. R. Clark & G. Neave (Eds.), *The encyclopaedia of higher education*. New York: Pergamon.

Clark, N. L., & Worger, W. H. (2004). *South Africa – The rise and fall of apartheid: Seminar studies in history*. Cape Town, South Africa: Pearson Education Limited.

Cross, M. (2020). Decolonising universities in South Africa: Backtracking and revisiting the debate. In I. Rhensburg, S. Motala, & M. Cross (Eds.), *Transforming universities in South Africa: Pathways to higher education reform* (pp. 101–114). Leiden, The Netherlands: Brill Sense.

Davids, N. (2019). Love in the time of decoloniality. *Alternation, 24*, 101–121.

De Oliveira Andreotti, V., Stein, S., & Ahenakew, C. (2015). Mapping interpretations of decolonization in the context of higher education. *Decolonization: Indigeneity, Education & Society, 4*(1), 21–40.

Fanon, F. (2004). *The wretched of the earth*. Cape Town, South Africa: Kwela Books.

Giroux, H. A. (2017). *Thinking dangerously: The role of higher education in authoritarian times*. https://truthout.org/articles/thinking-dangerously-the-role-of-higher-education-in-authoritarian-times/. Accessed 20 May 2020.

Hall, M. (2016). South Africa's student protests have lessons for all universities. *Higher Education Network*. https://www.theguardian.com/higher-education-network/2016/mar/03/south-africas-student-protests-have-lessons-for-all-universities. Accessed 20 May 2020.

Heleta, S. (2016). Decolonisation of higher education: Dismantling epistemic violence and Eurocentrism in South Africa. *Transformation in Higher Education, 1*(1), 1–8.

Maldonado-Torres, N. (2007). On coloniality of being. *Cultural Studies, 21*(2), 240–270.

Mamdani, M. (2016). Between the public intellectual and the scholar: Decolonization and some post-independence initiatives in African higher education. *Inter-Asia Cultural Studies, 7*(1), 68–83.

Panagia, D. (2000). Dissenting words: A conversation with Jacques Rancière. *Diacritics, 30*(2), 113–126.

Rancière, J. (2004). *The politics of aesthetics: The distribution of the sensible* (G. Rockhill, Trans.). London: Bloomsbury.

Rancière, J. (2010a). *Chronicles of consensual times* (S. Corcoran, Trans.). London: Continuum.

Rancière, J. (2010b). *Dissensus: On politics and aesthetics* (S. Corcoran, Trans.). London: Continuum.

Sanborn, H., & Thyne, C. (2011). *Learning democracy: Education and the fall of authoritarian regimes*. vmi.academia.edu/HowardSanborn/Papers/1149456. Accessed 21 Apr 2020.

Teferra, D., & Altbach, P. G. (2004). African higher education: Challenges for the 21st century. *Higher Education, 47*, 21–50.

Vihalem, M. (2018). Everyday aesthetics and Jacques Rancière: Reconfiguring the common field of aesthetics and politics. *Journal of Aesthetics & Culture, 10*, 1–11.

Chapter 6
Revolutionary Action

Abstract In this chapter, we are interested in the notion of revolution concerning practices of freedom, equality and novelty – that is, academic activism as 'perplexities of new beginnings' (Arendt H, On revolution. Penguin Books, London, 1963). Despite higher education suggesting a space where people might openly share and express their ideas without hesitancy and fear, we cannot assume that all universities provide open spaces for speech and disagreement, and we cannot assume that all people (academics, students, administrators) participate in this space equally or at all. The very pluralism of the public sphere means an array of diverse and conflicting views. It would seem, therefore, that if academic activism were to be revolutionary, it could not happen without aspiring to make the university a place where freedom holds sway. To think of academic activism as a revolutionary path towards what might not be possible, we contend, is to remain open to surprise and strangeness. Stated differently, to be open to the unexpected and the strange is to be concerned with what can yet unfold so that higher education institutions should remain open to adapt and respond to ongoing transformations.

Keywords Hannah Arendt · Revolution · Freedom · New beginnings

Introduction

Our attraction to Hannah Arendt's (1963) *On Revolution* is not so much that we are equating academic activism with the occurrence of a revolution but, rather, that the spirit of activism cannot ignore a revolutionary spirit. Based on Arendt's bold analysis of the term 'revolution', we examine what makes such an action what it is and how academic activism can gain a revolutionary drive in the sense of establishing new beginnings in higher education discourse. Thus, we analyse the notion of revolution, in particular, how the spirit of a revolution can arouse in academics an activism that embraces irresistibility and novelty (Arendt, 1963). We are specifically interested in the notion of revolution concerning practices of freedom, equality and novelty – that is, academic activism as 'perplexities of new beginnings' (Arendt, 1963: 208). Despite higher education suggesting a space where people might openly

N. Davids, Y. Waghid, *Academic Activism in Higher Education*, Debating Higher Education: Philosophical Perspectives 5, https://doi.org/10.1007/978-981-16-0340-2_6

share and express their ideas without hesitancy and fear, we cannot assume that all universities provide open spaces for speech and disagreement, and we cannot assume that all people (academics, students, administrators) participate in this space equally or at all.

The very pluralism of the public sphere means an array of diverse and conflicting views. It would seem, therefore, that if academic activism were to be revolutionary, it could not happen without aspiring to make the university a place where freedom holds sway. Our own perceptions experiences of universities in South Africa are somewhat perplexing. While one of us had more limited opportunities than the other due to the period when we accessed higher education, we both came to it with heightened political expectations. As already pointed out in this book, historically disadvantaged (black) universities, a few white 'liberal' universities, students and a number of academics played pivotal activist roles in protesting the obscenity of apartheid. Despite the intensely stratifying influence of apartheid, a number of universities remained intent in bringing about the change necessary for a socially just society. South Africa has un-mistakenly undergone a revolution – that is, political and social change – and the role of the university in this regard cannot be diluted. That the revolution unfolded peacefully bears testimony to the formidable reconciliatory spirit of revolutionary figures, such as Nelson Mandela, Oliver Tambo and Walter Sisulu. While growing up, and participating in endless student protests and rallies, it was difficult to always have hope that apartheid would end. It was difficult to always believe that our condition as an oppressed people could change. Yet, to think of academic activism as a revolutionary path towards what might be possible, we contend, is to remain open to surprise and strangeness. Stated differently, to be open to the unexpected and the strange is to be concerned with what can yet unfold so that higher education institutions should remain open to adapt and respond to ongoing transformations.

Revolution as Freedom

In Hannah Arendt's (1963) meticulous analysis of the concept 'revolution', she begins by juxtaposing it against war. While it might be necessary, to differentiate in theory and practice between war and revolution, she posits, we must remember that despite their close inter-relatedness, the mere fact that wars and revolutions are not even conceivable outside of violence is not enough to set them apart from all other political phenomena (Arendt, 1963). To Arendt (1963), violence is a common denominator, which is why wars so easily result in revolutions and why revolutions have shown inclinations to unleash wars. That being said, neither wars nor revolutions are ever only determined by violence. Violence, according to Arendt (1963: 8), is a marginal phenomenon – 'for man [or woman], to the extent that he [or she] is a political being, is endowed with the power of speech'; 'violence itself is incapable of speech, and not merely that speech is helpless when confronted with violence' (1963: 9). Because of this speechlessness, she asserts, political theory has little to say about the phenomenon of violence. And, continues Arendt (1963), although violence plays a predominant role in wars and revolutions, both, strictly speaking, occur outside the political realm.

Arendt (1963: 11), however, in her own words, is 'not concerned with the war question'. Whereas war wants to annihilate people, revolution hopes 'for the emancipation of all mankind [humankind]' (Arendt, 1963: 1), which, of course, *is* her concern. Revolutions, maintains Arendt (1963: 11), are 'the only political events which confront us directly and inevitably with the problem of beginning'. She believes that the term 'revolutionary' is only applicable if freedom is the objective (Arendt, 1963: 19). In her words:

> Crucial, then, to any understanding of revolutions in the modern age is that the idea of freedom and the experience of a new beginning should coincide. And since the current notion of the Free World is that of freedom, and neither justice nor greatness, is the highest criterion for judging the constitutions of political bodies, it is not only our understanding of revolution but our conception of freedom. (Arendt, 1963: 19)

Just as she differentiates between war and revolution, she distinguishes between liberation and freedom. While liberation 'may be the condition of freedom', she argues, liberation has always loomed large, and the foundation of freedom has always been uncertain, leading political theory to 'understand by political freedom, not a political phenomenon, but... the more or less free range of non-political activities' permitted and guaranteed (Arendt, 1963: 21). Arendt (1963) expounds that freedom as a political phenomenon arose with the Greek city-states and was first understood as 'a form of political organization in which the citizens lived together under conditions of no-rule' or isonomy. Isonomy was not equality of condition, but political equality. Men were not equal by nature but became equal through the law of the *polis*. As a result, freedom needed the place of the polis or political space in which the life of free men and women needs the presence of others for the advancement of their freedom (Arendt, 1963).

As an intersubjective space, the *polis* or public sphere is a place which should be open to all and, thus, holds the capacity for political engagement, deliberation as well as authority and judgement. Action and speech, she explains, 'create a space between the participants which can find its proper location almost any time and anywhere. It is the space of appearance in the widest sense of the word, namely, the space where "I appear to others as others appear to me, where men exist not merely like other living or inanimate things but proclaims their appearance explicitly"' (Arendt, 1998: 198). To Arendt (1963), the modern concept of revolution represents an attempt to change the public sphere; it represents an opportunity for history to begin anew, and this new beginning coincides with an idea of freedom.

Unlike some, who might consider freedom and equality as being in tension, Arendt contends that public freedom requires equality. People, she maintains, are not naturally equal; they are made equal in 'artificial' political spaces, 'where men [encounter] one another as citizens and not as private persons' (1963: 21). In turn, '[t]he life of a free man needed the presence of others. Freedom itself needed a place where people could come together – the agora, the market-place, or the *polis*, the political space proper' (Arendt, 1963: 22). For Arendt, explains Wellmer (1999: 219), 'the sphere of public freedom also signifies a sphere of action, of self-organization, of direct democracy. In such a sphere of public freedom, délibération and action are intertwined with each other; and an essential theme of délibération will be the constitution and préservation of public freedom itself'.

Towards a Revolutionary Spirit of Activism

In *The Promise of Politics* (2005: 136), Arendt asserts:

> As long as one understands politics to be solely concerned with what is absolutely neces-sary for men [or women] to live in a community so that they then can be granted, either as individuals or social groups, a freedom that lies beyond both politics and life's necessities, we are indeed justified in measuring the degree of freedom within any political body by the religious and academic freedom that it tolerates, which is to say, by the size of the nonpoliti-cal space of freedom that it contains and maintains'.

Significantly, in Arendt's (1963) opinion, thus far, revolutions (such as the French, Russian and American) have not succeeded in reaching its primary goal, which is to ensure a public sphere where all citizens enjoy the same rights of access and participation. Once authorities are established, revolutions come to an end. This is equally evident in a South African context – once the ANC achieved its objective to bringing an end to apartheid and assumed the role of the country's first demo-cratically elected government, it ceased in its role and purpose as an activist politi-cal party. The assumption is that the attainment of a democracy equates to a restoration of equality and socio-economic equity. Yet the effects of oppression and marginalisation and stratification have persisted, and not only because of the histori-cal role of apartheid but because the new democratic government very quickly lost sight that to the majority of South Africans, apartheid continues in abject living conditions, desperate unemployment and poverty as well limited access to the promises of a democratic society. As a result, the revolution might have ended, but the plight of people has not – as is evident in ongoing civil unrests against poor service delivery; demands for basic housing and living conditions, such as running water, sanitation and electricity; and, of course, increasing student protests, who view access to universities as the only route to a better and socially just life and lifestyle. As such, the university becomes a space not only of students from incred-ibly diverse contexts and ideologies, a melting pot of different and competing expectations, with equally disparate pressures and hopes, but a veritable social and economic fault line between those who can access and compete and those who cannot.

As a space in which academics, students and administrators from diverse back-grounds can come together, it provides a potential base for converging and diverg-ing views – where people might openly share and express their ideas without hesitancy and fear. And yet, we cannot assume that all universities provide open spaces for speech and disagreement; we cannot assume that all people (academics, students, administrators) participate in this space equally or at all. The very plural-ism of the public sphere means an array of diverse and conflicting views. It would seem, therefore, that if academic activism were to be revolutionary, it could not happen without aspiring to make the university a place where freedom holds sway. In the case of South Africa, it is not just that the ANC, since assuming the role of government, that has relinquished its role of activism. It is also a worrying trend that the ANC seeks greater control of universities than did the apartheid state (Higgins, 2000). Complaints from South African academics include that the state has become increasingly interventionist and that there is an ambivalent relationship between the academy and the state, underscored by the impression that the state does not trust the academy to transform itself to meet the demands of a democratic society (Habib, Morrow, & Bentley, 2008). Justifications of being 'well-meaning' by the demo-cratic state, argues Higgins (2000: 110), cannot be used to defend the abandonment of academic freedom.

On the one hand, the pace of transformation, which is tied to academic freedom, has not been as robust as the post-apartheid government had anticipated. Here the argument is that the inequalities and inefficiencies of higher education are the result of a disregard for accountability to the state and therefore necessitate state interven-tion. For as long as South African universities remain primarily dependent on state funding, maintains Du Toit (2000), any talk of effective institutional autonomy must, in principle, always remain significantly qualified. To this extent, he contin-ues, the structural conditions for possible state action threatening academic freedom in the sense of institutional autonomy remain in place. On the other hand, there are internal threats – those which Du Toit (2000: 99) describes as arising '*within* the university communities themselves'. These pertain to the new structures of univer-sity governance, the reconfiguration of faculties, financial devolution to faculty level, the transformation of the curriculum by the introduction of new academic programmes as well as downsizing and redeployment and the possibility of retrench-ments, which have not been imposed externally on the university (Du Toit 2000). Although he concurs that these internal developments might very well be in response to changes in the external environment (e.g. changes in government policies), the actions and circumstances of universities depend on institutional autonomy, rather than on any external interference with academic freedom. For this reason, Du Toit (2000: 103) believes that the challenge for South African institutions 'is the neces-sary and ongoing transformation of the institutional culture of the university; this is no external threat to academic freedom; on the contrary, it is needed to secure effec-tive academic freedom itself'.

Following Arendt (1963), the success of a revolution resides in its capacity to ensure the exercise of freedom, and not only the granting of freedom to citizens. Intrinsically, asserts Higgins (2000), the university is not an instrument of state policy to deliver on the needs of society; instead, the purpose of the university is the pursuit of truth. In this sense, academic activism manifests in the extent to which students and academics are free to exercise their views concerning whatever topic or issue they choose – nothing, to repeat Derrida (2005: 253), 'is beyond question'. More and more universities attach themselves to *the idea* of freedom of participation and expression, and not necessarily to the exercise and propagation thereof. Academics, for example, often find themselves constrained by institutional structures and policies, which not only impede their freedom to act as they choose but which force them into acting in ways with which they might disagree. Universities are certainly not free of social or moral injustices.

Regardless of geopolitical contexts, the university, as a social institution, produces and reproduces not only particular epistemologies but particular kinds of graduates and people. In this way, universities retain and perpetuate social and political inequalities – re-affirming societal hegemonies and binaries, which renders most people to the margins so that the centre, which is occupied by a few, remains intact. Students are not treated equally in terms of access, and even if they gain access, they are not treated equally as participants, and even if they do manage to participate, they are not afforded equal opportunities in terms of academic support, assessment or recognition. Seemingly, despite numerous and innovative attempts by our university, for example, to anonymise students, which has included a reliance on student numbers, rather than names on examination papers, biases cannot be addressed or remedied through external mechanisms and processes. Similar prejudicial encounters are witnessed during oral examinations of postgraduate students. Students, who do not have English as their mother tongue and, therefore, do not have a strong command of the language, are subjected to what can only be described as unfair interrogations of their work. The focus is often only on their inability to express themselves, rather than on whether they have actually demonstrated a clear understanding and presentation of a research study through their thesis writing. The humiliation that is, at times, experienced by these students is hard to ignore and clearly provides some evidence of why so many black postgraduate students do not see themselves as working in the academy.

Likewise, academics are not immune to discriminatory or marginalising practices. Depending on historical ties, or common ground – whether concerning academic disciplines, race, culture, religion, gender or sexuality – different rules apply when it comes to appointments, research funding or promotion. Appointment committees of universities offer profoundly disturbing insights into the mechanisms necessary for the retention of a particular institutional culture. While some academics might be subjected to rigorous criteria in terms of research outputs, postgraduate supervision and teaching, others bypass all of these based on historical ties. A recent experience of an interview panel by one of us laid bare just how unethical these practices can be. The chair of the committee had quite literally added an applicant from a designated 'diverse' group only for the sake of having some 'diversity' on the list. This action became apparent when he announced just before the interviews were about to commence that the 'diverse' candidate is not a serious contender and was added for the purposes of compliance. Adding to his shocking action was his apparent oblivion or apathy regarding the ethical questionability of his conduct. As disagreement and disgust erupted from no more than two members on an eight-member panel, it became apparent that his dichotomous construction between 'white' competence' and 'black' incompetence was just so deeply embedded that he was actually incapable of seeing the wrongness of his actions.

These are just some of the injustices, which perpetuate the university landscape, and which confront academics, depending on whether or not they choose firstly to see it and secondly to act against it. As academics, we occupy and inhabit institutions, which, through the enactment of particular injustices, can place our work and reputation at risk. While our silence can rightly be interpreted as complacency, our protest can be seen as opposition to the university. Each of these constitutes its own set of risks. But, if we are to begin anew, then we can only act freely by laying claim to our freedom. The degree of our freedom increases in relation to the extent to which we are prepared to act with fear and restraint and so that history might begin anew.

Activism as 'Perplexities of New Beginnings'

The rhetoric of apartheid relied extensively on an inseparability between the state and religion – specifically, Christian Nationalism, which, in turn, framed the national curriculum, known as Christian National Education. This explicit religious foundation is captured in the preamble of the Constitution, which renders all governments subordinate to 'the sovereignty and providence of God in guiding the affairs of nations'. Bloomberg (1990: xxiii) explains that what the Nationalist Party (responsible for propagating apartheid) stood for was not only 'white mastery' and 'white rule based on race'; it also stands propagated in 'a society modelled on Christian norms'. To this end, it justified all policies, including segregation, on the basis of the Christian Nationalist Protestant ethic (Bloomberg, 1990). Why are we writing about this? Firstly, because we lived and experienced this society – not as white masters, but as black subjects. Secondly, despite our subjection to Christian Nationalism, we worry about Arendt's assertion that secularisation is crucial in humans' revolutionary actions.

Secularisation, states Arendt (1963: 18–19), is the 'emancipation of the secular realm from the tutelage of the Church', and 'the separation of religion from politics and the rise of a secular realm is certainly a crucial factor in the phenomenon of revolution'. 'What we call revolution is precisely that transitory phase which brings about the birth of a new, secular realm'. Hence, Moyn (2008) concluded that it would not be too much to argue that Arendt placed secularisation at the very centre of her analysis of the revolutionary phenomenon and secularism at the core of her political hopes. 'Put simply, Arendt thought that what was at stake in modernity was leaving religion behind, at least as the foundation of public coexistence. Conversely, modernity took its most politically defective forms when (among other things) it had failed to make its necessary break with the religious civilization that preceded it'. As explained in the first half of this chapter, to Arendt, the term 'revolutionary' is only applicable if freedom is the objective. 'Crucial, then, to any understanding of revolutions in the modern age is that the idea of freedom and the experience of a new beginning should coincide' (Arendt, 1963: 19).

It is our contention, however, that unless religion and politics restrain humans from being free, we do not concur with her assumption that religion inhibits peoples' freedom or with her argument that secularisation is possible only as a revolution. The idea that religion inhibits people's freedom implies that people who ascribe to a particular religion surrender themselves to that religion so that they become constrained in their thoughts and actions. As such, they no longer operate as autonomous beings, but as subjects of religious doctrine and dogma. Yet, on the one hand, religion can also be used as a source and medium of freedom. During apartheid, religious authorities and communities often drew on their religious doctrine not only in support of their demands for justice and freedom but as a manifestation that the law of the state (apartheid) cannot be used to curtail or subjugate the freedom afforded to humanity. In this sense, religion itself can be interpreted and practised as a manifestation of freedom, which is different to the principle of freedom of religion. Instead, religion can be used as a language and medium through which to undermine and contest social injustice and oppression. We witness this in the works of Paulo Freire (whose ideas we coincidentally focus on in the next chapter).

Christianity had a profound influence on Freire's philosophy and vision. Kirylo (2017: xvii) explains that Freire reflectively filtered his thoughts through a spiritual lens so much so that his work was as influential outside the circle of education and had an impact on theological and religious circles. His work found a strong resonance in liberation theology, which, according to Gutiérrez (2005), seeks to provide a language for talking about God; it is an attempt to make the word of life present in a world of oppression, injustice and death. To Kirylo (2011: 186), liberation theology views God as 'acting in history' – suggesting that faith corresponds to real historical circumstances; liberation theology views history from the perspective of the marginalised and poor and symbolises a historical break with the Church being linked with the ruling oligarchy, the military and the government (Kirylo, 2011: 186). Freire's (1984: 73) education approach was critical in the formation of liberation theology, and thus, he provided theologians with a language of what it means to empower people at a grassroots level – that is, to 'reconcile Christian love with the exploitation of human beings'. He connected his faith to undermining oppression and inequality; he used his faith as a means to produce a more just and humane society. To Freire (1997), cultivating a more humane and just society can be realised through an awareness of self (conscientisation) and others, engaging in deliberative dialogue for purposes of transformation and becoming deeply committed to the struggle for social justice.

The association of theology with liberation is certainly not unique to Christianity or monotheism for that matter. The Qur'an is abundantly explicit in its insistence on justice as a foundational manifestation of faith: 'O you who have believed, be persistently standing firm in justice... even if it be against yourselves or parents and relatives' (Chapter 4: verse 135).

Of course, we cannot deny the persistence of dogma and indoctrination within all religions. However, it is imperative to draw clear distinctions between what religious source codes actually state and how these source codes are interpreted – that is, how text is understood and lived in contexts. Moreover, in our opinion, religion does not translate into a negation of individual autonomy. Instead, an ethics of individual autonomy, if positively exercised, can engender more tenable judgements based on negatively pursuing human understanding. Humanity is continuously encouraged to seek clearer understandings on the basis of exercising their individual autonomy as a positive pursuit for critical judgement and reflection and a negative inclination towards finding out things through mutual consultation, a matter of acting with collective understanding (Davids & Waghid, 2016).

On the other hand, even a secularised notion of religion liberated from politics can provoke people to act freely. People's very adherence to something secular can only happen as a consequence of their unwillingness to be dominated by religion or controlled by politics for that matter. In this regard, individual autonomy can do much to oppose and even eradicate authoritarianism often encountered in patriarchal practices and societies.

Concerning the academy, any act of freedom exercised by academics should be left unconstrained if such actions were to be recognised as free. For instance, freedom of speech can only be a free expression of human thoughts when it is left unconstrained. In this way, Amy Gutmann's (2003) enunciation that freedom of expression has its limitations when it unjustly discriminates against others is perhaps not a corroboration that freedom of expression should be restricted but rather that such expressions are not in themselves free. The exercise of freedom of expression is inherently about making freedom count, and if it is constrained, as Gutmann (2003) argues, then it is not apposite to talk about freedom of expression at all. The point is, why would one limit freedom in the name of freedom? Even pronouncing expressions freely that might be injurious to others is no justification for restricting freedom of expression per se. Unless of course, we are not talking about freedom of expression but rather something else. Thus to nurture unbridled freedom becomes a condition of freedom in itself.

Secondly, the notion of revolution also reveals humans' capacity for novelty or new experiences (Arendt, 1963: 24). Being revolutionary implies a 'pathos of novelty is present' – that is, revolutions are more than successful insurrections, and we are not justified in calling every coup d'état a revolution (Arendt, 1963: 24). The point about revolution bringing about something new 'spells the definite end of the older order and brings about the birth of a new world' (Arendt, 1963: 32). In this way, the metaphor of revolution carries with it an inclination to produce irresistible and irrevocable human experiences (Arendt, 1963). In this way, the novelty (newness) brought about through revolution is permanent. This implies that being revolutionary is concerned with a newness that things will not be the same and that the unexpected and improbable might still be possible. To think of academic activism as a revolutionary path towards what might not be possible is to remain open to surprise and strangeness. Stated differently, to be open to the unexpected and the strange is to be concerned about what can yet unfold so that higher education institutions should remain open to adapt and respond to ongoing transformations.

Likewise, being open to novelty is tantamount to being open to otherness. Here we are specifically thinking of other ways of university teaching, learning and even education itself. To think about teaching as revolutionary would be to think anew about teaching itself. For instance, if we consider teaching as a kind of rhythmic action according to which teachers withhold their judgments as students make sense of their learning and conversely when students are summoned to judge without being constrained by teachers, then such a form of teaching would open up more opportunities for engagement among teachers and students. This would be a new form of teaching in the sense that students learn based on making evaluative judgements of teachers' disciplinary content matter without holding back on being provocative, dissenting and even controversial. Novelty per se invites dissent and controversy, which also allows one to look at teaching as an otherly action.

Thirdly, for Arendt (1963), it is not adequate to describe revolution in relation to violence. For Arendt (1963), insurrections, rebellions, uprisings, civil wars and factional strife are all brought about by violence. However, violence in itself is inadequate to describe revolution, although there might be some aspects of violence in revolutions. If Arendt is correct that violence is not central to revolution, then we would like to infer that violence is used by Arendt in a metaphorical way, in the sense that revolutions are disruptive, tumultuous and moving. Moreover, for academic activism to be metaphorically speaking violent implies that such actions should be disturbing, vociferous and stirring – that is, to shift an individual from one point of view to another. Here we are not talking about indoctrination, which relies upon an uncritical acceptance of this belief or that argument. What we have in mind is provoking students into critically interrogating their own perspectives, so that we might become aware not only of their particular biases but the blinkers, which we all wear as we go through life. It is neither reasonable nor acceptable enough for academics to be aware of problematic views that might exist among a group of students, and not try to redress these views.

Often, in our faculty, as we convene departmental and committee meetings, we listen as certain academics complain about how cloistered and closed-off a number of our students are and how unexposed they are to the 'real' South Africa. The majority of our students have only ever experienced schooling and university life in the same town – a town, which is somewhat remote from the city centre, and seemingly untouched by the complexities of a country, which has transitioned from apartheid to democracy. Its geographical remoteness in what is considered as one of the wealthiest areas in South Africa has meant a relatively low influx of students from different racial and socio-economic communities. As a result, the university has largely managed to maintain its historical identity, character and architecture. Students here can easily go through an academic programme without ever encountering or engaging with students, who are different from themselves in terms of race, culture, language, ethnicity or class. No surprise, therefore, to find that even in a class like our PGCE, where there are students from diverse backgrounds and contexts, students naturally gravitate towards that which is familiar. As a result, when it comes to allocating these students to various schools around the university for the purposes of teaching practice, there is generally a flurry of insistence to be placed at schools, which are similar, if not the same, as the ones they attended.

Often, their perspectives and perceptions about diversity and the effects of apartheid on themselves and others (especially, those who have been oppressed) are disturbingly uninformed. This is not only because they see themselves as generationally detached from the ideology of apartheid, but they are dismissive of its residual effects, most notably encountered in schools and education. More problematic is the expression of certain views and prejudices that are clearly more suited to an apartheid context, than a democratic one. These views or the complacent attitudes of students cannot be left unchallenged – especially if one considers that these are not only students; these are students, who are on their way to becoming teachers. Unless they are awakened to their inherent biases, they will take these prejudices into their teaching and encounters with those they teach. In sum, they will cause unknown harm. Academic activism necessarily implies a willingness to call out these practices and to redirect students to a more just understanding – not only of the world in which they find themselves but of themselves in relation to others. This has very little to do with insisting that all students should perceive the world and its people in the way that we as academics do; it has to do with getting them to see the world as a diverse and different space; respect, rather than agreement, carries the highest value.

We can only imagine that transformation of universities in South Africa is metaphorically speaking unprecedented violent acts of permanent change. Students have been provoked into protesting against certain universities, which have seemingly chosen not to act in removing statues and busts of colonial and apartheid statesmen. Likewise, students find themselves in situations where their only resort is violence as institutions persist with authoritarian practices, which attempt to shut them down or restrict their access when they attempt to make their voices heard. Politically, it would be fair to describe South Africa's forced transition from apartheid to a democratic state as a revolution. The apartheid state certainly had no desire to end what they understood as a God-given right to supremacy and privilege. Instead, it was forced to do so by relentless forms of activism, violence and deaths, which eventually garnered enough international support and economic sanctions to force the apartheid defeat to relinquish its power.

Like Arendt's (1963: 11) revolution, the struggle for democracy was 'not concerned with the war question'. The only concern and objective of the struggle against apartheid were that of freedom – 'the emancipation of all mankind [South Africans]' (Arendt, 1963: 1) – which, of course, *is* her concern. Revolutions, maintains Arendt (1963: 11), are 'the only political events which confront us directly and inevitably with the problem of beginning'. Was this a successful revolution? Yes, insofar as it saw the ideological demise of apartheid. Did 'new beginnings' emerge? Yes, insofar as people are regarded as free from oppression, and in possession of a set of human rights, at least ideologically. Have people achieved their freedom, as is the objective of a revolution? No, if one considers only the higher education landscape as a microcosm of society, which is not only fraught with socio-economic inequalities and exclusion, but with a growing sentiment and attitude that student activism is an unnecessary obstruction.

What we have attempted to do with an Arendtian conception of revolution is to rethink academic activism along the lines of freedom, novelty and metaphoric violence. We contend that revolutionary academic activism can contribute towards the transformation of universities in the country, but then educational matters have to be looked at anew.

References

Arendt, H. (1963). *On revolution*. London: Penguin Books.
Arendt, H. (1998). *The human condition*. Chicago: The University of Chicago Press.
Arendt, H. (2005). *The promise of politics*. New York: Schocken Books.
Bloomberg, C. (1990). *Christian-Nationalism and the rise of the Afrikaner Broederbond, in South Africa, 1918–48* (S. Dubow, Ed.). London: The MacMillan Press Ltd.
Davids, N., & Waghid, Y. (2016). *Ethical dimensions of Muslim education*. New York/London: Palgrave Macmillan.
Derrida, J. (2005). The future of the profession or the unconditional university (Thanks to the "humanities," what could take place tomorrow). In P. P. Trifonas & M. A. Peters (Eds.), *Deconstructing Derrida* (pp. 11–24). New York: Palgrave Macmillan.
Du Toit, A. (2000). Critic and citizen: The intellectual, transformation and academic freedom. *Pretexts: Literary and Cultural Studies, 9*(1), 91–104.
Freire, P. (1984). *Pedagogy of the oppressed*. New York: Continuum.
Freire, P. (1997). *Pedagogy of hope: Reliving pedagogy of the oppressed*. New York: Continuum.
Gutiérrez, G. (2005, February 10). Paper presented at the first research seminar of the Centre for the Study of Religion and Politics (CSRP), School of Divinity, University of St. Andrews.
Gutmann, A. (2003). *Identity and democracy*. Princeton, NJ: Princeton University Press.
Habib, A., Morrow, S., & Bentley, K. (2008). Academic freedom, institutional autonomy and the corporatised University in Contemporary South Africa. *Social Dynamics, 34*(2), 140–155.
Higgins, J. (2000). Academic freedom in the New South Africa. *Boundary 2, 27*(1), 97–119.
Kirylo, J. D. (2011). *Paulo Freire: The man from Recife*. New York: Peter Lang.
Kirylo, J. D. (2017). *Paulo Freire: His faith, spirituality, and theology*. Rotterdam, The Netherlands: Sense Publishers.
Moyn, S. (2008). Hannah Arendt on the secular. *New German Critique (Political Theology), 105*, 71–96.
Wellmer, A. (1999). Hannah Arendt on revolution. *Revue Internationale de Philosophie, 53*(2), 207–222.

Chapter 7
A Pedagogy of Courage

Abstract In this chapter, we endeavour to re-read Freire in a post-critical way and to offer some view on how a Freirean notion of courage impacts our thinking of philosophy of higher education and our concern with academic activism. What is important for our post-critical analysis of Freire's seminal thoughts is that education is a courageous act in the sense of being open to the world and others, a risk of what is new and an awareness of our unfinishedness (Freire P, Pedagogy of freedom: ethics, democracy, and courage. Rowman & Littlefield, Lanham/Boulder/New York/Oxford, 1998a). We follow this with an analysis of Freire's (1994) conceptualisation of critical consciousness or conscientisation as a form of activist representational politics. Here, we pay careful attention to Freire's (Pedagogy of the city. Continuum, New York, 1993) articulation of a sensual body that cannot be disconnected from teaching, learning and, hence, freedom. In this regard, we reflect on the body as a choreographed form of protest and activism. We conclude by arguing that although activism presents itself as forms of resistance and antagonism, the very pursuit to act against that which is oppressive and harmful is in itself an act of love for humanity and justice.

Keywords Paulo Freire · Pedagogy of courage · Post-critical · Conscientisation · Representational politics

Introduction

Although difficult to limit ourselves, our interest in this chapter pertains to the reading of three of Paulo Freire's major works, namely, *Pedagogy of the Oppressed* (Freire, 1984), *Pedagogy of Freedom* (Freire, 1998a) and *Pedagogy of Hope* (Freire, 2004). One of the world's most celebrated education scholars, Freire did much to advance a critical perspective on (higher) education along the lines of democracy, freedom and liberation. He held that because of the different identities, histories, perspectives and struggles that humans bring to the world, the world and, hence, humans are constantly changing. Likewise, students and academics are part of the

© The Author(s), under exclusive license to Springer Nature Singapore
Pte Ltd. 2021
N. Davids, Y. Waghid, *Academic Activism in Higher Education*, Debating
Higher Education: Philosophical Perspectives 5,
https://doi.org/10.1007/978-981-16-0340-2_7

world; their lives unfold in relation to the world. They have certain needs, insecurities, vulnerabilities, fears, beliefs and hopes that live inside of them and that cannot be separated from the world. They have to be made aware of human suffering, which too often is viewed from a distance, and not seen as a concern of the student's world. University education cannot be used as means of and for insulated thinking and being; instead, it has to awaken students and academics alike to their interconnectedness and, hence, collective responsibility to ensure the pursuit of freedom from all manners of oppression.

In this chapter, we endeavour to re-read Freire in a post-critical way and to offer some view on how a Freirean notion of courage impacts our thinking of philosophy of higher education and our concern with academic activism. Informed by critique, a post-critical approach is open to alternative and different views; it desires to look beyond conservative and taken-for-granted assumptions and refuses to be boxed in by singular interpretations. In this regard, what is important for our own post-critical analysis of Freire's seminal thoughts is that education is a courageous act in the sense of being open to the world and others, a risk of what is new and an awareness of our unfinishedness (Freire, 1998a). We follow this with an analysis of Freire's (1993) conceptualisation of critical consciousness or conscientisation as a form of activist representational politics. Here, we pay careful attention to Freire's (1993) articulation of a sensual body, which cannot be disconnected from teaching, learning and, hence, freedom. In this regard, we reflect on the body as a choreographed form of protest and activism. We conclude by arguing that although activism presents itself as forms of resistance and antagonism, the very pursuit to act against that which is oppressive and harmful is in itself an act of love for humanity and justice.

On a Pedagogy of Courage

Humans, says Freire (1984), do not simply live in the world; they encounter the world as the history of humanity and as a historical struggle. As humans interact with others and their world, they give shape to themselves and how they understand themselves and how they perceive others in the world. Hence, Freire (1984: 69) asserts that '[t]o exist, humanly, is to name the world, to change it' – that is, as humans engage with the world, they bring themselves into the world through their being and action. The world, therefore, is constituted by humans with different histories, perspectives, perceptions and struggles, which means that there is no neutral understanding of the world or what it means to be human. Freire (1998a: 92) explains that humans 'are constantly in the process of becoming and, therefore, are capable of observing, comparing, evaluating, choosing, deciding, intervening, breaking with, and making options, we are ethical beings, capable of transgressing our ethical grounding'. As such, argues Freire (1998a), they are changing beings, who intervene in the world, on the basis of their political presences. To him (1984), knowledge emerges through inquiry, invention and re-invention. He maintains that '[t]he more radical a person is, the more fully he or she enters into reality so that, knowing it better, he or she can better transform it. This individual is not afraid to confront, to listen, to see the world unveiled. This person is not afraid to meet the other people or to enter into dialogue with them' (Freire, 1984: 21).

When humans are unafraid of engaging with others, they are courageous; they demonstrate a willingness to intervene in the world; they aspire 'for radical changes in society in such areas of economics, human relations, property, the right to employment, to land, to education, and to health, and to the reactionary position whose aim is to immobilize history and maintain an unjust socio-economic and cultural order' (Freire, 1998a: 99). To Freire (1998a: 91), education in itself is 'a form of intervention in the world', but only if this education is not characterised by processes of passive and compliant transmission and reception – that is, the 'banking concept of education', which is characterised by processes of passive and compliant transmission and reception. Freire (1984: 72) explains as follows:

> In the banking concept of education, knowledge is a gift bestowed by those who consider themselves knowledgeable upon those whom they consider to know nothing. Projecting an absolute ignorance onto others, a characteristic of the ideology of oppression, negates education and knowledge as processes of inquiry. The teacher presents himself to his students as their necessary opposite; by considering their ignorance absolute, he justifies his own existence.

Within the banking concept of education, there is 'the assumption of a dichotomy between human beings and the world: a person is merely *in* the world, not *with* the world or with others; the individual is spectator, not re-creator' (Freire, 1984: 75). The more this form of education is propagated, the narrower the chance for students to 'develop the critical consciousness which would result from their intervention in the world as transformers of that world' (Freire, 1984: 73).

In stark contrast to the banking concept of education, a libertarian education aspires to dismiss the dichotomy between teachers and students, so that 'both are simultaneously teachers and students' (1984: 72); it focuses on reconciling the efforts of teachers with those of students so that both 'engage in critical thinking and the quest for mutual humanization' (1984: 75). For Freire (1984: 79), authentic liberation is 'the process of humanization'; 'liberation is a praxis: the action and reflection of men and women upon their world in order to transform it'. He refers to this as 'problem-posing' education – an education which responds to the essence of consciousness, intentionality, which embodies communication. To this end, he associates praxis with dialogue; praxis does not simply interpret the world; it is a productive activity that brings about change, intervention and transformation. Through dialogue, explains Freire (1984: 80), 'the teacher-of-the-students and the students-of-the-teacher cease to exist, and a new term emerges: teacher-student with students-teachers'. As such, the role of the teacher is no longer only that of the-one-who-teaches but also one who is taught in dialogue with the students, who, in turn, while being taught, also teach. In this way, the teacher and her students connect: they pose problems to each other, and they seek to make sense of the world in which they find themselves and to intervene. Through engaging in dialogue, we maintain, teachers and students are conscientised into responding and acting against that which is unjust, so that what we emerges are new ways of affirming and preserving the humanity of the world in which we find ourselves.

Freire (1984: 81) clarifies that because both the teacher and students 'apprehend the challenge as interrelated to other problems within a total context, not as a theoretical question, the resulting comprehension tends to be increasingly critical and thus constantly less alienated'. The more students and teachers respond to challenges, the more they become aware of new challenges. They begin to recognise that they are not detached from their world and that their reality is not abstract. As they reflect upon their world, they become simultaneously conscious of themselves and the world, and as their sense of consciousness deepens, they begin to conceive of education as 'the practice of freedom', as opposed to 'education as the practice of domination'. For this reason, Freire (1984) contends that without inquiry, consciousness and praxis, individuals cannot be truly human. The idea of instilling consciousness as a purpose of education holds profound implications. It immediately suggests an awakening that otherwise might not be evident. At times, it is easy for students and academics alike to be caught up in their own ideas, perceptions and perspectives, to consider the world only from their own vantage points. To be conscious is to detach oneself from a singular point of view and to attach oneself to the perspective of the lifeworlds of others: to consider the possibility that things might not be as they seem and that what one understands about the world might only be one idea. To Freire (1984: 96), knowledge, he maintains, 'emerges only through invention and re-invention, through the restless, impatient, continuing, hopeful inquiry human beings pursue in the world, with the world, and with each other'. Moreover, says Freire (1984: 96), 'true education incarnates the permanent search of people together with others for their becoming fully human in the world in which they exist'.

As part of Freire's openness to the world, he conceives of pedagogy as a shared inquiry or praxis – 'action and reflection upon the world in order to change it' (1984: 17). Any situation that prevents others from engaging in the process of inquiry, contends Freire (1984), is one of violence. As such, he encourages teachers to stimulate 'critical curiosity in their students, [and] the taste of adventure', thus contributing to the building of a 'solid autonomy in their students' (Freire, 1998a: 100). Moreover, by autonomy Freire (1998a: 70) intimates that students and teachers ought to become open-minded persons who do not fear what is new, who are upset by injustice and hurt by discrimination and who struggle against impunity. Again, about open-mindedness and autonomy, Freire (1998a: 59) has the following to say:

> Respect for the autonomy and dignity of every person is an ethical imperative and not a favor that we may or may not concede to each other. It is precisely because we are ethical beings that we can commit what can only be called a transgression by denying our essentially ethical condition. The teacher who does not respect the student's curiosity in its diverse aesthetic, linguistic, and syntactical expressions; who uses irony to put down legitimate questioning … who is not respectfully present in the educational experience of the student, transgresses fundamental ethical principles of the human condition.

For Freire, only through respect and openness does education open up people to the world in which they encounter one another's differences and otherness. Humans, in fact, following Freire (1998a: 59), grow 'by confronting their differences' in open and respectful ways. When they act in this way – that is, with openness and respect, they show courage. Sometimes it is easier to remain silent; other times, we respond with aggression, anger and violence, which serve only to hinder the potential for dialogue before it has even begun. Confronting differences in a way that assures the other of one's regard takes courage and boldness. This is because when we confront differences within ourselves, and especially in others, it makes us vulnerable to the other, leaving us unsure about what response to expect.

Imagine a scenario in which a student confronts a teacher with the possibility that the teacher has been unfair in his or her assessment practices. This takes courage; the student places himself at risk of not receiving good results if the teacher experiences the question as an affront. However, courage, as Freire describes, is the human condition, if we are to conceive of ourselves as ethical beings. For academics, this means having the courage to speak out when they see a wrong – whether in relation to acceptance criteria and practices, teaching and assessment practices or how students are treated as a collective. If academics conceive of themselves in this way, then they should not only expect this same principle from their students, but they should nurture it.

Secondly, for Freire (1998a: 41), 'proper to right thinking is a willingness to risk, to welcome the new'. For us, philosophical thinking is a form of critical reflection in the sense used by Freire (1998a: 44) when he posits that having a disposition for critical change makes it possible for humans to imagine themselves as subjects in the process of becoming. And, this becoming involves risking 'to express appropriate anger [unlike rage and hatred] against injustice, against disloyalty, against the negation of love, against exploitation, and against violence' (Freire, 1998a: 45). For Freire (1998a: 87), humans will remain unfree if they do not take risks. For him, taking risks to come up with something new is to assume an ethical responsibility for one's actions. Moreover, this ethical responsibility that teachers have towards students is to risk admitting they are wrong when they do not have all the answers to pedagogical queries.

Put differently, teachers for Freire should run the risk of recognising the autonomy of students and that they can learn from them. This implies that teachers recognise students' right to question, to doubt and to criticise – that is they take the risk to be told that they can be wrong and that their authority lies in their ethical responsibility to concede their errors. This is what we think Freire implies when he states that one has to take risks in encouraging students to be open because there are things teachers do not know (Freire, 1998a: 120). So, taking risks involves critically reflecting as one risks welcoming what is new and to enact an ethical responsibility by risking being challenged by those who are assumed to have less authority than oneself. In his words, 'my role as a teacher is to assent the students' right to compare, to choose, to rupture, to decide' (Freire, 1998a: 68).

Thirdly, for Freire (1998a: 66), education is based upon critical reflections about the 'unfinishedness of our human condition'. In other words, the very possibility of being educated resides in a 'consciousness that gives rise to a permanent movement of searching, of curious interrogation that leads us not only to an awareness of the world but also to a thorough scientific knowledge of it' (Freire, 1998a: 66). By implication, the educational project for Freire is one of incompleteness and constant curiosity. It is education as a 'permanent movement of searching' that provokes humans to 'adapt to the world but especially to intervene, to re-create, and to transform it' (Freire, 1998a: 66). Education, seen as an unfinished adventure in the sense understood by Freire, takes issue with mechanical memorisation and transfers of knowledge to which Freire responds by claiming such 'so-called learning is a denial of critical epistemological curiosity' (Freire, 1998a: 67). One would not be able to see the substantiveness of our knowing if we were to rely extensively on simple lesson repetitions of things already given. For humans to learn and hence to engage in the unfinishedness of education 'is to construct, to reconstruct, to observe with a view to changing – none of which can be done without being open to risk, to the adventure of the spirit' (Freire, 1998a: 67).

Teaching, therefore, exists only in a Freirean (1998a, 1998b) realm of 'unfinishedness'; it can know no end since learning serves only to teach us what we do not know and, hence, that there must be more to know. It is in this regard that Freire connects the unfinishedness of education to a pedagogy of hope. In his words:

> Hope is something shared between teachers and students. The hope that we can learn together, teach together, be curiously impatient together, produce something together … Hope is a natural, possible, and necessary impetus in the context of our unfinishedness. (Freire, 1998a: 69)

Thus, for Freire, a pedagogy of courage accentuates the importance of remaining open-minded, taking risks and treating things as always unfinished. This in itself implies an activist approach to education in that it infers much more than the attainment of a qualification, but a renewed consciousness of how one sees and engage with others and the world. In this way, a pedagogy of courage is, in reality, a pedagogy of freedom and pedagogy of hope in a combined way as there is so much still to learn about our human condition. Freire (1998a: 69) conceives of hope as 'natural, possible, and [a] necessary impetus in the context of our unfinishedness. Hope is an indispensable seasoning in our human, historical experience … A future that is inexorable is a denial of history'. To us, this is what serves as the foundational premise of higher education – a steadfast belief and hope that the world could be otherwise and having the courage to act so that the world can indeed become otherwise. If we have the courage to continue on our substantive educational adventure Freire would posit, then there is always the possibility that we would not only see things anew but also bear witness to our own becoming.

In the ensuing discussion, we turn our attention to Freire's notion of critical consciousness or conscientisation as a form of activist representational politics.

Representational Politics as Conscientisation

As humans live and go through their world, they acquire certain understandings and perspectives about the world and those around them. Included in these understandings are social myths and perceptions, which might emanate from or promote certain biases. It becomes necessary for humans (teachers and students), therefore, to develop a critical awareness of their social reality through reflection and action – described by Freire (1984) as critical consciousness or conscientisation. To Freire (1984: 81), '[a]uthentic reflection considers neither abstract man nor the world without people, but people in their relations with the world. In these relations, consciousness and world are simultaneous: consciousness neither precedes the world nor follows it'. He explains '*I* cannot exist without a *non-I*. In turn, the *not-I* depends on that existence. The world which brings consciousness into existence becomes the world of that consciousness' (1984: 82).

As academics and students reflect upon themselves, they broaden what they know and understand about themselves and become aware of 'previously inconspicuous phenomena' (1984: 82). Upon reflection, things, ideas and arguments, which had previously been taken for granted as truths, begin to have deeper implications and begin, says Freire (1984: 83), to 'stand out', assuming the character of a problem and therefore of challenge. In his book, *Education, the practice of freedom*, Freire (1976: 19) asserts that critical consciousness awakens through the expression of social discontents, precisely because 'these discontents are real components of an oppressive situation'. Oppression suggests a disharmony or disequilibrium among people or between people and their natural world. To Freire (1993: 67), there is a dialectical relationship between the material world that generates the ideas and the ideas that can influence the world by which they are generated. As humans become awakened to these discontents of oppressions, they are agitated to act – that is, they want to act in response to the discontent. Implicit in Freire's (1984) conception of libertarian education is the connectedness and centrality of the body within the process of teaching and learning. The importance of the body, states Freire (1993: 86–87), 'is indisputable; the body moves, acts, rememorizes the struggle for its liberation; the body, in sum, desires, points out, announces, protests, curves itself, rises, designs, and remakes the world'. Whatever transformation might emerge, however, cannot be achieved through an individual body, because, explains Freire (1993: 87):

> The body is also socially constructed… And its importance has to do with a certain sensualism… There is a lot of sensualism contained by the body and made explicit by the body… I think it is absurd to separate the rigorous act of knowing the world from the passionate ability to know. I am passionately attracted not only to the world but also to the curious process of learning about the world.

Protests as a form of activism do not only find expression through the articulation of slogans and speeches, but they are also embodied in marches, sit-ins and stand-offs and an array of sensual forms of political representation and demonstration. Protesters often use their bodies as sensual pronouncements of resistance – whether by covering their mouths, tying their hands together or forming human chains – as an emulation of their imposed silencing and restriction. One of the more well-known examples includes that of the 'Standing Man in Istanbul', by the Turkish dancer and choreographer Erdem Gündüz. Gündüz's action of standing and looking at the Atatürk monument was originally a response to the ban on public assembly imposed after the 2013 protests in Gezi Park in Istanbul. Others followed his example and stood next to him. The subtle action of simply standing and not doing anything meant that Gündüz and others could subvert the ban on public assembly and demonstration (Berghausen, 2018).

In turn, while dance has a long history of a form of choreographed protest, politically motivated flash mobs and performances have been a common feature of contemporary activism. In South Africa, the toyi-toyi is a war dance, which dates back to the Mau Mau people in Kenya, and remains a defining feature of struggle politics. The dance involves rhythmic, stomping movements; for those oppressed and disenfranchised by the apartheid state, the only weapons black people had were their bodies.

Other embodiments of social and political protest take on more vivid forms of the objectification of the body as a means of making explicit experiences of injustice and oppression. At the height of the AIDS epidemic in the late 1980s, protesters in America piled their 'dead' bodies next to one another and then used the weight of their bodies to prevent police officers from forcibly removing them. Other extreme examples include hunger strikes, especially when an individual is imprisoned, making any other kind of protest impossible. In 2016, amidst the #FeesMustFall and #RhodesMustFall campaigns, students embarked on a series of protests, known as #EndRapeCulture movement, which soon merged with the global #MeToo movement. The movement started as a response to the increasing prevalence of rape on South African university campuses and soon escalated to protests against university policies, which were seemingly ineffective in responding to this scourge and, hence, seen to causing institutional harm by perpetuating a climate of under-reporting from victims.

Due to their overwhelming disproportionate exposure to gender-based violence, female students – and more specifically, black female students – were at the forefront of these protests. Here it is imperative to note that not only are black females in South Africa more at risk of rape because of their precarious living conditions but because the media coverage of their rape is not similar to that of white females. Moreover, the issue of violence against the bodies of black women cannot be separated from the broader campaign of decolonisation, which, in turn, cannot be limited to discourses within university settings, but should also refer to broader societal ills and concerns. Both as a means of using their bodies as a form of protest and in showing their outrage against the violation and exploitation of their bodies, the #EndRapeCulture protests were characterised by female students exposing their breasts, with the words 'this is mine' or 'enough' written on them. Their actions represented a simultaneous reclaiming of their bodies and public spaces in which they had the right to be as female bodies.

More often than not, says Darder (2018: 423), expressions of student resistance are enacted through counterculture alterations of the body – be they clothing, hairstyle, posturing, manner of walking, way of speaking, the piercing and tattooing of the body. These, she continues, 'represent not only acts of resistance but alternative ways of experiencing and knowing the world, generally perceived by officials as both transgressive and disruptive to the social order' (Darder, 2018: 423). Students' bodies are not the only ones regulated, restricted or harmed. Academics experience similar challenges when they are constrained and subjected to 'disembodied practices', which force them to 'consciously or unconsciously, reproduce a variety of one-dimensional authoritarian classroom practices' (Darder, 2018: 424).

Freire, according to Darder (2018: 425), recognised that such 'disembodiment serves to disable the formation of student voice, social agency, and democratic participation – a process that can be even more disabling to students from racialised working-class communities who seldom enjoy the resources and opportunities of their more affluent white counterparts'. If academics feel unheard and alienated from their own working environments, policies and practices, it follows that their teaching and engagement with students will be mechanical and dispassionate. They (academics) and their intellect and bodies risk becoming 'domesticated' in their workplace. The only way for teachers and academics to reject this domesticating role, argues Freire (1998b: 9), is 'by demythologizing the authoritarianism of teaching packages and their administration in the intimacy of their world, which is also the world of their students'.

Key to (re)-establishing the connections and intimacy between students and the materiality of the world is to bring the body of this world into teaching. One of the most challenging aspects of university education is the continuous obsession with the acquisition of qualifications. Many students and teachers in post-apartheid South Africa have become immersed in the idea that improved qualifications result in significant material gains for them. While the attainment of formal qualifications might not be a problem within itself, the urgency shown by many in the current university sector suggests that the desire for qualifications is inextricably linked to the advancement of a labour market economy that will favour individual prosperity and success based on competition and a craving for wealth. Seldom does one hear that the need for qualifications should be connected to the building of a society and its democratic ethos or that knowledge should be acquired to expand one's horizons into unknown spaces. Economic rationalism seems to be the main driving force behind the attainment of qualifications and the concern for lucrative employment, and job security has emerged as a real concern for many university students and academics.

One of the key goals of the National Plan for Higher Education in South Africa (2001) is to increase access to higher education and to redress past inequalities by producing graduates with the skills and competencies necessary, firstly, to meet the human resource needs of the country and, secondly, to address regional and national needs in the context of social and economic development (DoE, 2001). The achievement of equity and redress so prominent throughout the National Plan became secondary to the primary objective of 'making higher education more responsive to attending to economic labour market imperatives and concomitant neoliberal requirements for skilled and innovative knowledge workers and producers who …

can ensure unprecedented mobility of capital' (Waghid, 2003: 37). By implication, a clear economic rationalist agenda has come to characterise university education with a strong leaning towards neoliberalism with its economic labour market imperatives.

For almost a decade, our faculty's education programme was tied to a private company, Educore Learning, on the grounds of which thousands of students could complete their formal qualifications. The idea of linking university education to skills development and economic growth resulted in our institution having endorsed the idea of producing graduates with specific marketable attributes who can function as workers and professionals in the economy. In light of such a significant change in university education, many of the institutions in the country have adopted a corporatised agenda commensurate with their economic rationalist orientations.

Why is an economic rationalist approach to university education problematic? We are not denying that producing a better skilled and competitive labour force, especially in science, engineering and technology, would place South Africa favourably within a globalised market economy. However, when university education fails to emphasise in people (students and teachers) the capacities for thinking openly and anew and taking risks as if such an education can be acquired only through finished qualifications, then the university itself is in trouble. It would then urgently require a kind of academic activism that undermines a neoliberal conception of public university education. Economic-rationalist university education has to become more responsive to the requirements of what it means to cultivate a democratic citizenry. Academic activists would have to become far more sceptical about universities that are run as business enterprises and that produce courses for students now seen as customers – that is, exclusive corporatisation would be extremely harmful for universities in a country where equity and redress still require so much more attention. As Pierre Bourdieu (1998: 5) reminds us, economic rationalism is a negative effect of neoliberal education as it will exclude the already marginalised because it has 'as its only law the pursuit of egoistic interests and the individual passion for profit'.

University education cannot only be concerned with teaching to a prescribed curriculum. In turn, students need to be awakened to the idea of a university education that looks beyond the imperative of material gains – they have to, Darder (2018: 427) states, 'become free from the social and material entanglements of a society that imprisons them, both ideologically and corporally'. Students are part of the world; their lives unfold in relation to the world. They have certain needs, insecurities, vulnerabilities, fears, beliefs and hopes which live inside of them and which cannot be separated from the world. They have to be made aware of human suffering, which too often is viewed from a distance, and not seen as a concern of the student's world. University education cannot be used as means of and for insulated thinking and being; instead, it has to awaken students and academics alike to their interconnectedness and, hence, collective responsibility to ensure a pursuit of freedom from all manners of oppression.

In sum, it would be apposite for a democratic university education discourse in South Africa to be framed according to the academic activist aspirations of a renewed understanding of education. This would imply that current trends in university education ought to be reconceptualised in light of what it means to be open-minded and think anew; what it means to take risks in university education; and more importantly what it means to treat education as an unfinished project. If the latter were to be possible, and we have hope in its aspirations, then not only would academics have been actively engaged but they would have been courageous in the adventurous pursuits of knowledge and understanding.

Academic Activism as a 'Pedagogy of Contentment'

At first glance, it might be odd to associate a discussion or argument on academic activism with that of a pedagogy of contentment. Certainly, the concept of contentment, which has connotations of ease and serenity, would appear to be incommensurable with a concept of activism, which suggests practices of resistance, force and intervention. And yet, both contentment and activism reside in objectives of doing good or attaining good. Activism, therefore, although either a demonstration of resistance or promotion, is not driven by imperatives of devaluation, dismissal or othering.

If we accept that students are not merely passive recipients of knowledge who come to their learning in subjugated roles of compliance, then academics have to embody a teaching and a presence that dispels teaching as a series of mechanical gestures and repetitions. To Freire (1993: 88), 'the task of liberty, the task of liberation, the history as possibility, the understanding of the conscious and sensual body, full of life', and we would add, the task of academic activism 'necessarily demands a pedagogy of contentment'. Too often, teaching, and hence learning, as well as student supervision, is held hostage by the negative presence of teachers. In other words, when teachers come into their presence of teaching with a regulated, disinterested or sceptical body, they affect the (in)capacity of students to learn.

Who academics are, what they represent and how they understand themselves in relation to their teaching, supervision and research affect how students and others perceive and experience them. The sensual being of academics, therefore, cannot be disentangled from what they do. Hence, Freire (1998b: 48) contends that what is important in teaching is 'a comprehension of the value of sentiments, emotions, and desires … and sensibility, affectivity, and intuition'. 'This powerful assertion of our human faculties, beyond reason, in the struggle for our liberation is indeed a hallmark of Freire's revolutionary praxis', says Darder (2018: 424). For her, Freire's unwavering efforts 'to challenge the necrophilic grip of hegemonic schooling', simultaneously, provided a rightful place for engagement of the body in the classroom, which also entails an integral view of students as multidimensional human beings (Darder, 2018: 425).

In *Pedagogy of the City*, Freire (1993: 88) shares: 'firstly, love and affection do not weaken the seriousness of studying and of producing at all. Secondly, I don't think they can, in any way, be an obstacle to political and social responsibility. I have lived my life with love'. In breaking with the Cartesian mind/body dichotomy, which renders the heart and mind as antagonists to intellectual formation, Freire's (1984) problem-posing pedagogy or libertarian education, explains Darder (2018: 425), counters the limits of this Western pedagogical tradition, which abstracts knowledge and negates the role of the body in the process of teaching and learning. Freire (1993: 50) explains as follows:

> I think the role of a consciously progressive educator is to testify constantly to his or her students his or her competence, love, political clarity, the coherence between what he or she says and does, his or her tolerance, his or her ability to live with the different to fight against the antagonistic. It is to stimulate doubt, criticism, curiosity, questioning, a taste for risk-taking, the adventure of creating.

Following Freire, activism is enveloped in teaching, learning, writing and engaging with a love and passion for what and who is encountered and the courage to speak out and confront that which harms. In *Dialogue is Not a Chaste Event: Comments by Paulo Freire on Issues in Participatory Research*, Freire (1985: 19) is critical of university professors who are ignorant of the dialectical relationship between pedagogy and politics:

> I feel so sad concerning the future of these people who teach at universities and think that they are just professors. They don't put their hands into politics because they think that it is dirty. It's precisely in escaping from politics that you have to know that you are a politician, and that your tactics are not merely pedagogical ones. But we cannot escape from this fact that politics and education are interwoven. You must develop your tactics there in response to the situation you confront in the field, not here, in the university, unless you wish to stop the project.

To be a university professor or teacher or academic or to be an academic activist is to be aware of the politics of education and politics of the world, and that these two sets cannot be engaged as two separate entities. Education is always politicised, and to be in education is to live in and confront these politics. While Freire (1985) recognises that studying and learning are not easy endeavours, he does not dissociate the complexity of these undertakings from actions and manifestations of love. Instead, what one learns and gains from Freire is that commonly and traditionally, activism is couched in a discourse and action of resistance and conflict; yet to him, to demonstrate activism is to affirm a love for what one does – in the sense of not only being in love with the work of the academy but being in love with acting or speaking out when confronted with that which is interpreted as un-love, such as oppression, marginalisation and exclusion. In other words, it is because one loves the other, the cause, that one acts, perhaps not *with* love (as protests are seldom expressed as such), but *from* a place or sense of love. A pedagogy of contentment, therefore, is one which embodies a sense and intuition of peace in terms of what the academic does, says, writes and shares. It is also one which attunes the academic to students and the work he or she does in a language and experience of love. Remarkably, we find resonance in Freire's (1993: 91) assessment that the more one experiences love, the more one is able to give it. In this regard, we experience this in relation to colleagues who share not only a commitment to a pedagogy of contentment, but a sensual connection to a desire to learn, teach, write and aspire for how the world might otherwise be. The more academics can testify to their students their love for what they do – read, write, teach and confront that which is unjust and inhumane – the more students will begin to love the idea and action of studying for the purposes of freedom.

For Freire (1993: 87), love and revolution go together – described as follows:

> My love for reading and writing is directed toward a certain utopia. This involves a certain course, a certain type of people. It is a love that has to do with the creation of a society that is less perverse, less discriminatory, less racist, less *machista* than the society that we now have. This love seeks to create a more open society, a society that serves the interests of the always unprotected and devalued subordinate classes, and not only the interests of the rich, the fortunate, the so-called "well-born". (Freire, 1993: 140)

In the end, this is what activism has in mind – a society and world devoid of oppression and discrimination; where people are invited into spaces, rather than shut out; where openness is welcomed as a route to knowing about others in our world; and where dignity accompanies freedom. As a pedagogy of contentment, academic activism departs from premises of love and tolerance for all conceptions and enactments of peace and equality while expressing a simultaneous willingness and commitment to confronting those aspects and practices of the world, which aim to cause harm and dehumanisation.

References

Berghausen, N. (2018). *Choreography as a form of protest*. https://www.goethe.de/en/kul/tut/gen/tan/21327381.html. Accessed 3 June 2020.

Bourdieu, P. (1998). Utopia of endless exploitation: The essence of neoliberalism. *La Monde Diplomatique*, 1–6. http://mondediplo.com/1998/12/08bordieu. Accessed 15 Apr 2020.

Darder, A. (2018). Freire and a revolutionary praxis of the body. *Review of Education, Pedagogy, and Cultural Studies, 40*(5), 422–432.

Department of Education. (2001). *National plan for higher education*. Pretoria, South Africa: DoE.

Freire, P. (1976). *Education, the practice of freedom*. London: Writers and Readers Publishing Cooperative.

Freire, P. (1984). *Pedagogy of the oppressed*. New York: Continuum.

Freire, P. (1985). *Dialogue is not a chaste event: Comments by Paulo Freire on issues in participatory research*. Amherst, MA: University of Massachusetts.

Freire, P. (1993). *Pedagogy of the city*. New York: Continuum.

Freire, P. (1998a). *Pedagogy of freedom: Ethics, democracy, and courage*. Lanham, MD/Boulder, CO/New York/Oxford, UK: Rowman & Littlefield.

Freire, P. (1998b). *Teachers and cultural workers: Letters to those who dare to teach*. Boulder, CO: Westview Press.

Freire, P. (2004). *Pedagogy of hope*. New York: Continuum.

Waghid, Y. (2003). Deliberative democracy and higher education policy discourse in South Africa: In defence of equitable redress. In Y. Waghid & L. Le Grange (Eds.), *Imaginaries on democratic education and change* (pp. 31–40). Pretoria, South Africa: South African Association for Research and Development in Higher Education.

Chapter 8
A Feminist Critique of University Education

Abstract In this chapter, we highlight some of Judith Butler's main pronouncements about the university and offer some ways to think differently about philosophy of higher education and academic activism. We consider three ways in which the idea of a university of critique intertwined with notions of non-mastery and 'error-living' education might be possible. Firstly, an open and speculative university should cultivate forms of education where making mistakes is considered not only as routine *to* learning but as a necessary process *for* learning. Secondly, a university grounded in academic freedom is not only pertinent for free, critical engagement that is unafraid but can play a pivotal role in calling into question existing norms and hegemonies, policies as well as political structures and discourses. It also opens up the possibility of free and critical thought, including intellectual positions. And thirdly, dissent is critical not only as a recognition of alternative or controversial views but for the very cultivation of academic activism.

Keywords Judith Butler · Feminist critique · Bodies · Non-mastery · Dissent

Introduction

Our decision to focus on Judith Butler's ideas in this chapter emanates from two intertwined reasons: her standing and reformulation of philosophy through a feminist lens and her tireless commitment and activism in ensuring that her writing is made visible in our world. Like so many other scholars we have thus far drawn and expanded upon in this book, Butler's work symbolises the kinds of activism university education can no longer do without. This chapter has two points of interest. Firstly, we pay attention to Butler's (1993) contention that 'bodies matter' and, specifically, that while certain bodies enjoy legitimacy and value, others do not and are instead (re)produced as objects. The idea that bodies signify a world beyond themselves holds particular implications for university spaces and education. Secondly, we turn to her conversation with Facundo Giuliani (2015), in which Butler offers some remarks about the university and its relationship with philosophy of education.

N. Davids, Y. Waghid, *Academic Activism in Higher Education*, Debating Higher Education: Philosophical Perspectives 5, https://doi.org/10.1007/978-981-16-0340-2_8

We continue by highlighting some of her main pronouncements about the university and offer some ways to think differently about philosophy of higher education and academic activism. We consider three ways in which the idea of a university of critique intertwined with notions of non-mastery and 'error-living' education might be possible. Firstly, an open and speculative university should cultivate forms of education where making mistakes is considered not only as routine *to* learning but as a necessary process *for* learning. Secondly, a university grounded in academic freedom is not only pertinent for free, critical engagement that is unafraid but can play a pivotal role in calling into question existing norms and hegemonies, policies as well as political structures and discourses. It opens up the possibility of free and critical thought, including intellectual positions. And thirdly, dissent is critical not only as a recognition of alternative or controversial views but for the very cultivation of academic activism.

A Feminist Critique of the University as Corporeal and Embodied Education

Butler's (2015) account of a new philosophy of (higher) education interrelates with three primary ideas that we examine in this chapter. To begin with, Butler is particularly concerned with encouraging new readings around human engagements that allow resistance and disruption to manifest. In one instance, she offers an account of the university as an open place where criticism should unfold:

> The University has to be the place where we have open critical debate, and we can't have open critical debate unless we know what criticism is. And those skills – practices or exercises, like the exercise of criticism – are precisely what is supported and possible through the University. I would say that the capacity for criticism – here, thinking about critical literature analysis and also philosophical criticism – is crucial to open democratic debates on values. In what direction we should be going? (Butler in Giuliano, 2015: 185)

Through criticism, Butler envisages that the university becomes a place of potentiality – that is, the potential to become 'a scene of an empowering contact' (Butler in Giuliano, 2015: 186). By claiming that the university should be an empowering educational space, Butler has in mind the potential of the university to cultivate an 'embodied, corporeal, and social' education. When education becomes embodied, it no longer just focuses on individual 'excellence' and productive subjects. Rather, university education invites students and teachers to become 'non-conforming' beings who present themselves as embodied beings who take risks and looks at possibilities for thinking and acting otherwise (Butler in Giuliano, 2015: 190).

Long before students arrive at the universities, they would already have been socialised into particular codes of speech and conduct. This, says Butler (Butler in Giuliano, 2015: 188), would have involved knowing how to sit, how to raise your hand and wait your turn to be called upon, how to use your voice, when to be loud and when to whisper – 'you learn all these modes of bodily performativity to learn how to be'. These codes are not only applicable to conduct, but to conduct in relation to a binary construction of male and female students to Butler (Butler in Giuliano, 2015: 188):

> Education is training in gender and is training in citizenship, and there are punishments that go along with it; there are also modes of excitement that emerge at the prospect of transgressing those rules. You can develop an entire mode of sexuality that is dedicated to the breaking of the rules in a mad effort to gain some freedom from that kind of disciplinary apparatus.

How students and academics conceive of themselves – as corporeal beings – concerning their spaces, whether in lecture theatres, libraries, laboratories, seminar groups or supervision encounters, has implications for their learning and questioning. While some are noticeable and seen as present, others are not. Furthermore, even when certain are indeed seen, they are not seen as they are, but rather through a distortion of prejudice and preconceived ideas. Bodies, as Butler (1993) maintains, 'do matter':

> The body posited as prior to the sign, is always *posited* or *signified* as *prior*. This signification produces as an *effect* of its own procedure the very body that it nevertheless and simultaneously claims to discover as that which *precedes* its own action. If the body signified as prior to signification is an effect of signification, then the mimetic or representational status of language, which claims that signs follow bodies as necessary mirrors, is not mimetic at all. On the contrary, it is productive, constitutive, one might even argue *performative,* inasmuch as this signifying act delimits and contours the body that it then claims prior to any and all signification. (Butler, 1993: 6)

Of concern to Butler (1993) is not the only that the corporeal matters but how the world – through its signification – perceive, construct and respond to bodies. To Butler (1993), the power dynamics which plays out in a matrix of gender relations, for example, forces us to ask ourselves who we are and how we have come to know what we know in relation to bodies – more importantly, how the 'we' has been constructed in relation to a question of knowledge. Certain constructions, she asserts, appear constitutive – that is, they 'have this character of being that without which we could not think at all' (Butler, 1993: xi). Thanks to social codes and discourses, the result is a stark binary between certain bodies, which have been rendered as valuable and legitimate – such as white, heterosexual and male – as opposed to others which have been (re)produced as an object, such as black, lesbian and female. How the body is experienced is materialised through particular normative discourses. In this sense, explains Butler (1993: ix), not only do 'bodies tend to indicate a world beyond themselves, but this movement beyond their own boundaries, a movement of boundary itself, appeared to be quite central to what bodies are'. This might begin to explain why women in particular use their bodies as a form of protest when demonstrating against gender-based violence. It allows them to use the physicality of who they are as a weapon against abuse.

The idea that social settings, as well as educational environments, assign recognition and value to some physical bodies, while not to others, is one which has long impacted upon how students access their learning and their relationship with learning. There are many signifiers of what determines legitimacy and value – from race, gender, ethnicity and class to embodiments of beauty and sexuality. The domain of ontology, which assigns legitimacy to some bodies, while withholding it from others, is regulated, states Butler (Meier & Prins, 1998: 280) – 'what gets produced inside of it, what gets excluded from it in order for the domain to be constituted is itself an effect of power'. The effects of this domain are profound, yet often invisible, under-reported and unknown. Students neither enter nor similarly participate in their university education. Depending on race, ethnicity, religion, ability and sexuality, students not only encounter different responses from peers, but they are forced to find different ways of presenting themselves – this either means an insertion of the self via assimilation, or standing on the periphery, and gazing in. While race has always been a determining factor of legitimacy, and hence recognition and inclusion, signifiers of religion, gender and sexuality are increasingly (re)interpreted through discourses of antagonism.

Consider, for example, what is often described as the feminisation of the teaching profession, which stems from an uncomfortable and misleading conception of teaching as 'women's work' – a signifier steeped in sexual bias. Seemingly, the issue is not only the predominance of female teachers in schools and there the effects thereof on pedagogy and classroom culture but that the absence of male role models creates problems for boys in terms of motivation, discipline and social interaction. Feminism has created an apparent shift towards the privileging of female learning styles, assessment practices, modes of discipline and so forth (Skelton, 2002: 86).

More worrying is the assumption that 'feminised' teaching spaces ought to be remedied through the 'masculinisation' of the profession. Can we conceive of a world, for example, in which the masculinisation of the corporate world is held to question and interrogation? Ironically, the perceived need for an increase in male bodies in teaching – so as to de-feminise teaching and presumably provide positive role modelling for male bodies – does not pertain to male bodies who are also gay. The normative centrality of heterosexual identity discounts the option or appeal of gay male bodies as teachers – exposing 'the ways in which homophobia polices the boundaries of the teaching profession in relation to masculinities' (Mills, 2004: 28). The full effects of both the boundaries and the policing cannot be fully comprehended unless directly experienced. In Butler's words (Butler in Giuliano, 2015: 193):

> Sometimes it is in the way it's looked at, or the way power structures the visual fields, so that certain bodies are stigmatized, so let's remember that. Power can work to efface bodies so that we do not see them, or it can work to stigmatize bodies so that we see them in a hyperbolic way, or in a way that fits a stereotype or fetish. A vulnerable population can suffer from being overexposed in the visual field, or being effaced by the visual field, or being regulated according to categories that are restrictive or false in certain ways.

We are aware, for example, of a few student teachers on our PGCE programme, who identify as non-binary, who experience great difficulty during teaching practice. Their difficulty starts before they even go to the respective school to which they have been assigned. They express anxiety as to whether they will encounter a welcoming school environment; whether they will be provided with the necessary mentoring support; whether they will be assessed fairly; and, indeed, whether they have any prospects of being appointed into a teaching post. None of these anxieties have anything to do with their knowledge or skills as teachers – yet they know that their bodies will predetermine how they are perceived and judged as teachers.

Bodies Matter Because They Do

It is worth spending a bit more time on Butler's (1993: xi) assertion that bodies matter and, in particular, her argument:

> For surely bodies live and die; eat and sleep; feel pain, pleasure; endure illness and violence; and these 'facts', one might skeptically say, cannot be dismissed as mere construction. But their irrefutability in no way implies what it might mean to affirm them and through what discursive means. Moreover, why is it that what is constructed is understood as an artificial and dispensable character?

Specifically, it is worth revisiting her articulation that 'discourses do actually live in bodies. They lodge in bodies; bodies in fact carry discourses as part of their own lifeblood. And nobody can survive without, in some sense, being carried by discourse' (Meier & Prins, 1998: 282). In her interview with Meier and Prins (1998: 282), Butler contends that 'we also have to worry about certain ways of describing orientalism and especially describing orientalism as it pertains to women, women's bodies, and women's self-representations'. She explains that there are many complex debates about the veil, yet there is little clarity on who 'the veiled woman' refers to – 'In what context, for what purpose? What is the action, what is the practice that we are thinking about? In what context are we trying to decide whether or not the veiled woman is an example of the abject?' (Meier & Prins, 1998: 282).

We find this point of discussion particularly pertinent not only in relation to growing trends among liberal democracies to regulate or prohibit the veil (or *hijab*), as worn by Muslim women, but also in relation to higher education spaces. From our own experiences, there is an increasing differentiation between Muslim women and veiled Muslim women – where the latter seems to suggest something more than the former. More importantly, the body of a veiled Muslim woman is seemingly more contentious, more alienating to herself and to others, than a non-veiled Muslim woman. Who decides this, as Butler (Meier & Prins, 1998) ponders, is unclear, except to consider the predominance of norms, which relies on marginalisation and subjugation in order for the centre to hold.

As a veil-wearing Muslim woman, one of us enjoys first-hand experience of being subjected to scrutiny about religious beliefs, which would not be asked of someone else. There is a particular suspicion which accompanies the veil – which precedes the voice of the subject. Stated differently, the veil on the body speaks before the subject does – whether in lecture theatres or conferences. Not surprising, Muslim women in the academy are often reluctant to wear their veils in university or conference spaces – even if they wear it in other contexts. They feel 'less seen' without the veil and prefer it not to interfere with what they have to say. In other cases, Muslim women worry that wearing a veil will impede their chances of appointment or promotion. These experiences and actions confirm a particular abjection of who these women are as whole beings – not only as academics.

The irony is that inasmuch as the veil has been misperceived and misconstrued as a symbol of backwardness or oppression of Muslim women, enforced by patriarchal hegemonies, rather than Muslim women's autonomous action, Muslim women themselves have abdicated to this very biased understanding. When they remove it for any reason other than their own imperative, then by so doing, they are bowing to social pressures and biases. Of course, in this regard, we are not including those contexts – as encountered in a number of liberal democracies – which have established legal frameworks with the express purpose of regulating Muslim women or students in the public sphere, which includes educational spaces.

We would concur with Butler (in Meier & Prins, 1998: 282) that the veil can, in fact, be an exertion of power – but only if Muslim women (academics and students) reclaim the narrative by reclaiming their bodies. When Muslim women remove their veils for fear of questions or judgement, or because of a need 'not to be seen' and to become invisible through sameness, they allow their bodies to be held hostage by norms that are neither their own nor in recognition of who they are as Muslim women. By contrast, the veil can be used as a form of embodied activism – without necessarily assuming abjection. Muslim women or students, therefore, do not only wear the veil as an enactment of their religious identities, but they also wear it as a defiance against being objectified as sexual objects (Golnaraghi & Dye, 2016) or as an 'act of resistance' (Khiabany & Williamson, 2008: 71). Here, the resistance is not only a refusal to adhere to a set of prescribed norms, which dictate how women ought to dress in the public sphere, but it also pertains to maintaining control and power over how one's body is interpreted as a body, and not as a symbolic object.

This argument is certainly not limited to Muslim women – it pertains to any individual or group that succumbs to normative discourses at a cost to individual subjectivity and voice. The purpose of enforcing a regulated school uniform, for example, is not only a demonstration of a physical attachment to and representation of a particular school. It is also about ensuring regulated conduct and thinking. Notably, school uniforms extend beyond a prescribed tie, blazer or tunic. They include long lists of sports attire, satchels, tog bags, shoes, as well as regulated haircuts, and dress or tunic lengths. In turn, this attire is not only symbolic of a school identity and ethos, but it is often steeped in particular histories, which are either disconnected from present-day politics or fundamentally at odds with the politics of people. A number of historically advantaged schools continue to emulate dress codes reminiscent of colonialist influence. So, too, are the sporting codes, school songs and general climate of the structure and organisation of the school. We mention this example, because the kind of compulsory regulated dress and thinking, which define 12 years of schooling, are not simply left behind once these school learners transition to university students. Much of the uncertainty that accompanies the first year of university education and life has to do with undoing the stifling hold, which had been sustained through education as regulation and conformity. This begins to explain why even as postgraduate candidates, sometimes, students continue to struggle to find their voice, and to formulate their own arguments, preferring instead to rely on academics or supervisors to think for them and to tell them what to do.

The University as Unregulated

Now that we have looked at using the body as a means to resignify how it is perceived, we turn our attention to Butler's assertion that the university offers an education that is 'not regulated' but instead interrupts (Butler in Giuliano, 2015: 194). A university education that is regulated points to mastering this or that such as students mastering their examinations or results, as opposed to immersing themselves in the subject and its content. We witness this kind of approach in students' requests for not only what texts they should read or what specific sections of the text they should focus on so that they do well in this or that assessment or assignment.

It is similarly evident in postgraduate students – even at PhD level – who have no interest in reading for the sake of grasping a concept or argument, but, rather, only for the purposes of being able to cite whatever section of writing is pertinent to their own research. Here, it would appear that the driving imperative is about attaining a degree – often for the purposes of career advancement – rather than a love or desire to study. In this way, it is not only the university that regulates teaching and learning, as might be evident in a concentration on learning outcomes, or only using certain theorists, but students, too, impose their own self-regulation by not approaching their studies with an openness to learning, reading or a willingness to struggle with their writing and studies. Where students are encouraged to look beyond the prescribed texts of a module or course, they often resist such invitations and persist in only engaging with the bare minimum of what they require to get through. In this sense, mastery of a particular subject is often associated with merely repeating what has been learnt, rather than attempting to reconsider ideas or arguments. For this reason, it is not unusual to find students who, despite having a postgraduate qualification, struggle to speak with confidence on their research.

Unlike most other universities in South Africa, our university considers the formal assessment of a PhD to comprise an examination by three examiners (two of whom should be external to the university) and a *viva voce*. It is interesting to note how differently students perform in these two assessment processes. Students who attain a good report based on their written thesis do not necessarily perform well during the *viva voce*. The concern here is not that of student anxiety or nervousness; instead, while students might be able to write coherently and logically, they might be less articulate and clear in the presentation or substantiation of their research hypothesis and argument. From engaging with these students – even outside of the context of the *viva voce* – there is seemingly a gap in the internalisation of their research.

In other words, their understandings of concepts or theories remain on a surface level; any sort of interrogation of their knowledge of their own research study leaves them unconfident and incoherent. To us, this raises serious concerns not only about how mastery is understood, but indeed what the doctoral journey suggests and entails. Why do these gaps arise? Why do most students not have a comfortable command of their research? One answer resides in the pressure of completing a PhD within a stipulated time-frame – in South Africa, this is 5 years; failure to do so results in a loss of government subsidy. Students are obligated to complete and successfully defend their proposals within their first year of registration. Thereafter, they are under pressure not only to conduct whatever empirical work they have set out to do but to read extensively while also producing drafts of writing on a regular basis. In turn, supervisors are under pressure not only to attend to a study but to continuously remind students of an emptying hourglass.

One infers from a Masters or a PhD that the student has reached a level of mastery on a specific research topic. From the discussion at hand, it becomes apparent that mastery can be misinterpreted so that it is seen as a means to an end, rather than as a process. In this way, mastery can result in curtailing the potential of students – in terms of not only their grasp of a particular research topic but indeed how they are invited into the ethos and field of research. Here, the role of the supervisor is critical. It is common for academics or supervisors to direct students to their own field of research. Quite correctly, academics explain that in order to supervise students adequately, they need to be experts on a topic.

However, we cannot ignore the reality that some academics direct students only to certain theorists or theories, because of their own familiarity with that theory. In other words, some academics do not want to be bothered with having to read new texts or engage with new ideas. The problem, however, with a practice of repeating the same theoretical and conceptual frameworks, or research methodologies, is that it means that students have to fit into a research area, which is predetermined by an academic. Students do not have a say or space to decide on their own research topic. As such, students do not have autonomy, and research is not open, bringing into contention the idea of research contributing and advancing new debates and reimagined thinking. Furthermore, what such a narrow understanding of research and supervision implies is that academics, too, might only end up working within one research area, thereby curtailing their own growth. Moreover, there is a risk that the kinds of knowledge in an academic department or faculty stagnate, without the possibility of opening new kinds of debates and thinking.

Of course, we are not arguing that academics should always be able to work across disciplines or that they need to have many specialisations. The very idea of a specialisation implies mastery, which is how professional appointments in universities are made. We are, however, concerned that not only do certain supervisors only allow certain research topics for their students, but they initiate their students into the same theorists and research paradigms year after year. In this regard, mastery stunts the possibility to see things as they could be otherwise, which closes university education to anything new that might arise. Knowledge conceived in a mastery way has already been finalised, and no educational spaces are left to see things differently. To Butler (in Giuliano, 2015: 186), 'education allows us to not become a master subject aware of all the disciplines or to just simply stay in our self-interested or instrumental modes of living, but to take into account larger versions of power that have produced the world that we live in'. Quite differently, an unregulated university education involves 'the surprise that happens in the midst of education and in the midst of formation. It's a way of responding to the world or realizing what a certain encounter can bring, and that's very different from ... mastery ... as control' (Butler in Giuliano, 2015: 195).

In turn, Butler (Butler in Giuliano, 2015: 198) claims an 'error-living education'. By this, she means that university education should be concerned with making mistakes and lauding one's mistakes. In her words, university education should be about 'living error as a way of accepting our perceptible, limited frame, accepting that as part of what is to be living, to becoming, to be in process' (Butler in Giuliano, 2015: 198). This implies a willingness to engage with the unfamiliar and to venture into unknown and new debates. As we write these words, the global pandemic (COVID-19) has forced universities as well as most other sectors to reconfigure how it functions. In the case of universities, traditional contact sessions of lectures, tutorials, seminars as well as conferences have been replaced by widespread digital learning and communication platforms. In most instances, this presents a new terrain and methodology of teaching and learning. While encouraged and affirmed for its capacity to maintain the academic programme, online learning is not without its pitfalls. Key among these is the absence of physical engagement, which has implications not only for student and academic wellbeing but also for how students as well as academics engage with divergent viewpoints and, more importantly, how to sustain human connection in a world of unprecedented connectivity. The point is, inasmuch as there have been gains in teaching and learning through technology, there is room for error and, hence, revisiting. When university teachers and students pursue an 'error-living education', they do not look at themselves as actualised beings who can learn nothing more or who are infallible. Instead, being educated with error is a recognition that our human fallibility can arouse in us an urgency to take risks as we would not be chastised if we err.

Quite frankly, it is indeed the case that we stand to learn more from our mistakes and our failures – in this way we are forced to reflect not only on the error itself but on ourselves and the thinking and actions which led to the error. In most cases, it would be equally true to describe the writing process as an 'error-living' education – we write, convinced that we have expressed ourselves in a coherent way and that we have taken account of any potential criticism or counter-argument. But, a few days later when we read the text again, or when we subject our work to scrutiny and review, we might be surprised to find just how weak or illogical our writing has been. This speaks to the rhythmic ebbing and flowing of writing, a continuous back and forth, if the writing is to get to a point of standing on its own. Moreover, it confirms the necessity and importance of peer review – we cannot know the worth of our work unless it is seen and critiqued by others.

Towards a University of Criticism, Non-mastery and Fallible Truths and Their Implications for Academic Activism

Following the above, taking risks involves opening ourselves to engaging with different viewpoints and a willingness to engage from different perspectives. As aptly put by Maxine Greene (1995: 120), university education should aim 'to find ways of enabling the young [students] to find their voices, to open their spaces, to reclaim their histories in all their variety and discontinuity'. This can only unfold if the university has an ethos, which affords hospitality to diverse communities of students and where students recognise and experience a sense of belonging where their respective identities, histories and stories enjoy the same legitimacy as all others. Now if university education is about cultivating 'error-living' practices, then such an education cannot be about resolving this or that, or to direct students in this or that way, or to improve on this or that matter. 'Error-living' demands more in terms of time and emotion – it demands patience, which allows for students to come into their own without simply providing all the tools and knowledge. At times, it is easier to simply correct students or to provide articles for their research than to step back and invite them in and allow them to follow their own journey, which might involve going back and forth, or getting it wrong, or decide against continuing with a certain module or programme.

Postgraduate students, particularly those who are interested in establishing careers in higher education, are often under the illusion that they need to follow the same steps as their mentor academics. This illusion is often propagated and perpetuated by the academic, who will also insist that the student has to first do X, before moving onto Y. Yet, no two experiences are exactly the same, and what is the value of expecting students to embark on a similar path as a mentor? Such an approach is not only restrictive of the student's potential to be different but suggests that mentor-student encounters are exclusively one-directional – that is, that while only the student learns, the mentor only guides. 'Error-living' implies a recognition that what academics or mentors know is neither all there is to know nor without faults. The student has to be exposed to the full value of education – this includes an acceptance of errors as necessary to self-understanding. This can happen in a context of university education where making mistakes is considered not only as routine *to* learning but as a necessary process *for* learning. Even our ability to persist, explains Butler (Butler in Giuliano, 2015: 186), 'depends upon a certain kind of contact, what we call potential, which cannot be actualized without a contact, without a reaction from the world that allows it'. To Butler (Butler in Giuliano, 2015: 186), it is necessary to conceive of education as a scene of an empowering contact:

> [T]eachers empower students. Teachers are aware of this, although sometimes we notice that students are going in the wrong direction, because we don't control that, we can't. All we can do is produce the space for thinking in a key of relative safety within educational institutions, and this must be thought as something that is not always accomplished.

In sum, Judith Butler (2015) reminds us that an open and speculative university should cultivate forms of education commensurate with criticism, non-mastery and learning by mistakes. This is possible and can happen in a context of university education where making mistakes is considered not only as routine *to* learning but as a necessary process *for* learning. If university education were to be enacted in such ways, the possibility is there that a philosophy of higher education would be about reconstituting criticism, non-mastery and the recognition of human fallibility. Moreover, an open and speculative university has to both emanate from and sustain the fundamentals premises of academic freedom. In emphasising the criticality of academic freedom, Butler (2017: 857) draws a careful distinction between freedom of thought or freedom of expression and academic freedom. While related, they are not the same, argues Butler (2017). Individuals have the right or not to express certain views (freedom of expression); the university has a certain obligation to uphold academic freedom – 'academic freedom implies a right to free inquiry within the academic institution, but also an obligation to preserving the institution as a site where freedom of inquiry can and does take place, free of intervention, and censorship' (Butler, 2017: 857).

To Butler (2017: 858), 'higher education is not only a public good that every state should provide, but higher education based on principles of academic freedom is necessary for an informed public, a public that can understand and evaluate issues of common concern and form judgements on the basis of a knowledgeable understanding of the world'. A university grounded in academic freedom is not only unafraid but can play a pivotal role in calling into question existing norms and hegemonies, policies as well as political structures and discourses. It opens up the possibility of free and critical thought, including intellectual positions. Within the academy, contends Butler (2017: 858), a 'critical' position is defended on the basis of academic freedom:

> From the perspective of public life, that critical position may well count as dissent. Thus, viewpoints pursued within the academy ought rightly to be protected and supported by the principles of academic freedom; viewpoints that constitute political dissent in public life ought rightly to be protected and supported within democracies as freedom of expression. (Butler, 2017: 858)

The emphasis for Butler (2017) is on the possibility and preservation of dissent. Dissent is not just a matter of holding an alternative or controversial opinion; dissent is about a willingness to consider what else might be possible.

Consider a recurring debate about the place or value of statues of certain historical figures, who, depending on an individual's context and perspective, evoke different responses from different people. At the time of writing and against a highly vocal background of 'Black lives matter', a group of protesters in Bristol toppled a statue of the seventeenth-century slave trader, Edward Colston, and dumped the effigy in the nearby harbour. The removal of statues as a symbolic enactment of political change is, of course, not new – from the dismantling of Russian Tsar Alexander III after the 1917 revolution that led to communist rule in Russia; the breaking down of Stalin's statue during the Hungarian revolution in 1956; to the destruction of Saddam Hussein's statue in Baghdad in 2003.

In South Africa, the issue of statues remains mired in controversy. Leading up to the eventual removal of the statue of Cecil John Rhodes from the campus of the University of Cape Town were not only waves of protest but vandalism which saw the statue covered in faeces. Significantly, this was not the first time that the statue of Rhodes had provoked anger and demands for its removal. Similar calls had been made in the 1950s by an entirely different group of students, but for the same reason – Afrikaans students had wanted it removed because it symbolised British colonial rule and the oppression of Afrikaners. Not surprisingly, the successful removal of the Rhodes statue emboldened actions against other statues, which included the defacement of more statues, including the smearing of green paint on the statue of Queen Victoria; the statue of King George VI being spray-painted at the University of KwaZulu-Natal; and the defacement of the Mahatma Gandhi monument.

The removal of the Rhodes statue, as well as the ensuing acts of vandalism against statues across South Africa, opened necessary debates about how South African society ought to deal with the symbols of its horrific history. Of course, the statues of Rhodes or Colston are abhorrent because of their representation of discrimination and oppression – at least, to those who agree with this description. Few, therefore, would disagree with a view that there is legitimate anger directed at the actions of these individuals. But, as Habib and Leisegang (2020) point out, whatever one's ideological orientation, 'questions have to be asked about these attacks on statues. Who decides which ones fall and which ones stand? What are the public deliberations that underlie these decisions, and what are the legitimate parameters on making judgements on historical figures?' And, in line with Butler's (2017) call for the necessity of dissent in university education, what would be the harm in retaining these statues and symbols? Would the world be a better place if there were no symbolic reminders of historical oppressors?

In the academy, posits Butler (2017: 859), we are free 'to imagine alternative forms of society and of the very relation between society and the state, to develop new accounts of justice and freedom in response to historical realities that compel our thinking'. In this way, it is possible to (re)conceptualise and (re)construct to extend historical memory and inform public consciousness, so that some experiences are never repeated. 'This is more than simply learning history in a narrow sense; it is really about public conscientisation and the transmission of values and memory from one historical epoch to another' (Habib & Leisegang, 2020). As Butler (2017: 859) maintains, 'when we develop forms of thought concerning a historical crisis, our thought becomes critical – critical in the sense that it is a form of questioning presuppositions, tracking forms of power, but also imagining possibilities of transformation'. To Butler (2017: 859), the freedom to imagine the transformation of society is part of academic freedom. Transformation, like imagination, cannot hinge on one interpretation or a singular perspective; both transformation and imagination rely on the existence and expression of divergent views and truths. The university has to accommodate and tolerate divergence and dissent – even if it is against its own truth.

References

Butler, J. (1993). *Bodies that matter: On the discursive limits of sex.* New York: Routledge.

Butler, J. (2017). Academic freedom and the critical task of the university. *Globalizations, 14*(6), 857–861.

Giuliano, F. (2015). (Re)thinking education with Judith Butler: A necessary meeting between philosophy and education (interview with Judith Butler). *Encounters in Theory and History of Education, 16*(3), 183–199.

Golnaraghi, G., & Dye, K. (2016). Discourses of contradiction: A postcolonial analysis of Muslim women and the veil. *International Journal of Cross Cultural Management, 16*(2), 137–152.

Greene, M. (1995). Art and the imagination: Reclaiming the sense of possibility. *The Phi Delta Kappan, 76*(5), 378–382.

Habib, A., & Leisegang, A. (2020). *Analysis: We shouldn't simply break down offensive statues, but we can reimagine them.* https://www.news24.com/news24/analysis/analysis-we-shouldnt-simply-break-down-offensive-statues-but-we-can-reimagine-them-20200625. Accessed 23 June 2020.

Khiabany, G., & Williamson, M. (2008). Veiled bodies – Naked racism: Culture, politics and race in the sun. *Race & Class, 50*(2), 69–88.

Meier, I. C., & Prins, B. (1998). How bodies come to matter: An interview with Judith Butler. *Signs, 23*(2), 275–286.

Mills, M. (2004). Male teachers, homophobia, misogyny and teacher education. *Teaching Education, 15*(1), 27–39.

Skelton, C. (2002). The "feminisation of schooling" or "remasculinising" primary education? *International Studies in Sociology of Education, 12*, 77–96.

Chapter 9
Academic Activism and the Postmodern Condition Revisited

Abstract In this chapter, we turn to Jean-Francois Lyotard's (The postmodern condition: a report on knowledge (trans: Bennington G, Massumi B). Manchester University Press, Manchester, 1979) influential book, *The Postmodern Condition*, which had an enduring effect on the understanding of knowledge in the contemporary world. We are drawn to some of his main claims about knowledge, performativity and managerialism and how a philosophy of higher education and academic activism in universities could be reconsidered. Lyotard accentuates the argument in defence of a speculative university by insisting that scientific knowledge should be intertwined with narrative knowledge that will actualise learning possibilities for humanity. In reflecting on higher education in South Africa, we raise concerns about its explicit preoccupations with massification and performativity without due cognisance of the risks of student alienation and neglecting a responsibility to social justice. The attention seems to be only on graduate production, with scant consideration of the kinds of students being passed through a system. We raise similar concerns about slippages into practices of functionalist technical training, as opposed to immersing students into thinking about what they know so that they might reimagine things anew.

Keywords Jean-Francois Lyotard · Narrative knowledge · Performativity · Unity

Introduction

In this chapter, we turn to Jean-Francois Lyotard's (1979) influential book, *The Postmodern Condition*, which had an enduring effect on the understanding of knowledge in the contemporary world. To Lyotard (1979), knowledge cannot just be subjected to criteria of truth, validity and those of efficiency. Knowledge, he asserts, is also composed in the narratives, opinions, customs, ideologies and myths of humans. To this end, knowledge is also 'embodied in a subject' (Lyotard, 1979: 27). Our decision to focus on Lyotard's seminal ideas in this chapter stems, on the one hand, from his contention that science is obliged to produce 'a discourse of legitimation with respect to its own status, a discourse called philosophy' (1979: xxiii).

© The Author(s), under exclusive license to Springer Nature Singapore Pte Ltd. 2021
N. Davids, Y. Waghid, *Academic Activism in Higher Education*, Debating Higher Education: Philosophical Perspectives 5,
https://doi.org/10.1007/978-981-16-0340-2_9

On the other hand, we are drawn to some of his main claims about knowledge, performativity and managerialism and how a philosophy of higher education and academic activism in universities could be reconsidered. Lyotard accentuates the argument in defence of a speculative university by insisting that scientific knowledge should be intertwined with narrative knowledge that will actualise learning possibilities for humanity. In reflecting on higher education in South Africa, we raise concerns about its explicit preoccupations with massification and performativity without due cognisance of the risks of student alienation and neglecting a responsibility to social justice. The attention seems to be only on graduate production, with scant consideration of the kinds of students being passed through a system. Critical questions need to be asked about the students we are producing. Who are they, not only as university graduates, and future professionals, but as citizens and human beings? Implicit to these questions is a particular understanding of the university as a space of ethical responsibility. We raise similar concerns about slippages into practices of functionalist technical training, as opposed to immersing students into thinking about what they know so that they might reimagine how things might be otherwise.

Narrative Knowledge as an Enactment of Academic Activism

Lyotard (1979: xxiii) uses the term 'modern to designate any science that legitimates itself with reference to a metadiscourse of this kind making an explicit appeal to some grand narrative, such as the dialectics of Spirit, the hermeneutics of meaning, the emancipation of the rational or working subject, or the creation of wealth'. By contrast, Lyotard (1979: xxiv) defines the term 'postmodern' as 'incredulity towards metanarratives', where metanarratives are understood as totalising stories about history and the goals of the human race that ground and legitimise knowledge and cultural practises. To Lyotard, the two metanarratives that have been most important in the past are history as progressing towards social enlightenment and emancipation and knowledge as progressing towards totalisation. To Lyotard (1979: xxv), postmodern knowledge 'is not simply a tool of the authorities; it refines our sensitivity to differences and reinforces our ability to tolerate the incommensurable'. In sum, if modernity is the age of metanarrative legitimation, then postmodernity is the age in which metanarratives have become bankrupt.

For Lyotard, the most challenging problem that faces the university today is the problem of the commodification of knowledge. In his words, '[k]nowledge in the form of an informational commodity indispensable to productive power is already, and will continue to be, a major – perhaps the major – stake in the worldwide competition for power' (Lyotard, 1979: 5). This 'mercantilization of knowledge' would invariably result in 'communicational transparency' that would be difficult for nation-states and their universities to control, and, ultimately, it results in 'new forms of the circulation of capital that go by the generic name of multinational corporations' (Lyotard, 1979: 5). Three matters pertaining to the university emanate from Lyotard's analysis. Firstly, if knowledge becomes commodified, then the notion that 'scientific knowledge' is the only legitimate form of knowledge becomes questionable. Secondly, Lyotard (1979: 44) contends that 'technology is a game not to the true, the just, or the beautiful, etc., but to efficiency'. And, it is when science combines with technology that it becomes 'a force of production; in other words, a moment in the circulation of capital'. Thirdly, research, as understood in the parlance of performativity, implies that the discourse has to be managerialised (Lyotard, 1979: 46).

In returning to the first matter, knowledge, asserts Lyotard (1979: 7), 'does not represent the totality of knowledge; it has always existed in addition to, and in competition and conflict with another kind of knowledge, which [he calls] narrative in the interests of simplicity'. His contention is not that narrative knowledge can prevail over science but rather that the narrative model 'is related to ideas of internal equilibrium and conviviality next to which contemporary scientific knowledge cuts a poor figure' (1979: 7). The narrative function, he asserts, 'is losing its functors, its great hero, its great dangers, its great voyages, its great goal' (Lyotard, 1979: xxiv). Lyotard (1979: 18) posits that knowledge cannot just be subjected to criteria of truth, validity and those of efficiency. Rather, knowledge is also 'embodied in a subject' – that is, knowledge is also composed in the narratives of humans, that is, opinions, customs, ideologies, fables, myths and legends (Lyotard, 1979: 27). Humans (academic and students) do not live in vacuums; they live in relation to others and are shaped and influenced by others as much as by their environments. It is not enough, therefore, to simply look at students as someone enrolled for this or that course; all students come with their own stories and narratives; these stories cannot be separated from what they bring into the classroom. Similarly, academics do not enter lecture theatres or the supervision encounter without their own histories, worldviews and identities. In South Africa, the racial and social disparities cemented through apartheid continue to present serious implications and impediments for relations and understandings between students and academics. Historically universities have predominantly been occupied and dictated to by white males, who not only have little insights into the lived experiences of black students, as well as black academics, but often continue to engage with minority groups with bias and prejudice.

Firstly, says Lyotard (1979: 20), narratives 'allow the society in which they are told, on the one hand, to define its criteria of competence and, on the other, to evaluate according to those criteria what is performed or can be performed within it'. Secondly, the narrative form, unlike the developed forms of the discourse of knowledge, lends itself to a great variety of language games. Thirdly, narration usually obeys rules that define the pragmatics of their transmission – that is, narrators' only claim to competence for telling the story is the fact that they have heard it themselves; 'it is claimed that the narrative is a faithful transmission' (Lyotard, 1979: 20–21). And fourthly, narrative form follows a rhythm. It exhibits, states Lyotard (1979: 22), a surprising feature: 'as meter takes precedence over accent in the production of sound (spoken or not), time ceases to be a support for memory to become an immemorial beating that, in the absence of a noticeable separation between periods, prevents their being numbered and consigns them to oblivion'.

Of course, the kinds of dichotomies between scientific knowledge and other knowledge forms, such as narrative knowledge, are deeply established in common separations of disciplines. In our own faculty, for example, curriculum studies are considered as distinct from philosophy of education. So, too, in our own department (Education Policy Studies), certain academics insist upon separating philosophical and sociological thought. At the time of writing this chapter, we became aware of yet another controversy surrounding the publication of an article, entitled 'Why are black South African students less likely to consider studying biological sciences?' – written by Nicoli Nattrass and published in the *South African Journal of Science* (2020). An excerpt from the introduction reads as follows:

> An exploratory survey of University of Cape Town (UCT) students in mid-2019 drew attention to an important, but under-researched, question: why do conservation biology, zoology and the other biological sciences subjects struggle to attract black South African students? A large part of the answer is obviously that persisting inequalities in the schooling system make it less likely that they will meet the entrance requirements for science courses. Yet there are likely to be other reasons too, notably materialist values and aspirations (pertaining to occupation and income) as well as experience with pets and attitudes towards wildlife – all of which are likely also to be shaped by a student's socio-economic background. Given the 'Fallist' protests of 2015/2016, another possibility is that wildlife conservation itself might be regarded as colonial, and students might perceive a trade-off between social justice and conservation. The survey, conducted by researchers from the Institute for Communities and Wildlife in Africa (iCWild) at UCT, explored these possibilities. (Nattrass, 2020)

Nattrass' (2020) table below shows that the list of 7 questions which the 'opportunistic survey' of 211 students were required to answer (Table 9.1).

Nattrass' (2020) study finds that the low enrolment of students in the biological sciences might be because of the materialist values of black students; lack of pet

Table 9.1 Nattrass' (2020) 'Opportunistic survey'

	Black South Africans	Other students	Total sample	Fisher's exact (Pr)
Considered studying the biological sciences	32.4%	49.5%	40.3%	0.016
Agrees 'Addressing social inequality is more important than wildlife conservation'	43.4%	31.6%	38.0%	0.087
Agrees 'I support wildlife conservation but have no interest in having a career in it'	76.1%	60.0%	68.8%	0.016
Agrees that 'Humans evolved from apes'	19.9%	57.1%	36.3%	0.000
Likes having starlings around at UCT	44.3%	68.0%	55.2%	0.001
Agrees that disciplines like conservation biology are colonial and should be scrapped at UCT	7.1%	3.1%	5.3%	0.199
Agrees that many of South Africa's national parks should be scrapped and the land given to the poor	10.6%	5.3%	8.2%	0.281

ownership; attitudes toward wildlife; 'fallism' and anti-colonialism; and black students' perceived trade-offs between social justice and conservation. In response, UCT executive issued a statement in which it expressed its concern with regard to 'the methodological and conceptual flaws that raise questions about the standard and ethics of research at UCT', stating further:

> The paper is constructed on unexamined assumptions about what black people think, feel, aspire to and are capable of. The commentary by Professor Nattrass offers an example of research that is unable to examine the historical and ideological roots of academic disciplines, and that is equally unaware of the role that power differentials have in closing or opening possibilities and choices in the life of individuals and communities. The paper is offensive to black students at UCT; black people in general and to any academic who understands that the quality of research is inextricably linked to its ethical grounding.

In a more scathing response, the Black Academic Caucus at UCT expressed their 'outrage' by highlighting that Nattrass (2020) fails to take account 'the socio-economic inequalities that restrict black students from entering this field, the historical deprivation of access to land and its associated ecological systems which conclude in the very deprivation of food, shelter and clothing for black bodies which are the locations of myriad forms of biological violence'.[1] In addition to questioning the hypothesis of the study, they expressed criticism against Natrass' reference to black students as 'fallist' students – accusing her of trivialising students who were part of the #RhodesMustFall and #FeesMustFall movements. The statement continued that '[w]hile this kind of research is presented as a study into the attitude of black students, the irrelevant hypothesis and arbitrary manner in which the questions are posed and tested tell us that it is meant to lead a larger narrative. A narrative that is neither kind nor charitable to black people'. The Black Academic Caucus concludes their statement as follows:

> Let us not have more of this kind of patronising and dehumanising research. Instead let us have research that affirms the humanity of all and doesn't seek to insidiously fault black people for institutionally racialised structures that are beyond their control. If enrolments are down in the biological sciences, then you need to first address the socioeconomic inequalities that prevent black people entering this field, the historical deprivation of access to land, the violence of colonial biological sciences and the denial of the deep spiritualities of the land and its ecologies in the biological sciences.

Putting aside the obvious ethical concerns in terms of linking a social construction of race to a student's choice of a university programme, this particular controversy presents an apt space for the elucidation of Lyotard's (1979) illustrative importance of narrative knowledge. As Lyotard (1979: 7) contends, it is not his intention to argue that narrative knowledge can prevail over science but, rather, that the model of narrative knowledge 'is related to ideas of internal equilibrium and

---

[1]According to its Facebook page, the Black Academic Caucus (BAC) is a platform that advocates for inclusive and diverse academic institutions that also prioritise black academics and their knowledge. Committed to transformation and decolonisation of UCT primarily, and influencing the higher education landscape in South Africa, BAC will advocate for curriculum and research scholarship that is linked to social justice and the experiences of black people.

conviviality next to which contemporary scientific knowledge cuts a poor figure'. Few would disagree with Nattrass' (2020) intention to understand why there are significantly fewer black students who choose to study biological sciences at UCT. Clearly, students are influenced by various reasons why they opt for certain programmes and careers. During apartheid, bursaries available to students of colour were limited to the professions of teaching and nursing. Many young people embarked on teaching and nursing programmes, not because they had any interest or excitement about these programmes or professions, but because it was the only way to qualify for a state bursary. In most instances, programme choices are influenced by particular interests and passions, which, at times, arise from homes, role models or painful life experiences. All of these decisions live in and emanate from lived experiences.

To discount these narratives is not only neglectful but risks distorting the findings – as is evidently the case in Nattrass' (2020) study. Black students would agree with the statement that 'Addressing social inequality is more important than wildlife conservation', not because they are averse to wildlife conservation, but because they are profoundly more affected by social injustice than any other group. Similarly, it is somewhat predictable that black students would agree 'that many of South Africa's national parks should be scrapped and the land given to the poor' – again, not because they do not care about national parks, but because the majority of black people live on scraps of land, not conducive to humane living conditions. Can a researcher expect an individual to care about the existence or maintenance of a national park, when this same individual has never enjoyed the privilege (let alone the right) to living in an actual house, with running water, sanitation and electricity?

Academic activism as a form of narrative knowledge recognises that we all bring our past into what we do, say and write. It is imperative, therefore, that who academics, researchers and students are are taken into account and recognised as voices in academic as well as human encounters. Inasmuch as students come into the academy with their pasts – how they have come to know what they know – so, too, researchers can never lay claim to objectivity. At best, they are subjectively neutral. There is a reason Nattrass (2020) conducted this study; there were certain understandings and perceptions, which prompted her to ask the kinds of questions she did. As such, she brought her own subjectivity and narrative into the hypothesis of her study.

Similarly, we are motivated to write this book – not only as an academic project but as two individuals, who have lived through particular experiences of marginalisation and oppression, which not only have attuned us to those experiences in relation to ourselves and others but have enhanced our uncompromising position on a need for activism as embedded in the responsibilities of the university. This is true for all the texts where we have written – that is, our past is never excluded. A narrative's reference, explains Lyotard (1979: 22), 'may seem to belong to the past, but in reality it is always contemporaneous with the act of recitation'. It is the present act that on each of its occurrences marshals in the ephemeral temporality inhabiting the space between the 'I have heard' and the 'you will hear'.

Of course, our potential critic might claim that if a professor or researcher, such as Nattrass (2020), were not allowed to tell her story from her subjective vantage point, that in itself would be a denial of her academic freedom. And we would concur with this view. However, when a professor selectively constructs a narrative on the basis of being remiss of other perspectives that might elucidate the story, then she seems to constrain her own academic voice to illuminate and, in a Lyortadian sense, legitimise the story. The point is, making claims about 'black' students without considering the broader context that underscores their narrative is to undermine one's own academic liberty to do so. What is most crucial to educational research is that narratives are not just told without deeper insight into what framed such stories. It cannot be assumed that a particular racial or ethnic group acts in a particular way because of certain responses to a questionnaire. Rather, one would expect that more rigorous narratives be legitimised on the basis of more credible and inclusive evidence.

Based on this non-dichotomous understanding of knowledge, Lyotard (1979: 27) argues that that the university should orientate its constituent element of science (knowledge of argumentation and proof) in relation to the speculative discourse of philosophy. In his words:

> The University is speculative, that is to say, philosophical. Philosophy must restore unity to learning, which has been scattered in laboratories and in pre-university education; it can only achieve this in a language game that links the sciences together as moments in the becoming of spirit [narrative knowledge], in other words, which links them in rational narration, or rather meta-narration.

Lyotard accentuates the argument in defence of a speculative university by insisting that scientific knowledge should be intertwined with narrative knowledge that will actualise learning possibilities for humanity. In this way, the university becomes 'the home of … metadiscourse, owes its knowledge to people whose historic mission is to bring metadiscourse to fruition by working, fighting, and knowing' (Lyotard, 1979: 37).

The legitimacy of humanities and social sciences in the context of science, engineering and technology becomes even more credible according to such a Lyotardian notion of the university. As Nussbaum (2010: 7) highlights, the humanities creates a spectrum of abilities – to think critically, to transcend local loyalties, to imagine the predicament of another person sympathetically and to approach world problems as a 'citizen of the world'. When practised at their best, says Nussbaum (2010: 7–8), other disciplines, such as economics and science, 'are infused by what we might call the spirit of the humanities: by searching critical thought, daring imagination, empathetic understanding of human experiences of many different kinds, and understanding of the complexity of the world we live in… Science, rightly pursued, is a friend of the humanities rather than their enemy'. A university would be postmodern when it does not prejudice against the human sciences as has been the case for the last few decades in South Africa. Instead, a postmodern university is sensitive to that which is different; it 'reinforces our ability to tolerate the incommensurable' (Lyotard, 1979: xxv).

The Risk of 'Performance Maximisation'

Lyotard (1979: 44) contends that 'technology is a game not to the true, the just, or the beautiful, etc., but to efficiency'. And, it is when science combines with technology that it becomes 'a force of production; in other words, a moment in the circulation of capital' (Lyotard, 1979: 45). Lyotard (1979: 45) explains that it was more the desire for wealth than the desire for knowledge that initially forced upon technology the imperative of performance improvement and product realisation – that is, 'the "organic" connection between technology and profit preceded its union with science. Increasingly universities have played into "the imperative of performance improvement and product realization … technology [with science] became important to contemporary knowledge … through the mediation of a generalized spirit of performativity"' (Lyotard, 1979: 45).

In South Africa, major research universities have structured their academic programmes around technological applications of knowledge to ensure what Lyotard refers to as 'the best possible input/output [of capital] equation' (1979: 46). University authorities explicitly invoke the criterion of performance in the country in line with the idea of 'performance maximisation' (Lyotard, 1979: 47). Universities have become more concerned with producing more skilled graduates so that 'the transmission of knowledge is no longer designed to train an elite capable of guiding the nation towards its emancipation, but to supply the system with players capable of acceptably fulfilling their roles at the pragmatic posts required by the institutions' (Lyotard, 1979: 48). While not a new phenomenon, the issue of massification of students in higher education is considered as a significant marker of transformation in South Africa, insofar as massification is centred on including historically excluded groups. What is often not given adequate attention, however, is whether the massification has been able to redress historical inequalities or whether the South African economy is able to accommodate the increasing number of graduates. It would seem that an unbalanced emphasis on massification and graduate production has led universities to focus on producing large numbers of technicians of learning – referred to by Lyotard (1979: 49) as the 'technical intelligentsia' – who might not necessarily seek to connect their academic qualifications to a social justice agenda or responsibility.

One of the biggest concerns persistently raised by students during protests is the alienating institutional culture of many universities in South Africa. Students are conceived as commodities, which ought to be passed through a system. Scant attention is given to the organic experience of what it means to experience higher education or what kinds of students universities actually produce. At the end of each year, as our university prepares for its December graduation (the other (smaller) one takes place in April), we listen as the university pats itself on the back for producing yet another record number of graduates. This is generally followed by a breakdown of what is referred to as BAIC students – an acronym designed for 'black', 'African', 'Indian' and 'coloured' students. Here, too, one witnesses great satisfaction among university governance structures as they applaud themselves for 'embracing transformation' and 'becoming more diverse'. Even in years where the university might have experienced student protests (which, although significantly less pronounced at our particular institution, is still an annual occurrence), there is never any deliberation or reflection of what the university needs to do so that there is a deeper attunement between university governance structures and students.

The limited discussions that *are* held – whether in relation to decolonising the university curriculum, food insecurity among students, gender-based violence or racism – never move beyond that of policy fixation. There seems to be no attempt to take into account the narrative knowledge, which so clearly can provide insights not only into the lived experiences of students and academics but also in assisting universities in providing more humane responses. The result is that students neither witness nor experience the university as an open and deliberative space; they are not immersed in the discourse of democratic engagement, disagreement and justice. As such, it is fairly common for most students to pass through 3–5 years of a degree programme without once pondering on social justice issues or actually considering their role and responsibility as citizens in a democratic society. There is seemingly an entirely inward focus on individual achievement and prosperity, with little, if any, sense of a collective responsibility to society.

Performativity is so ubiquitous in universities that knowledge is 'served a la carte to adults who are either already working or expect to be, for the purpose of improving their skills and chances of promotion ... allowing them to widen their occupational horizons and to articulate their technical and ethical experience' (Lyotard, 1979: 49). In our faculty where teachers are supposed to be prepared for the profession, our teacher education programmes have taken the form of functionalist technical training whereby knowledge is merely transmitted to passive students seemingly concerned only about their professional competence to teach in schools. Teacher education has mostly taken the route of technical professionalism in terms of which knowledge of the teaching profession seems to reside mostly in 'new techniques and technologies' (Lyotard, 1979: 49). Already we see that a university teacher's role has been realigned with one who can technologise learning. Such a teacher is competent to translate learning into a computer language of video clips and audio podcasts placed at the students' disposal. The only learning that students seemingly acquire is to download pre-packaged ideas and regurgitate them in improving their technical performance-oriented skills. Unless university teachers begin to challenge these performative procedures of learning, Lyotard (1979: 53) cautions on what role the professor would assume:

> [T]he predominance of the performance criterion ... is sounding the knell of the Professor: a professor is no more competent than memory bank networks in transmitting established knowledge, no more competent than interdisciplinary teams in imagining new moves or new games.

Thirdly, research, as understood in the parlance of performativity, implies that the discourse has to be managerialised (Lyotard, 1979: 46). And, by managerialism, it meant that universities are run as hierarchies informed by centralised decision-making, teamwork, calculation of individual and collective returns, the development of saleable academic programmes and marketable research (Lyotard, 1979: 46). In other words, following Lyotard, in a managerialist university, academics are 'technicians, and instruments are purchased not to find the truth, but to augment power' (Lyotard, 1979: 46). To keep the university functioning in such a hierarchical manner implies that 'there will be a growth in demand for experts and high management executives' to manage the research in the university and 'to encourage professional advancement' (Lyotard, 1979: 50). The implication of such centralised control of the university has the effect 'that practically nowhere do [university] teachers' groups have the power to decide what the budget of their institution will be; all they can do is to allocate the funds that are assigned to them, and only then as the last step in the process' (Lyotard, 1979: 50). We concur with Lyotard that the managerialist attack on the university will leave the institution paralysed.

The finances in our faculty, for example, are not managed by the dean and the faculty executive. Instead, it is managed by a faculty manager, who, in addition to attending to the budget of the faculty, seems to make all key decisions about what the financial priorities of the faculty are. Of course, we understand that the faculty manager takes his cue from university management and that he does not simply act autonomously. But, the fact that academics are excluded from financial planning and decision-making has had serious repercussions for the faculty. Over the past 5 years, for example, departments in our faculty have received minimal operational funding. There are no funds for academics in terms of supporting conference attendance, or arranging conferences, or advancing any aspect of their teaching or research areas. Despite these concerns being raised in faculty meetings, there is no way of knowing whether the faculty manager understands the work of academics or whether he indeed takes these concerns to the university executive, as expected. To the extent that the power of the faculty has shifted to the non-academic or managerialist sector, power has similarly been centralised by the institution's management. Academics in the sense used by Lyotard are treated like 'terrorists' because they have been silenced or coerced to consent on the grounds that their ability 'to participate has been threatened (there are many ways to prevent someone from playing)' (Lyotard, 1979: 64).

In a way, performative university managers exercise 'terror' because their decision-making, following Lyotard (1979: 64), is based on 'arrogance, which in principle has no equivalent in the sciences … It says: Adapt your aspirations to our ends – or else'. So it appears that even research at universities have become centralised and often academics are told to align their intellectual pursuits with consensual themes of research. Our concern is not so much with a university discourse based on consensus because genuine academics would welcome 'a dialogue of argumentation' or discourse (Lyotard, 1979: 65). Instead, we are concerned about an overemphasis on a consensus that can inhibit further deliberation. And, when this happens, there is no place for dissent and by implication what Lyotard refers to as 'paralogy' (1979: 66). If university academics are not recognised for their capacities to act with dissent, then there is no reason why a university should exist. If a university does not recognise the educational value of dissent, it will never 'respect the desire for justice and the desire for the unknown' (Lyotard, 1979: 67). Such a university would be in a state of paralysis. To avoid such a situation of paralysis, Lyotard argues that there has to be a move towards such established ways of seeing things – that is, paralogy should be invoked. This means that new ideas have to be conjured up by going against established traditions of thinking or language games – what Lyotard (1979: 68) refers to as the legitimation of knowledge by paralogy.

On Philosophy as a Restoration of Unity

In sum, we have made an argument for the notion of a postmodern university in line with the seminal thoughts of Lyotard premised on the following: the university should invoke understandings of both scientific and narrative knowledge that will contribute towards cultivating humanity; it should also be concerned with counter-acting the performative; and it should encourage the pursuit of the legitimation of reason by paralogy. If a university fails to do the above, it would have succumbed to a discourse of performativity and managerialism that would be difficult to combat without serious academic activism. It might just be that university leaders would become those who allocate the funds and control the capital. In fact, this would spark the death of the speculative university.

Already in South Africa, educational research has succumbed to the legitimation crisis to which Lyotard (1979) refers. In other words, universities are funded according to the levels of production, and often a university that is highly productive in terms of research output and student throughput would be financially rewarded for its quantified academic outputs. This itself is beginning to show signs of fatality as only the established universities, those institutions with huge capital and experienced staff, have actually played the performative game well. And, there seems to be little end in sight for such performative research games. In a South African context, there are even more dire implications to consider as the institutions, which have the huge capital and experienced staff, are those that have been designated as historically white. This means that institutions, which have historically been marginalised and under-resourced, are at serious risk of continuing on a trajectory of historical disadvantage. The cliché publish or perish has gained much more currency in a post-apartheid South Africa where the functionality of a university is looked at in terms of the numbers it produces. There is little interest in the legitimacy of scholarship but more of an inclination towards increasing institutional academic outputs. Academics are under tremendous pressure not only to produce outputs (including postgraduate students) but to embark on collaborative research projects, which involve writing up proposals to access limited funding. In turn, academics are required to apply for 'research rating' from the National Research Foundation (NRF).

The NRF describes itself as a key driver to build a globally competitive science system in South Africa and as a valuable tool for benchmarking the quality of South African researchers against other international researchers. The rating of academics is based primarily on the quality and impact of their research outputs over 8 years.

Generally, South African universities use the outcomes of the NRF evaluation and rating process to position themselves as research-intensive institutions, while others provide incentives for their staff members to acquire and maintain a rating and give special recognition to top-rated researchers. Whether or not an academic has an NRF rating has an influence on a number of prospects, such as promotion and access to research funding. One of the key criticisms levelled at the NRF rating system is that it violates academic ethics by not ensuring the anonymity and confidentiality of applicants. Callaghan (2018) explains that unlike a typical review process, an academic applying for rating is not anonymised, making him or her vulnerable to bias. Another concern, says Callaghan (2018: 3), is a lack of transparency in terms of the methodology, which creates a potential for harm 'particularly in a context that seems to prioritise research in promotion rather than teaching, notwithstanding the societal imperatives associated with massified higher education and the dramatic inequalities in access to opportunities in our society'.

There is also another downside to a lack of legitimation of knowledge by paralogy. The privatisation of universities has begun to escalate all over the world, and many established institutions of higher learning have established satellite campuses in especially underdeveloped countries. Top American universities have established campuses in major African cities such as the Carnegie Mellon University in Kigali (Rwanda), Stanford Seed institution in Ghana, the American University in Cairo and the Columbia Global Centers in Nairobi (Kenya) and Tunis to 'export' higher education to Africa. There can be no denial that African economic development is important for the continent and that privatising university education provides access to many local students to university education. And, undoubtedly, many African students would acquire new skills and capacities to improve efficiency in their nation-states, especially if such universities partially fund private higher education. But the problem with privatisation in such a way seems to increase commercialised opportunities for established universities from outside of Africa rather than focusing on eradicating pressing socio-economic problems on the continent.

The point is, it seems even more challenging to delegitimise knowledge by paralogy as private universities are more concerned about the production of capital than the actual re-skilling of local students. We say this on account that unemployment, job creation and economic growth on the African continent remain in peril despite almost two decades of privatisation of higher education in Africa. Privatisation seems only to commercially benefit those universities intent on expanding their legitimate knowledge interests with very little, if any, regard for the local concerns. How would cybernetics and artificial intelligence and courses in robotics – dominant discourses of private higher education in Africa – benefit the business interests of African societies if the provision of electricity is a major concern for the continent? Our point is, educating students in accounting and management to run efficient civil services in African countries is not sufficient as such a private higher education merely seems to consolidate legitimation of knowledge. Students should also be educated to engage in paralogical discourses whereby they learn to rethink established traditions and norms of work and learning. Privatisation of universities in Africa seems to be mere dumping sites to further legitimise commercial knowledge interests in the name of efficiency.

Research and learning, contends Lyotard (1979: 34), 'are not justified by invoking a principle of usefulness'. To him, 'The idea is not at all that science should serve the interests of the State and/or civil society. The humanist principle that humanity rises up in dignity and freedom through knowledge is left by the wayside'. He explains that German idealism has recourse to a meta-principle that simultaneously grounds the development of learning, of society and of the state in the realisation of the 'life' of a subject. From this perspective, 'knowledge first finds legitimacy within itself, and it is the knowledge that is entitled to say what the State and what Society are' – but only if knowledge becomes speculative. In this regard, says Lyotard (1979: 34), philosophy 'offers a particularly vivid representation of one solution to the problem of the legitimacy of knowledge'. To Lyotard (1979: 33), the great function to be fulfilled by the universities is to 'lay open the whole body of learning and expound· both the principles and the foundations of all knowledge. For there is no creative scientific capacity without the speculative spirit'. Because the university is speculative, it has to be philosophical. To this end, philosophy can be used to 'restore unity to learning' (1979: 33) so that the separations between sciences can be dissolved and, more importantly, so that humane action, teaching and research can take its rightful place in the focus and responsibility of the university.

References

Callaghan, C. (2018). A review of South Africa's National Research Foundation's ratings methodology from a social science perspective. *South African Journal of Science, 114*(3/4), 1–7.

Lyotard, J. F. (1979). *The postmodern condition: A report on knowledg* (G. Bennington & B. Massumi, Trans.). Manchester, UK: Manchester University Press.

Nattrass, N. (2020). Why are black South African students less likely to consider studying biological sciences? *South African Journal of Science, 116*(5/6), 1–2.

Nussbaum, M. (2010). *Not for profit: Why democracy needs the humanities*. Princeton, NJ: Princeton University Press.

Chapter 10
Through the Agency of the Muselmann

Abstract In this chapter, we take the opportunity to reflect on the kinds of stigma and shame students and academics can and do experience in higher education – from experiences of discrimination and marginalisation to violence. As troubling as these might sound, higher education has always been a convergence of hope and academic performance, on the one side, coupled with the struggles and tensions created by issues of race, ethnicity, culture, religion and gender, on the other side. It is important, therefore, to take stock of the potential experiences of stigmatisation and shame. Immediately, however, it is equally important to ask who bears testimony to and takes responsibility for the shame and stigma, as symbolised through Agamben's (Remnants of Auschwitz: the witness and the archive (trans: Heller-Roazen D). Zone Books, Brooklyn, 2012) Muselmann. To us, this is the role of academic activism – the act of bearing witness or testimony resides in a preparedness to do so on behalf of others. To bear testimony, we argue, is to make manifest our humanity and our activism.

Keywords Giorgio Agamben · Stigma · Shame · Testimony · Humanity · Responsibility

Introduction

We are attracted to Giorgio Agamben's (2012) thoughts and expositions on the Muselmann for various reasons – not only because it offers glimpses into the parallel condition of inhumanity and humanity but because it provides profound reflections on conceptions of shame, stigma, testimony and responsibility. As our concluding chapter, we take the opportunity to reflect on the kinds of stigma and shame which students and academics can and do experience in higher education – from experiences of discrimination and marginalisation to violence. As troubling as these might sound, higher education has always been a convergence of hope and academic performance, on the one side, coupled with the struggles and tensions created by issues of race, ethnicity, culture, religion and gender, on the other side.

© The Author(s), under exclusive license to Springer Nature Singapore   127
Pte Ltd. 2021
N. Davids, Y. Waghid, *Academic Activism in Higher Education*, Debating
Higher Education: Philosophical Perspectives 5,
https://doi.org/10.1007/978-981-16-0340-2_10

It is important, therefore, to take stock of the potential experiences of stigmatisation and shame. Immediately, however, it is equally important to ask who bears testimony to and takes responsibility for the shame and stigma as symbolised through Agamben's (2012) Muselmann. To us, this is the role of academic activism – the act of bearing witness or testimony resides in a preparedness to do so on behalf of others. To bear testimony, we argue, is to make manifest our humanity and our activism. Academic activism, therefore, does not exist separate to who we are as academics; academic activism resides in our very being. To be an academic activist means to act when we witness shame and stigma; it means to speak out when others will not; and it means to assume responsibility for the 'zones of non-responsibility' (Agamben, 2012: 21), which perpetuate the experiences of higher education. In this regard, we conceive the very writing of this book as a manifestation of our activism. This is not simply an academic text, which speaks *about* the criticality of academic activism; the text embodies our own lived experiences as activists.

The Muselmann and Bearing Witness to Inhumanity

One of the key concerns for Agamben (2012), in *Remnants of Auschwitz: The Witness and the Archive*, is the act of witnessing – in terms of both what is meant by 'witnessing' and who does the 'witnessing'. He distinguishes between the Latin testis, which suggests a third party in a trial, superstes, which refers to someone 'who has experienced an event from beginning to end and can therefore bear witness to it' (Agamben, 2012: 17). In his exploration of the prisoners in the Auschwitz concentration camps, while he turns to the act of superstes, he asserts that those who survived might not be able to bear witness to their experiences. This is because what they had been subjected to had stripped them of all notions of what it means to be human and, hence, to see the humanity in others. In other words, the depth of debasement experienced at Auschwitz was such that it had left its survivors without the tools and words to bear witness.

In response to this dilemma, Agamben (2012) turns to the notion of the Muselmann (plural, Muselmänner) – a term initially used by Primo Levi (1988). The Muselmann described prisoners who had been reduced to absolute exhaustion, hopelessness and misery due to hunger and the horror of concentration camps – 'one hesitates to call them living: one hesitates to call their death death' (Levi, 1988: 33). In *Remnants of Auschwitz: The Witness and the Archive*, Giorgio Agamben (2012) explores the concept of the 'bare naked man' and writes about Muselmann as 'a bare, unassigned and unwitnessable life': the body stripped and devoid of all humanity and being. When translated from German, Muselmann means Muslim, but this is not to be confused with the Muslim, as an adherent of Islam. The most likely explanation, writes Agamben (2012: 45), can be found in the literal meaning of the Arabic word Muslim: the one who submits unconditionally to the will of God – 'It is this meaning that lies at the origins of the legends concerning Islam's supposed fatalism, legends which are found in European cultures starting with the

Middle Ages'. From a distance, continues Agamben (2012), the prisoners looked like Arabs or Muslims, because of their kneeling and rocking motion – as if they were participating in the ritual of Islamic prayers.

Agamben (2012: 51) describes the 'tortured bodies' of the Muselmänner as proof of the Nazis' atrocities – that is, 'a group of prisoners crouched on the ground or wandering on foot like ghosts ... who have survived by some miracle or, at least, prisoners very close to the state of Muselmänner ... [more specifically] naked ... half-living beings ... unbearable to human eyes'. In a way, the Muselmann represents the transfiguration of human into non-human through atrocious extermination (Agamben, 2012: 52). In other words, the Muselmann is 'the one who has abdicated his inalienable freedom and has consequently lost all traces of affective life and humanity' (Agamben, 2012: 56). The Muselmänner in the extermination camps have reached a 'point of no return' – that is, they have been dehumanised and lost all their dignity in the camps (Agamben, 2012: 61). When humans no longer exercise their freedom through communication, they have been subjected to domination against their will, and the only freedom they still have (but might not actually demonstrate it publicly) is their conviction in a God. As stated by Agamben (2012: 63):

> The *Muselmann* has, instead, moved into a zone of the human where not only help but also dignity and self-respect have become useless. But if there is a zone of the human in which these concepts make no sense, then they are not genuine ethical concepts, for no ethics can claim to exclude a part of humanity, no matter how unpleasant or difficult that humanity is to see.

By a lack of dignity and self-respect, Agamben alludes to the conditions of Auschwitz as a radical refutation of obligatory communication. Any attempt to engage the persecutors and torturers in the camp resulted in a beating of the Muselmänner with 'the place of communication being taken by the rubber whip' and not being talked to became the norm in the camp (Agamben, 2012: 65). When human dignity becomes lost, then humans lose their decency beyond imagination (Agamben, 2012: 69). Agamben explains the loss of human dignity and the rise of inhumanity in the following passage:

> In Auschwitz, people did not die; instead, corpses were produced. Corpses without death, non-humans whose decease is debased into a matter of serial production. And, according to a possible and widespread interpretation, precisely this degradation of death constitutes the specific offense of Auschwitz, the proper name of its horror. (2012: 72)

The point about speaking of corpses instead of deceased humans is that extermination has been induced by executioners of humans so that death has been degraded. When the dignity of death is negated for humans, they did not really die but are merely produced as corpses (Agamben, 2012: 75). The Muselmänner who had been denied the possibility of communication, and ultimately been subjected to inhuman torture and horror, could not have died in the camp of Auschwitz – that is, they only bore witness to non-human atrocities (Agamben, 2012: 75). Communication had been denied to them, and the only recourse to anything was to themselves and, by implication, their innate connection to a God to whom they either appealed for assistance or rebuked as a consequence that no help was forthcoming as they endured the horror of inhumane torture and persecution. Despite their subjection into inhumane actions, and despite being stripped of their humanity, the Muselmänner are still human. As living corpses, they are neither living nor dead. It is at this point, according to Bernstein (2002: 2), that we can begin to see the larger ramifications of Agamben's inquiry:

> Auschwitz shows us that it is possible to lose one's dignity and decency beyond imagination, but that there is still life in this most extreme degradation. Indeed, this paradoxical knowledge becomes the touchstone for judging all morality and all dignity. The Muselmann is the threshold of a new ethics, an ethics of a form of life that begins where dignity ends.

To Agamben (2012: 52), the idea that the *Muselmann* is the true witness of the camps reveals that 'the value of testimony lies essentially in what it lacks; at its centre it contains something that cannot be borne witness to and that discharges the survivors of authority'. While we have clear historical accounts of what unfolded in the camps, and what the legal circumstances were, and implications are, the same cannot be said for the ethical and political significance of the extermination – 'Not only do we lack anything close to a complete understanding: even the sense and reasons for the behavior of the executioners and the victims, indeed very often their words, still seem profoundly enigmatic' (Agamben, 2012: 11).

Although paradoxical, what we gain from Agamben (2012: 41) is that the act of bearing witness resides in a preparedness to do so on behalf of others:

> We may say that to bear witness is to place oneself in one's own language in the position of those who have lost it, to establish oneself in a living language as if it were dead, or in a dead language as if it were living – in any case, outside both the archive and the corpus of what has already been said

.

The disjuncture between the human as living being and speaking being, argues Agamben (2012), is the condition of possibility of testimony – 'if there is no articulation between the living being and language, if the "I" stands suspended in this disjunction, then there can be testimony' (Agamben, 1999: 130). As Mills (2003) explains, 'testimony arises in the intimate non-coincidence of the human and inhuman or the speaking being and the living being, the subject and non-subject'. More succinctly, testimony appears as the practice of remaining human, since testimony marks the trial by which the human being undergoes 'the double process of appropriation and expropriation in speaking, in which the human endures the inhuman and survives beyond its own expropriation or desubjectivation in language' (Mills, 2003).

In continuing, we are in no way suggesting that the experiences of Agamben's (2012) Muselmänner are akin to that of students. While it is indeed the case that numerous parents and family members of South African students were subjected to the dehumanising brutality of apartheid, including torture and death, our particular interests here reside in the experiences and emotions of stigma, shame as well as testimony and responsibility.

On Shame

We are interested in Agamben's understanding of shame as being consigned to something from which we cannot in any way distance ourselves (Agamben, 2012: 105). He provides the following explanation:

> To be ashamed means to be consigned to something that cannot be assumed. But what cannot be assumed is not something external. Rather, it originates in our own intimacy; it is what is most intimate in us (for example, our own physiological life). Here the 'I' is thus overcome by its own passivity, its own most sensibility; yet this expropriation and desubjectification is also an extreme and irreducible presence of the 'I' to itself. It is as if our consciousness collapsed and, seeking to flee in all directions, were simultaneously summoned by an irrefutable order to be present at its own defacement, at the expropriation of what is most its own. In shame, the subject thus has no other content than its own desubjectification; it becomes witness to its own disorder, its own oblivion as a subject. This double movement, which is both subjectification and desubjectification, is shame. (Agamben, 2012: 105–106)

There are numerous complex factors, which serve as sources or which perpetuate shame and dehumanisation in university settings. Firstly, although students from poor backgrounds gain access to university, equitable participation and substantive equality often do not follow (McLean, 2018: 116). Statistics show that 55.5% of South Africans are not able to sustain their needs within their income levels. Within this group, 25.2% of South Africans live in conditions of extreme poverty where they are unable to meet their daily dietary requirements or fulfil their basic sanitation or housing needs (Statistics South Africa, 2017). Students from disadvantaged backgrounds usually have insufficient and precarious financial resources (often going without food and other basic necessities); sometimes feel they do not 'belong' and do not always experience teaching and learning that is confidence-enhancing and imparts critical knowledge (Caltiz, 2018; Calitz, Walker, & Wilson-Strydom, 2016).

Although often under-reported, students experience significant psychological distress as they attempt to conceal their poverty, borne from shame and internalised oppression and the desire to avoid the stereotyping and stigma that they perceive they would receive as a result of being labelled poor (Firfirey & Carolissen, 2010). These students, as McLean (2018: 116) shares, are often first-generation. As such, they are often full of hope for themselves and their families, who hope to benefit from their education. Their biggest fear is not just that they will not succeed at university but that their failure will force them back into generational poverty. However, the transition to university, continues McLean (2018: 116), is often punishing for a range of economic, academic, linguistic and social reasons. As a result, students from impoverished family backgrounds have higher rates of dropping out of university and lower rates of throughput to graduation (Letseka & Maile, 2008).

A second major theme is that of race, racialisation and institutional racism, as well as classism, sexism, homophobia and xenophobia (Kerr & Luescher, 2018: 218). That these different categories of discrimination are couched together speaks to the intersectionality of these experiences. According to Kerr and Luescher (2018:

219), research on racialisation and institutional racism comes mainly from historically white universities (or merged components thereof). Overall, research 'gives a view of universities as enduringly racialised and segregated spaces in which black students repeatedly come up against the normative power of whiteness' (Kerr & Luescher, 2018: 219):

> The pervasive racism that appears to bedevil black–white relations in the historically white institutions is not the only form of discrimination in residences at higher education institutions. Equally pervasive, it appears, are (i) sexual harassment, which cuts across the divide of historically black and white institutions, (ii) xenophobia, which lurks in the background in some of the historically black institutions, as well as (iii) racial tension between African, Coloured and Indian students at the latter. The different forms of discrimination and the associated pathologies are the products of differences in the social, cultural and economic backgrounds of the students. (DHET, 2008: 75–76)

At one university, Kerr and Luescher (2018: 219) report, parts of the white university community continue to offer active and sometimes violent resistance to racial integration of residences (Kerr & Luescher, 2018). The series of student protests, which commenced in 2015, characterised by the slogans, #FeesMustFall, and '#RhodesMustFall', speak, on the one hand, to the economic disenfranchisement and, on the other hand, to the alienating ('white') spaces of certain university campuses. The widespread prevalence and reporting of institutional racism and sexism at a number of universities led to the establishment of a government-commissioned probe, which culminated in the 'Report of the ministerial committee on transformation and social cohesion and the elimination of discrimination in public higher education institutions' (DHET, 2008), also known as the Soudien Report (Prof Crain Soudien, former Deputy Vice-Chancellor of UCT, served as the chairperson of the committee).

The tipping point for the initiation of the commissioned inquiry was when the leaking of a video made by four young white Afrikaner male students of the Reitz Residence at the University of the Free State (UFS) came into the public domain in February 2008. It showed the students forcing a group of elderly black (cleaning) workers, four women and one man, to eat food into which one of the students had apparently urinated. The video had ostensibly been made under the auspices of an initiation ceremony. However, an investigation into the incident found that its real intent was to protest against the university's recently introduced policy to integrate the student residences (DHET, 2008). Unsurprisingly, the video provoked widespread outrage and disgust:

> It [the video] demonstrated white supremacy (extreme forms of racial prejudice and disrespect), and enacted direct and subtle discrimination through the weaving together of multiple forms of inequality. Its abuses invoked racism, ethnic and cultural supremacy, classism and sexism through the dehumanising debasement of four middle-aged, working-class, black cleaning women and a man, by what is assumed to be privileged young white male students. (Lewins, 2010: 127)

Disciplinary proceedings instituted by the university were not only found to be insufficient but seemingly fuelled more anger among the student body as well as the broader public. Beyond this specific incident, the commission of inquiry exposed an inhospitable institutional culture at many universities – characterised by racial discrimination, harassment, a pervading sense of whiteness, colour-blindedness and an aspiration to Western ideals and a refusal to redress historical identities and contexts (Lewins, 2010: 129). Significantly, in a number of cases, the experiences of students were not any different to that of academics. The commission of inquiry (DHET, 2008: 57–58) found:

> The role of an institutional culture that remains white and the pervasive racism that it engenders … is the source of immense unhappiness and frustration amongst black staff across institutions. The Committee was struck by the almost ubiquitous sense of disenchantment, alienation and anger amongst them, and by the fact that they did not feel at home in the institution. The full extent of the pain and hurt and humiliation that black staff members have had to endure is indicated by the observation by black staff… (they) are treated as 'unknowns' if their status and name is not known.

Perpetuating these painful and dehumanising experiences is a 'culture of silence', which permeates institutions because of the fear of victimisation. 'Black' academics choose to remain silent, because they fear not being promoted or not being given a good reference should they leave the institution (DHET, 2008: 58). This fear was equally prevalent among participants during the interview process of the commission of inquiry, with one academic (signed as anonymous) submitting the following:

> We make this submission on the understanding that confidentiality would be preserved and our identities not be made available to the University … or the public. In doing so we note our concern with respect to negative consequences in the form of possible victimisation. (DHET, 2008: 58)

The third major theme is that of gender-based violence. Like poverty and issues of race, gender-based violence also intersects with other forms of othering and discrimination. It emanates from an array of intersectional points and norms, which include culture, religion, economics, age, gender, sexuality, space, community as well as education or a lack thereof. While there appears to be consensus on the understanding that culture, religion, economics, age, gender, sexuality, space and community patriarchal norms play significant roles in legitimising gender-based violence, there is less consensus on the understanding of the role and influence of education or lack of education as a causal factor for gender-based violence. The seemingly unrestricted environments offered by university campuses, insofar as students are away from their homes, add to misperceptions around associations between sexuality and violence and the right by men to have sexual intercourse (Phipps, Ringrose, Renold, & Jackson, 2018: 1).

Echoing the 'culture of silence' that inhibits the reporting or resistance to racism in university settings, gender-based violence, too, is shrouded in veils of underreporting – predominantly due to the shame associated with being a victim of this scourge. Contrary to widespread 'stranger-rape' myths, in the majority of gender-based violence cases, the victim and the assailant are known to each other as an acquaintance, friend or date (Rennison & Addington, 2014). The commission of inquiry (DHET, 2008: 85), for example, found that with a few exceptions, there has been a deafening silence on sexual harassment in general and in residences in particular. From the few cases where it was raised, it is clear that sexual harassment, of women and gays and lesbians, is rife – as reported by one academic:

> Our student thugs are also mostly male, also racist – believing themselves to be superior to other human beings of different colours/ethnic groups, different sexual orientations, and gender... [O]ur thugs have beaten up gay men, including black gay men, beaten up and raped female students, raped lesbian women to 'cure' them, ridiculed and denigrated all homosexual people. (DHET, 2008: 85)

The shame and stigma attached to being a victim of gender-based violence are often reinforced by the social and institutional discourse and norms. Programmes and initiatives aimed to prevent GBV are regularly directed at women or victims of these crimes and place the responsibility of stopping this violence on them, rather than the perpetrators, or the contexts that might facilitate these crimes (Rentschler, 2015).

In terms of reporting, the experiences of students and academics are not dissimilar. Even when students want to report incidents of gender-based violence, contends Ahmed (2015), they are actively discouraged from doing so: 'if you complain you will damage your career (this can work as a threat, you *will* lose the very connections that enable you to progress); or if you complain you will damage the professor; or if you complain you will ruin a centre or collective' (Ahmed, 2015). Once complaints are made, more walls come up: an injury to the student or professor's reputation.

Furthermore, according to Jackson (2019: 698), women may not frequently or openly discuss experiences of gender-based violence, even if these are commonplace for them, because of early/initial experiences where such sharing – particularly about experiences that border on sexual harassment – is met primarily with objections and/or scepticism. Moreover, complaints about sexual harassment are not made public as a way of protecting the organisation from damage (Ahmed, 2015). Notably, despite the distinctive differences among South African universities in terms of historical identities, infrastructure and institutional cultures, they seemingly share one common feature – that is, a perpetuation of hegemonic masculinity, which maintains both the stigma and silence on gender-based violence.

Academic Activism as Testimony and Responsibility

Following Agamben, the purpose of a philosophy of (higher) education, we would argue, is to see the world 'from an extreme situation' (2012: 50). When seen from the dilemma of the Muselmann, philosophers (as academic activists we would assert) ought to find ways to procure the freedom and self-respect of humans. Such a philosophy would then be concerned with the acts of inhumanity, indignity and disrespect that seemed to have negated an ethics of communication everywhere. If philosophy and philosophy of higher education deepen analyses into inhumane actions and situations, then the possibility might be there to juxtapose such analyses against what can be perceived as humane. So how can this be done?

Certainly, our university courses should become more aligned with challenging what unfolds as inhumane practices everywhere. This would involve, first of all, identifying and bearing testimony to inhumane occurrences in the world and then to set out on a path of offering potential philosophical responses to how inhumanity and suffering in the world should be restrained. Here we specifically think of bringing philosophy of higher education into conversation with actions that can be considered as inhumane, for example, human trafficking, human displacement and forced migration and ongoing wars. In agreement with Agamben (2012: 99), a philosophy of higher education, and, by implication, academic activism, ought to be concerned with the revocation of the spirit of revenge and resentment. In his words:

> It is no longer a question of conquering the spirit of revenge … nor is it a matter of holding fast to the unacceptable through resentment. What lies before us now is being beyond acceptance and refusal, beyond the eternal past and eternal present … Beyond good and evil lies not the innocence of becoming but, rather, a shame that is not only without guilt but even without time.

It is shameful that we do very little, if anything, when students come to university without a meal or without having paid their tuition fees or without knowing where the next place of shelter will come from – all socio-political realities of a democratic South Africa. If academic activism cannot assist in bringing to disgrace such deplorable acts to which we bear witness, then our commitment to a philosophy of higher education is questionable. The destruction of the human being and the reemergence of the Muselmann are imminent if not already present. The Muselmann in itself should be freed from that which undermines his or her *humanitas*. And, for the latter to happen, philosophy of higher education ought to be looked at in a renewed (radical) way, such as to make political liberation even more possible.

To Agamben (2012), the possibility of testimony discerns between the human as living being and speaking being is the condition of possibility of testimony. When humans bear testimony through speech, they lay claim to their humanity – their testimony bridges the 'fracture between the living being and the speaking being, the inhuman and the human' (Agamben, 2012: 135). Academics and students alike see, observe and, at times, even participate in inhumane practices. It is not enough to stand in silence, knowing but not acting. Activism requires the action that makes knowledge, objection and resistance visible and audible. Academics, for example, are often fully aware of the precarious situations of students – whether related to adverse poverty or institutional marginalisation. So, too, they are often aware of colleagues who embark on dubious relationships with students – such as sexual favours for improved results or skewed assessment practices in relation to race, culture, nationality or religion.

When academics and students turn against these practices, they turn both against the inhumanity of what they have witnessed and against their own inhumanity in remaining silent. The point here is that opting to remain silent is in itself an act of inhumanity in that it refuses to acknowledge the inhumanity being witnessed, thereby allowing it to continue. Hence, Agamben's (2012: 155) assertion 'with its every word, testimony refutes precisely this isolation… of survival from life'. To him, an ethics of witnessing and bearing testimony is separate from a juridical responsibility, simply because, as Mills (2003) explains, it cannot be presumed that the law exhausts the question of responsibility. To Agamben (2012), there are 'zones of non-responsibility', which speaks to 'a confrontation with a responsibility that is infinitely greater than any we could ever assume. At the most, we can be faithful to it, that is, assert its unassumability' (Agamben, 2012: 21).

To us, academic activism ought to be embedded in actions of ethical responsibility and demands an unassumable responsibility. What this means is that as activists, we assume responsibility for that to which no responsibility has been assigned. Who takes responsibility for poor and hungry students at universities? Who takes responsibility for students who have been subjected to inhumane 'initiation' practices in university residences or for students who have been debased because of their sexual orientation? Who takes responsibility for students who are at risk of attrition because of student debt or who cannot graduate because of outstanding fees? Who takes responsibility for students when they have been subjected to racism, xenophobia or other forms of marginalising practices? Who takes responsibility for the culture of sexism and harassment, which often pervades departmental or faculty meetings?

Policies, no matter how well-intentioned and well-designed, can neither respond to nor alleviate inhumane and unjust experiences; policies cannot undo the harm of the inhumanity of others. Moreover, even when faculties and departments have modules specifically focused on matters and experiences of social justice, that which is taught theoretically in the confines of lecture theatres seldom find expression in how academics treat or respond to the plight of particular students. There is a clear disjuncture between what students are taught, and what they should be doing in relation to the world in which they find themselves, and what students actually experience at the hands and words of the same academics who teach them.

In South Africa, for example, we note the increasing criminalisation of poverty and homelessness. Those who are most vulnerable and in the greatest need of social and economic assistance are brutally evicted from makeshift shacks; homeless people are issued with fines for living on the streets or 'obstructing the sidewalk'. Earlier this year, as the world embarked on a series of lockdowns in response to the global pandemic of COVID-19, provincial authorities of Cape Town established a tent facility on a desolate piece of land. Approximately 2000 homeless people were relocated. Despite being justified as conditions necessary for the lockdown, it quickly became evident that the facility lacked a capacity for proper social distancing; had inadequate healthcare access; lacked food, water and ablution facilities; and was beset by allegations of sexual assaults. The appalling conditions of the facility resulted in the Human Rights Commission comparing it to concentration camps and demanded its immediate closure (Mahomedy, Boggenpoel, Van der Sijde, & Tlale, 2020).

Despite being found instructed by the Cape High Court to desist from fining, harassing and abducting homeless people in the city centre, and unfairly discriminating against the poor, the Cape Metro police have continued with their actions under the guise that homeless people are contravening COVID-19 regulations (Farr & Green, 2020). According to Farr and Green (2020), the astonishment now being expressed at the levels of city-authorised violence should be read as a testimony to the lack of national oversight of city policing and the erosion of public engagement in city and provincial decision-making about what constitutes safety and security. These are the 'zones of non-responsibility' – 'a confrontation with a responsibility that is infinitely greater than any we could ever assume' (Agamben, 2012: 21), which are the unassumable responsibilities of academic activism.

References

Agamben, G. (1999). *The man without content* (D. Heller-Roazen, Trans.). Stanford: Stanford University Press.

Agamben, G. (2012). *Remnants of Auschwitz: The witness and the archive* (D. Heller-Roazen, Trans.). Brooklyn, NY: Zone Books.

Ahmed, S. (2015). *Sexual harassment.* https://feministkilljoys.com/2015/12/03/sexual-harassment/. Accessed 12 June 2020.

Bernstein, R. J. (2002). Review of *remnants of Auschwitz: The witness and the archive* (D. Heller-Roazen, Trans.). *Bryn Mawr Review of Comparative Literature, 3*(2), 1–5.

Calitz, T. (2018). *Enhancing the freedom to flourish in higher education: Participation, equality and capabilities.* London: Routledge.

Calitz, T., Walker, M., & Wilson-Strydom, M. (2016). Theorising a capability approach to equal participation for undergraduate students at a South African university. *Perspectives in Education, 34*(2), 57–69.

Department of Higher Education and Training (DHET). (2008). *Report of the ministerial committee on transformation and social cohesion and the elimination of discrimination in public higher education institutions.* Pretoria, South Africa: Government Printers.

Farr, V., & Green, L. (2020). *Amid escalating gang violence, the City of Cape Town wages war on the poor.* https://www.dailymaverick.co.za/article/2020-07-08-amid-escalating-gang-violence-the-city-of-cape-town-wages-war-on-the-poor/#gsc.tab=0. Accessed 14 June 2020.

Firfirey, N., & Carolissen, R. (2010). 'I keep myself clean … at least when you see me, you don't know I am poor': Student experiences of poverty in South African higher education. *South African Journal of Higher Education, 24*, 987–1002.

Jackson, L. (2019). The smiling philosopher: Emotional labor, gender, and harassment in conference spaces. *Educational Philosophy and Theory, 51*(7), 693–701.

Kerr, P., & Luescher, T. (2018). Students' experiences of university life beyond the curriculum. In P. Ashwin & J. M. Case (Eds.), *Higher education pathways: South African undergraduate education and the public good* (pp. 216–231). Cape Town, South Africa: African Minds.

Letseka, M., & Maile, S. (2008). *Higher university drop-out rates: A threat to South Africa's future.* Pretoria, South Africa: Human Science and Research Council.

Levi, P. (1988). *If this is a man: A truce* (S. Woolf, Trans.). Royal Tunbridge Wells, UK: Abacus.

Lewins, K. (2010). The trauma of transformation: A closer look at the Soudien report. *South African Review of Sociology, 41*(1), 127–136.

Mahomedy, S., Boggenpoel, Z., Van der Sijde, E., & Tlale, M. (2020). *The Strandfontein relocation camp highlights how the rights of the homeless are being violated.* https://www.dailymaverick.co.za/article/2020-07-05-the-strandfontein-relocation-camp-highlights-how-the-rights-of-the-homeless-are-being-violated/#gsc.tab=0. Accessed 16 June 2020.

McLean, M. (2018). How higher education research using the capability approach illuminates possibilities for the transformation of individuals and society. In P. Ashwin & J. M. Case (Eds.),

Higher education pathways: South African undergraduate education and the public good (pp. 112–124). Cape Town, South Africa: African Minds.

Mills, C. J. (2003). An ethics of bare life: Agamben on witnessing? Review essay of Giorgio Agamben remnants of Auschwitz: The witness and the archive (Stanford UP, 1999). *Borderlands E – Journal: New Spaces in the Humanities, 2*(1), E-E.

Phipps, A., Ringrose, J., Renold, E., & Jackson, C. (2018). Rape culture, lad culture and everyday sexism: Researching, conceptualizing and politicizing new mediations of gender and sexual violence. *Journal of Gender Studies, 27*(1), 1–8.

Rennison, C. M., & Addington, L. A. (2014). Violence against college women: A review to identify limitations in defining the problem and inform future research. *Trauma, Violence & Abuse, 15*, 159–169.

Rentschler, C. (2015). #Safetytipsforladies: Feminist twitter takedowns of victim blaming. *Feminist Media Studies, 15*(2), 353–356.

Statistics South Africa. (2017). *Poverty trends in South Africa.* Pretoria, South Africa: Statistics South Africa.

Postscript: Constraints and Impediments to Academic Activism

Abstract In the postscript, we look at the possibility of the Muslim university cultivating resistance and dissent through its educational agenda. We argue that such a possibility is perhaps premature considering that autocracy and a reluctance to implement a genuine non-dichotomous view of knowledge seem to work against what it means to be an institution that is reflexive and open. In this way, academic activism might still be an elusive practice at a Muslim university. In response, and in recognising the criticality of cultivating academic activism within Muslim spaces of higher education, we argue for the importance of a pedagogy of resistance and dissent that could enhance the intellectualism so needed in the Muslim university; a willingness to respond to broader social malaises as a fulfilment of education as a human responsibility; an integration with the broader educational aspirations of the democratic state; and a preparedness to being reflectively open to new considerations and fusions of knowledge.

Keywords Constraints; Impediments; Muslim higher education; Democratisation

Introduction

The arguments of this book have fundamentally and predominantly focused on the imperatives and possibilities of academic activism; we have engaged extensively on the role and responsibility of the academic as an individual with autonomous, independent, curious and critical agency. In turn, we have consistently referenced the university as an engaging and rigorous space, unafraid of bold speech and disruptive thought, always pushing and moving beyond that which presents itself, always looking outward, while framed and immersed in a language of autonomous critique and interrogation. Yet, even within our own South African context – a relatively

© The Author(s), under exclusive license to Springer Nature Singapore
Pte Ltd. 2021
N. Davids, Y. Waghid, *Academic Activism in Higher Education*, Debating
Higher Education: Philosophical Perspectives 5,
https://doi.org/10.1007/978-981-16-0340-2

young and eager democracy – we are not remiss of increasing hiccups and impediments, as universities strain to detach themselves from infringing threats on their autonomy and academic freedom. We are also aware of the inseparable impact of political tractions on the capacity of universities to stay the course on not implementing its academic programmes, but in sustaining their roles as critical custodians of democracy. We can only assume, as we cast our eyes over other contexts, that higher education in South Africa is not unique in its pressures and struggles, and we can only imagine the additional burdens, constraints, frustrations and fears in contexts where democracy does not hold sway.

There are necessary questions, therefore, whether academics are indeed capable of fulfilling the kinds of roles we have discussed, advanced and advocated for in this book. On the one hand, even when academics are able to play active roles in the public sphere, they might choose not to participate in these; they might opt not to adopt a role of activism. In other words, even with the capacity to do so, academics might decide to impose self-censorship instead. On the other hand, capability does pertain not only to intellect and voice but also to how academics conceive of themselves in relation to their institutions and how they position themselves to their broader political and social contexts. Concomitantly, capability is equally reliant on how universities and broader political contexts conceive of role and responsibilities of academics – that is, the extent to which academics are allowed to adopt positions and articulations of critique.

Saliba (2018: 313) explains that prior to 2011, in some countries throughout the Arab world, universities were relative safe havens of free speech and, at times, even critical debate in an otherwise dominant picture of heavily censored public political discourse. Many researchers in the Middle East and North Africa (MENA), continues Saliba (2018: 313), had hoped that the spark that lit the wave of mass protests during the spring of 2011 and the political change (where it was manifested) could also reignite the light of academic freedom and end widespread political control over and censorship in higher education and research throughout the region's universities. Nearly a decade later, however, it would seem that academic freedom in the MENA region has suffered a downward and restrictive trend. As we have touched on in the preface to this book, in certain contexts, academic freedom and, hence, academics are at risk. Universities, academics and students are subjected to regulatory interference in the governance of higher education institutions, retaliatory discharge of researchers or students, arrests of students or university personnel or more severe infringements of their physical integrity, as well as safety (Grimm, 2018; Saliba, 2018).

As a continued manifestation of our own activism, we thought it apposite, therefore, to include a coda that looks specifically at the possibility of the Muslim university cultivating resistance and dissent through its educational agenda. We argue that such a possibility is perhaps premature considering that autocracy and a reluctance to implement a genuine non-dichotomous view of knowledge seem to work against what it means to be an institution that is reflexive and open. In this way, academic activism might still be an elusive practice at a Muslim university. In response, and in recognising the criticality of cultivating academic activism within Muslim spaces of higher education, we argue for the importance of a pedagogy of resistance and dissent that could enhance the intellectualism so needed in the Muslim university; a willingness to respond to broader social malaises as a fulfilment of education as a human responsibility; an integration with the broader educational aspirations of the democratic state; and a preparedness to being reflectively open to new considerations and fusions of knowledge.

A Philosophy of Muslim Higher Education

Throughout this book, we have been concerned with a (re)constructed and deconstructed understanding of academic activism in relation to a renewed philosophy of higher education. After having completed our chapter on academic activism in the context of a notion of Muselmann, we thought it might further advance our take on academic activism if we were to stretch our argument towards a philosophy of higher Muslim education. In other words, if Muslim higher education is so prominent in some parts of the world today, what would be the implications of such an understanding of higher education for academic activism? One of the world's renowned Muslim intellectuals from the Malaysian archipelago, Professor Syed Muhammad Naquib al-Attas (1991), offers an account of a philosophy of Muslim higher education that embodies the idea of a university. For him:

> the Islamic university must reflect the Holy Prophet [Mohammad] in terms of knowledge and right action; and its function is to produce men and women resembling him as near as possible in quality; each one according to his[/her] inherent capacities and potentials; to produce *good* men and women; to produce men and women of *adab*. (al-Attas, 1991: 40)

In light of the above, al-Attas further explains that the Muslim university articulates two kinds of knowledge: God-given or religious knowledge (*fardu 'ayn*) and acquired or rational, intellectual and philosophical knowledge (*fardu kifayah*). For him, on the one hand, religious knowledge is at the core of the university and should include sciences such as the Holy Quran, its recitation and interpretation (*tafsir* and *ta'wil*); the *Sunnah*, the experiences of the Prophet through the study of *hadith*; the *Shari'ah*, jurisprudence and law; *al-Tawhid*, theology and the concept of God; *al-Tassawuf*, Islamic metaphysics; and the grammar, lexicography and literature of the Arabic language (al-Attas, 1991: 42). On the other hand, but not separated from religious sciences, are the rational, intellectual and philosophical sciences such as human, natural, applied and technological sciences; comparative religion; Western culture and civilisation; linguistics; and Islamic thought, culture and civilisation (al-Attas, 1991: 43). What is important about al-Attas' non-dichotomous view of knowledge is that the rational, intellectual and philosophical sciences ought to be subjected to Islamisation that refers to 'the liberation of man [and woman] first from magical, mythological, animistic, national-cultural tradition, and then from secular control over his reason and his language' (al-Attas, 1991: 45–46).

Although we recognise al-Attas's insistence that knowledge has to be Islamised, we are somewhat concerned that such attempts would invariably dichotomise knowledge – an understanding against which he advocates. al-Attas's view that knowledge be conceived as universal seems somewhat ambivalent in the sense that knowledge in itself is also contextually grounded, thus invoking the local cultural dimensions of knowledge as well. Moreover, if Islamisation is about universalising knowledge, such an understanding would invariably seem to be remiss of the potentialities within the national-cultural (local) that can impact the universal view of knowledge he espouses. Moreover, it would seem that the very notion of Islamisation is in itself a contentious educational ambition.

A summary of the progress of Islamisation in the three major Muslim-majority regions in the world – the MENA region, Iran and Malaysia – reveals that Islamisation has been implemented along a continuum from not having been implemented successfully (having assumed a supplementary orientation) to having been maximally implemented as an integrated curriculum. There are several Muslim-majority countries, such as Turkey, Egypt, Indonesia and Pakistan, that have responded to the Islamisation idea in different forms but suffice it to say that these countries have either adopted a supplementary or integrated curriculum approach to the idea of the Islamisation of knowledge. Consequently, these countries would not necessarily be in a position to offer an understanding of how Muslim-majority countries that have responded to the Islamisation agenda have actually embraced the idea. Their understandings would be limited to one of three positions: having adopted an undesirable stance, as in the case of the MENA region; a supplementary position, as in the case of Iran; or a maximally integrated approach as is encountered in Malaysia.

Education can broadly be considered as an enactment of human encounters. When academics and students engage in collective action, they can be said to participate in educational practices on the grounds that they engage in deliberation in response to one another's claims and how their open and reflexive understandings can influence their human actions in society. When a concept of Islamisation envisages emancipating humans from pursuing their reasoned justifications from secularism and language, we are beginning to wonder how this is actually possible. The use of language is necessary in the articulations and understandings of people as they endeavour to make sense of themselves and the world in which they live.

What are the implications of the above understanding of the Muslim university for academic activism? Firstly, the exposure and engagement with a non-dichotomous view of knowledge could enhance an openness to that which is new and unexpected. This is not to suggest that such openness actually manifests in many Muslim universities. On the contrary, the obstinacy of several Muslim institutions of higher learning in several parts of the world causes them to resist an openness to what is other and appears to be intrusive. In such university contexts, it seems unlikely that academic activism would flourish. Secondly, a comprehensive understanding of knowledge that integrates both the local and universal for that matter would often bring dissenting and different views into conversation with one another. Such an understanding of knowledge could foreground the local in terms of the universal and vice versa so that universities could become more reflexive about their own practices in a dialectical way. That is the possibility that exists for the local to inform the global and be informed by the global as well, and vice versa. In this way, isolation and exclusivism could be thwarted.

Thus, academic activism starts with an introspective analysis of what is embedded in one's established traditions with the possibility that changes can ensue – a matter of acting reflexively. In other words, the global can also impact what is locally decided on. Thirdly, what Islamisation offers is for us to think anew about the university in that exclusionary and hegemonic practices ought to be looked at critically and even eradicated, if possible. Without being oblivious of the palpable fallibilities associated with Islamisation, it could arouse in us a thinking of resisting what is parochial and exclusivist.

Of course, the concern about the Muslim university of today is legitimate in the sense that the institution has become more disinclined towards dissent and resistance. Rosnani Hashim (2015: 111) posits that the current Muslim university fails in its goal to produce graduates who 'can articulate today's pressing issues of democracy, civil society, human rights, gender, environment, non-Muslim, pluralism, language, and globalisation to the extent that they can guide the masses'. Quite adamantly, she claims that many Muslim graduates 'are not critical, creative, or original in their thinking. They lack the Islamic intellectualism … to articulate a lot of pressing contemporary issues especially in a multi-faith society … [and] our Islamic [higher] education system has failed to bring the Islamic traditional sciences to bear on other spheres of life' (Hashim, 2015: 112). Hence, it seems as if the Muslim university is not ready to play a significant role in cultivating forms of resistance and dissent – especially when considering that such an institution appears to be averse to criticality and innovation in and about the diversity of knowledge and its dissemination. Hence, it is not surprising that Hashim (2015: 123) speaks about the decline of Muslim intellectualism as 'nowhere are they [students and teachers] encouraged to question, discuss, debate, challenge, or argue over ideas'. In our view, when a university no longer holds as sacred the practices of argumentation, dissent and resistance, then such a university is at risk. Furthermore, as Hashim (2015: 135) puts it, the inertia shown by many Islamic Studies graduates demands that philosophy be reintroduced into the university system.

Activism as Democratisation

We contend that philosophical inquiry would invariably orientate students and teachers towards argumentation, deliberation and a dissonance of thinking that can foster critical intellectualism once again in the Muslim university. However, the autocracy shown by many Muslim governments suggests that this might not be possible in the near future because such an 'undertaking requires great determination and sacrifice on the part of educationists, faculty members, teachers, curriculum designers and even politicians' (Hashim, 2015; 137).

Ahmad Akgunduz (2015: 158) reminds us that contemporary Western civilisation with her diverse Muslim minorities should have a Muslim university that can 'educate the new generation of Islamic scholars who will be able to participate within all fields concerning the Muslim communities, build the necessary bridges in intellectual, communicative as well as social fields'. For this to happen, he proposes that the Muslim university aims:

> [t]o promote learning from the perspective of the [I]slamic tradition within a modern society with growing cultural diversity; ... distinguish itself as a University with a diverse, socially responsible learning community of high quality scholarship and academic rigour sustained by faith that brings justice; ... work for the achievement of harmony, dialogue and balance in life, production and reproduction of knowledge within an Islamic paradigm; ... act as a leading model of an Islamic Science Institution based on the principles of integration of knowledge coupled with a comprehensive excellence for the progress of ... [all] ... communities; embark on a never ending quest for the truth: The truth emanates when both conscience and mind are brought together ...'. (Akgunduz, 2015: 158–159)

While we agree with Akgunduz (2015), we remain concerned about a number of factors he seemingly neglects to consider. These include, firstly, the importance of a pedagogy of resistance and dissent that could enhance the intellectualism so needed in the Muslim university. Muslim higher education cannot simply assume that students will succumb to its hegemonic practices. Such an assumption belies the autonomy and freedom of academics and students to act in relation to their own subjective experiences. Academics and students have a capacity and power to think critically about the educational space and society in which they find themselves. As such, they should not be expected or required to consensual understandings and arguments. Instead, resistance and dissent should be conceived as critical to the enhancement and advancement of knowledge. In the absence of dissenting arguments and views, there is no room for new ways of thinking and being. It is imperative that an embedded reliance on uncritical practices of unidirectional and compliant teaching and learning practices are replaced with pedagogical practices that are open and receptive to dissent and resistance.

Secondly, Muslim higher education should depart from a willingness to respond to broader social malaises as a fulfilment of education as a human responsibility. Not only does it seem parochial and self-deterministic to disengage and isolate into enclaves of exclusion and self-control, but such an understanding of the purpose of education is in itself un-educational. If education fails to address dystopias of exclusion, marginalisation and forms of violence so prevalent in many communities, then such a form of education has not fulfilled its human responsibilities. If education does not reflect a real and substantive engagement with socio-political issues of the day, it does not convince us to talk about education at all.

Finally, unless Muslim education becomes reflective and open to its own understandings and with which Muslim communities can engage together with extending such reflective openness with what is still to come through a fusion of knowledge, there seems little opportunity for such an education to be sustainable. Muslim education itself requires a form of critical inquiry that can deal adequately with what undermines its authenticity as a form of education. More specifically, it requires a willingness and reflectiveness to be open about that which constrains enhanced forms of collective and democratic human living, an openness about non-dichotomising different knowledge interests and, more poignantly, a self-reflectiveness about its relevance as a form of education that can engender acts of human responsibility. Thus, when a renowned Muslim philosopher of education, Wan Mohd Nor Wan Daud (2018: 35), posits that Muslim thought and practice should be re-Islamised intelligently and progressively towards the realisation of morality and ethics, we understand him to mean that Muslim education ought to be reconceptualised along the lines of an imaginary that provokes academic activism of relevance to all of humanity as it (humanity) endeavours to re-establish virtuous societies. As articulated elsewhere:

> [Muslim] education ought to cultivate in all students the skills and virtues of universal justice, including the capacity to deliberate about the demands for justice for all individuals, not only for citizens of any specific country. Deliberating about the demands for justice is a central virtue of [Muslim] … education, because it is primarily, rather than exclusively, through our empowerment of good persons that we can further the cause of justice around the world. (Waghid, 2018: 59)

In the end, if Muslim education, or any other education for that matter, is not open to the possibilities of how things might be otherwise, or how human encounters might serve in the interest of mutually just societies, then renewed questions have to be asked about what the purpose of this education is in the first instance.

References

Akgunduz, A. (2015). The role of Islamic higher education for communities in Europe: A case study of the Islamic University of Rotterdam (IR). In R. Hashim & M. Hattori (Eds.), *Critical issues and reform in Muslim higher education* (pp. 140–161). Gombak, Malaysia: IIUM Press.

Al-Attas, S. M. N. (1991). *The concept of education in Islam: A framework for an Islamic philosophy of education.* Kuala Lumpur, Malaysia: L ISTAC.

Grimm, J. (2018). *Authoritarian Middle East regimes don't like academics – Ask Matthew Hedges.* https://www.opendemocracy.net/en/policing-research-shifting-tides-for-middle-east-studies-after-arab-spring/. Accessed 23 June 2020.

Hashim, R. (2015). The decline of intellectualism in higher Islamic traditional sciences: Reforming the curriculum. In R. Hashim & M. Hattori (Eds.), *Critical issues and reform in Muslim higher education* (pp. 110–139). Gombak, Malaysia: IIUM Press.

Saliba, I. (2018). Academic freedom in the MENA region: Universities under siege. In *IEMed Mediterranean yearbook, 2018* (pp. 313–316).

Waghid, Y. (2018). Reconceptualising madrasah education: Towards a radicalised imaginary. In M. Abu Bakar (Ed.), *Rethinking madrasah education in a globalised world* (pp. 105–117). London & New York: Routledge.

Wan Daud, W. M. N. (2018). The timelessness of Prophet Muhammad and the nature of the virtuous civilisation. *TAFHIM: IKIM Journal of Islam and the Contemporary World, 2*(1), 1–38.

Index